Ann C. Dunbar

from Bill & Kim

Christmas 1990 -

ARIZONA
THE LAND AND
THE PEOPLE

ARIZONA
THE LAND AND
THE PEOPLE

EDITED BY TOM MILLER

THE UNIVERSITY OF ARIZONA PRESS TUCSON

Publication of this volume was made possible in part with financial support from the University of Arizona Centennial Committee and the Marshall Townsend Memorial Fund. Their assistance is acknowledged with gratitude.

Photographs by Ansel Adams on pages 84 and 181 are used by courtesy of the Trustees of the Ansel Adams Publishing Rights Trust. All rights reserved.

Edward Weston's photographs (Copyright © 1981, the Arizona Board of Regents, Center for Creative Photography) on pages 110 and 226, as well as those by Louis Carlos Bernal on pages 6, 194, 206, 208, 211, and 216 and by Ann Simmons-Myers (Copyright © 1986) on page 268 are used by permission of the Center for Creative Photography, the University of Arizona, Tucson.

THE UNIVERSITY OF ARIZONA PRESS

Library of Congress Cataloging-in-Publication Data

Arizona : the land and the people.

   Bibliography: p.
   Includes index.
   1. Arizona—Description and travel. 2. Arizona—History. 3. Natural history—Arizona. I. Miller, Tom.
F811.5.A76   1986   979.1   86-4275
ISBN 0-8165-1004-0 (alk. paper)

CONTENTS

Introduction: A Proud Beginning   *Tom Miller*   2

PART ONE: THE LAND

Introduction: The Land   *Stephen Trimble*   14

1. Mountain Islands   *Steve W. Carothers*   18

2. The Colorado Plateau   *Stephen Trimble*   44

3. The Mojave Desert   *Larry Stevens*   72

4. The Sonoran Desert   *Gary Nabhan*   90

5. The Chihuahuan Desert   *Peter L. Warren* and
                            Cecil R. Schwalbe   114

6. The Elusive Interior   *Stephen Trimble*   132

PART TWO: THE PEOPLE

Introduction: The People   *Thomas E. Sheridan*   158

7. Arizona's Indians   *Alvin M. Josephy, Jr.*   162

8. Hispanic Heritage   *Armando Miguélez*   194

9. Anglo Settlement   *Thomas E. Sheridan*   218

10. Modern Arizona   *Tom Miller*   248

Suggested Readings   280

About the Authors   288

Index   289

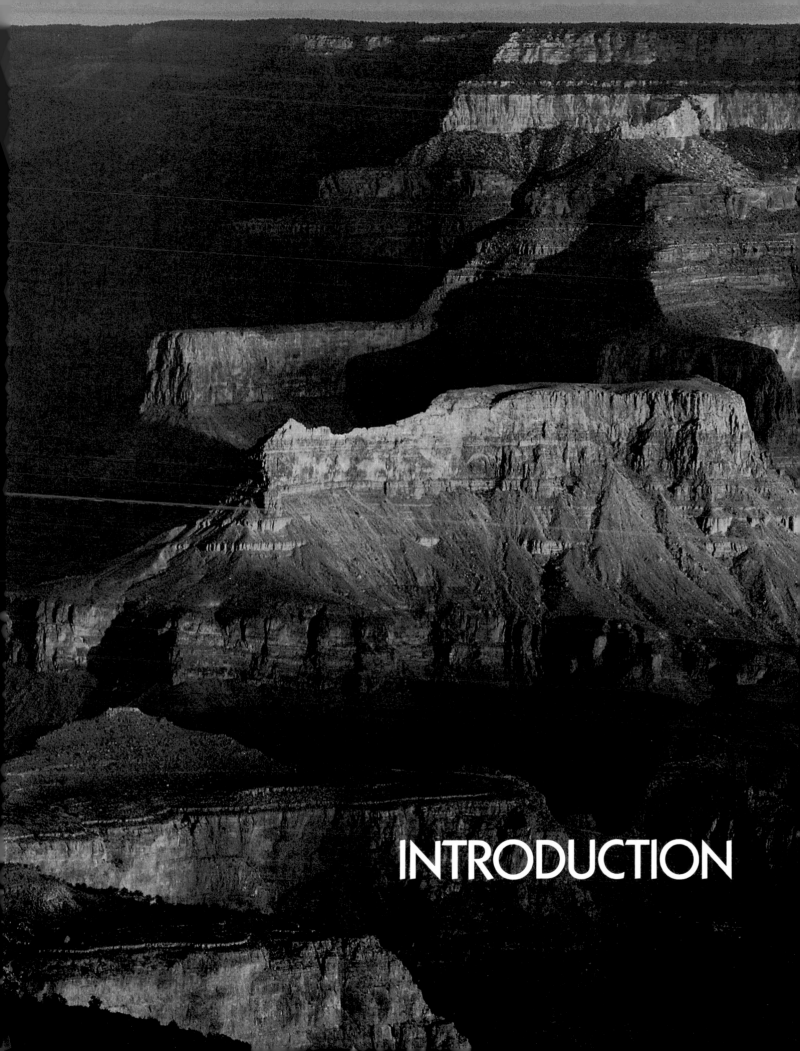

INTRODUCTION

A PROUD BEGINNING

Until 1848, the land we call the Rocky Mountain West, the Southwest, and California was the Mexican Northwest. The Treaty of Guadalupe Hidalgo, which ended the war against Mexico, changed all that by ratifying the seizure of present-day California, Nevada, and Utah, most of New Mexico and part of Wyoming, Colorado, Kansas, Arizona, and Oklahoma. Five years later, with the Gadsden Purchase, the U.S. bought from Mexico a sliver of New Mexico's southern edge and its boot heel, and all of Arizona south of the Gila River. From those annexations on, through the establishment of the Territory of Arizona by President Abraham Lincoln in the middle of the Civil War, and up through statehood in 1912, Arizona has mystified and intrigued eastern writers and editors. Unexplored terrain largely populated by Indians and Mexicans, vast potential for crops, cattle, and minerals, and land rugged and stunning in the extreme, spurred the eastern press to publish all it could about the new Southwest. Travelers obliged with material often more flamboyant than accurate, but always entertaining.

Read these words by travel writer J. Ross Browne in the October 1864 issue of *Harper's New Monthly Magazine*: "At the period of its purchase Arizona was practically a *terra incognita*. Hunters and trappers had explored it to some extent; but . . . . few people in the United States knew anything about it. . . . An impression prevailed that it was a worthless desert, without sufficient wood or water to sustain a population of civilized beings, and for the most part destitute of any compensating advantages. Mr. Gadsden was ridiculed for his purchase. . . . The most desperate class of renegades from Texas and California found Arizona a safe asylum from arrest," Browne warned, and "Tucson became the headquarters of vice, dissipation, and crime. . . . Murderers, thieves, cutthroats and gamblers formed the mass of the population," and "scenes of bloodshed were of everyday occurrence in the public streets." Tucson's garrison, Browne reported, "confined itself to its legitimate business of getting drunk or doing nothing. Arizona was perhaps the only part of the world . . . where all assumed the right to gratify the basest passions of their nature without restraint." It was literally, readers of *Harper's* learned, "a paradise of devils."

Overleaf: Grand Canyon sunrise at Shoshone Point. STEPHEN TRIMBLE.

Above left: Saguaro blossoms, signs of approaching harvest. TOM WEISKOTTEN.

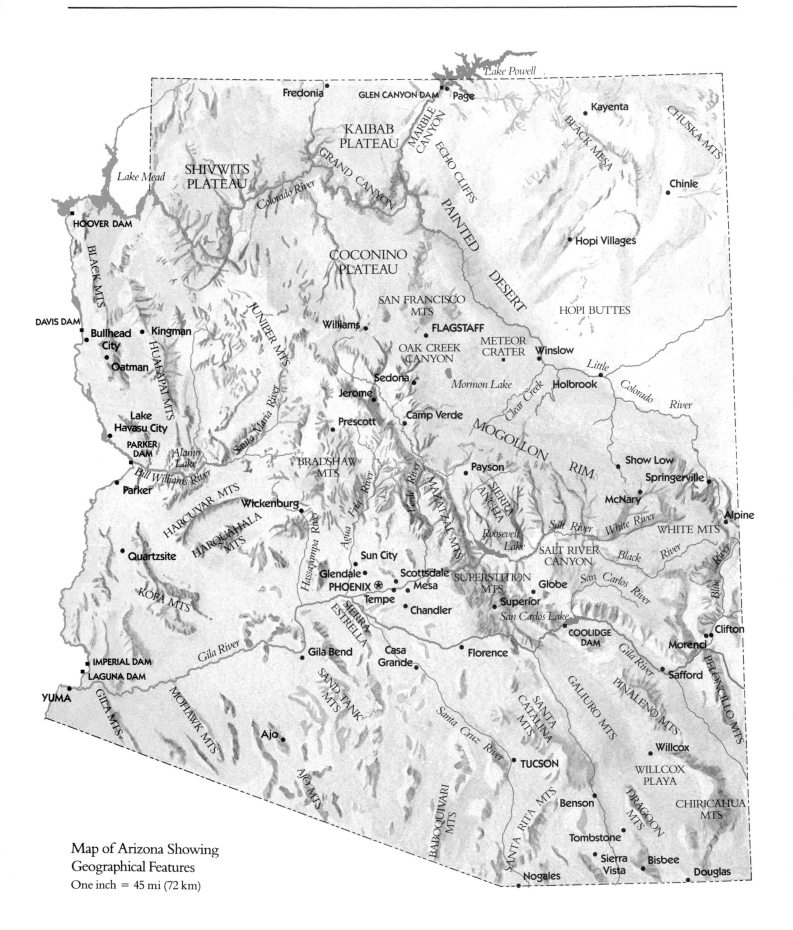

Map of Arizona Showing
Geographical Features
One inch = 45 mi (72 km)

Territorial Secretary Richard C. McCormick countered the following year with a glowing report on the land. "[T]here is not a section in the United States," he wrote, "which more abounds in glades and vales, and widespreading plains, suitable for cultivation, and only awaiting the hand of industry to blossom as the rose." In a lengthy dispatch to *The New York Herald*, he continued: "The climate, considered either in relation to health and longevity, or to agricultural or mining labor, is unrivaled in the world. Disease is unknown...."

McCormick served later as Governor and then Territorial Delegate to Congress from Arizona, but in every capacity he was known as its most enthusiastic booster. He complained of Washington's "exasperating ignorance and prejudice" about Arizona—a feeling many still sense in the closing decades of the twentieth century.

In 1871, Arizona's legislature—then meeting in Tucson—published the first of a succession of government-sponsored works about their land. That first thirty-one-page booklet was updated and expanded a couple of years later by Governor Anson P. K. Safford, with the laborious title *The Territory of Arizona; A Brief History and Summary of the Territory's Acquisition, Organization; and Mineral, Agricultural and Grazing Resources; Embracing a Review of its Indian Tribes—Their Depredations and Subjugations; and Showing in Brief the Present Conditions and Prospects of the Territory.*

During the next few years some hyperbolic books about Arizona were privately published. The most ambitious public effort was not printed until 1881 when the legislature—back in Prescott after ten years in Tucson—put up money for Patrick Hamilton's *Resources of Arizona*, subtitled *A Manual of Reliable Information Concerning the Territory*. Hamilton fell in step with the growing literary tradition, calling Arizona "a land of marvels for the scientist and the sightseer. Nowhere on the globe can the operations of nature be traced more clearly and distinctly...." Born in Ireland and raised in New York City, Hamilton eventually became Arizona's Commissioner of Immigration, in charge of luring new settlers to the territory. About the young Maricopa County seat, population 1,500, he boasted, "With its splendid water facilities and rich soil, with its fine farms, beautiful gardens, and shady groves, Phoenix is a handsome and a prosperous town, with a bright future before it." Salt River Valley land, he noted, could be bought, with water rights, "for $5 and $10 per acre, depending on quality and situation." Florence, Hamilton wrote, "with rich mines north, south, and east, will always be a prosperous town." Of Yuma: "its unrivaled climate for those troubled with lung diseases will always insure its permanency and prosperity." Tucson's Mexican neighborhoods, however, had streets "narrow and tortuous, and the houses make very little pretensions to architectural beauty. The advent of the railroad, however, has drawn hither an active, energetic American population, and the old order of things is being rapidly done away with." Finally, after 119 pages extolling Arizona's strengths, coaxing readers to move there, Hamilton admits, "Of lawyers and doctors the Territory has more than enough, and an influx of the 'learned professions' is not desireable." Now, more than a century later, Hamilton's conclusion still resonates with reason.

Westbound travelers found copies of *The Resources of Arizona* at eastern railroad depots. Reports reached Arizona that the book circulated in Canada and Great Britain. Thousands of letters poured in requesting information about settling there. Hamilton's slim volume was so well received that during the following three years, both privately and again at the behest of the legislature, it was updated and expanded three times. The last edition contained 414 pages, including illustrations, a map, and advertising. Patrick Hamilton had become Arizona's first Chamber of Commerce.

Others followed Hamilton as Commissioner of Immigration. John A. Black, who filled that post in 1890, wrote in his pamphlet about changes the state had undergone: "For years the very word 'Arizona' has had a gruesome sound to the Easterner. At the mention of the name of this Territory visions of bloodthirsty Indians, white desperadoes, barren mountains, and alkalai deserts would spring up before one's eyes.... But a marvelous change has come, and there is no State or Territory in the Union today where human life is more sacred, where crimes are less frequent, than in this same Arizona." None of this impressed the U.S. Congress, which denied statehood to the develop-

Opposite: Dirt road through Saguaro National Monument, west of Tucson. TOM WEISKOTTEN.

Left: "Barrio Portrait H Ave.," Douglas. LOUIS CARLOS BERNAL.

Opposite: Apache rodeo rider. RICO LEFFANTA.

ing Territory. "I do not think that Arizona has sufficient population, wealth or commercial importance" for statehood, sniffed a Massachusetts congressman during one debate in 1893.

Contributing to the Territory's reputation was a penchant for duels, occasionally between newspaper editors. One involved Territorial booster Patrick Hamilton, who served briefly as editor of *The Tombstone Independent*. Hamilton had been challenged by the editor of the competing *Tombstone Epitaph*, Samuel J. Purdy, with whom he had been carrying on a vicious fight through the pages of their respective journals. They squared off one morning near the Mexican border; when they could not agree on which weapons to use—Hamilton favored Colt .45 revolvers, Purdy claimed insufficient strength to handle a Colt and produced lighter guns, which Hamilton declined—they and their seconds went home, their mutual animosity intact. Another duel pitted Edward Cross, editor of the Tubac *Weekly Arizonan*, the Territory's first newspaper, against Sylvester Mowry, who lobbied for Territorial recognition in Washington and coveted its delegate seat in Congress. (The *Weekly Arizonan* printing press reached Tubac from Philadelphia via ship around South America, north to Guaymas on the coast of Sonora, and overland to Tubac.) Using Burnside rifles, Cross and Mowry faced each other, aimed, and fired. "At the last fire Mr. Mowry's rifle did not discharge," went one account, and he was allowed to try again, while Cross, who had fired and missed all his shots, stood defenseless. Mowry shot his last round into the air. Although firearms aren't used today, the ongoing spirited battle between the state's largest daily and its largest weekly, *The Arizona Republic*, founded in 1890, and *New Times*, born eighty years later, carries on that Territorial tradition.

The state's best-known advertising now is *Arizona Highways*, whose more than 350,000 monthly copies are sent to subscribers throughout the United States and twenty foreign countries. Through its pages visitors are lured by spectacular sunsets and glimpses of the state both rugged and rewarding.

Many visitors make their own impressions of Arizona. Ever since staff artists attached to mid-nineteenth-century government explora- tory missions sketched their versions of the land and the life it supports, Arizona has attracted outsiders who have taken on the task of recording its features, both permanent and ephemeral. Some, such as Thomas Moran's 1873—74 oil of the Grand Canyon and Dean Brown's photog- raphy on the Navajo Reservation almost a century later, draw on the spirit of the land. Other works, including a 1937 painting of a destitute household by Lew Davis and a Dorothea Lange photograph three years later of a migrant cotton picker, have revealed Arizona's poverty to the rest of America.

Photographs of Indians and their rituals have long been a source of controversy when taken by non-Indians. Some document, others dis- tort, but most photographers agree that their works have a distance from the subject which can only be bridged by Indians photographing themselves. For this reason, "Seven Views of the Hopi," a 1983 collec- tion of photographs by and of Hopis, was of particular note, especially because so many people saw it during its exhibition at the Smithsonian Institution in Washington, D.C., and elsewhere around the country.

Can the same be said of the written word? The school at Rock Point, serving fewer than five hundred students in a Navajo commu- nity of fifteen hundred, assembled a remarkable collection of poetry, historical essays, art work, and practical advice into a bilingual book, *Between Sacred Mountains*. Its contents teach and cajole, entertain and enlighten, none of which could have been accomplished by *biligáana*— the white man, in Navajo. Mainstream knowledge of Navajo and other Four Corners tribes comes from popular works such as Tony Hiller- man's series of detective stories, each of which involves solving reserva- tion crimes using ordinary police work and extraordinary native lore.

World War II gave the nation Arizona Marine Ira Hayes to sing about. Hayes was one of the soldiers who raised the flag at Iwo Jima in 1945; an unwilling hero, the Pima Indian was trotted about the country promoting war bonds, but he never really developed skills needed to readjust to a white society in peacetime America. A decade after his famous stand, Arizona's international hero died an alcoholic on the Gila River Indian Reservation.

In the 1970s another Arizona figure, also a Marine, was subjected to international hoopla surrounding his return from overseas. Sergeant James M. Lopez of Globe had the unfortunate luck to be on guard duty when the U.S. embassy in Iran was overtaken in 1979, and he, along with more than seventy others, was held hostage for 444 days. Known intimately to millions of strangers as Jimmy, Sgt. Lopez appealed to America because of his youthful appearance, his quick-wittedness, and his solid, working-class background. Recognizing the overblown nature of the many business offers made him, Lopez returned as quickly as possible to another overseas post, and out of the limelight. His comments on the ordeal were limited to sketches he drew and to suggestions he and his family made to two Phoenix writers whose

Opposite: Monument Valley, north- east Arizona. TIM FULLER.

play, *Made in America*, showed the anxiety and press overkill in Globe during the captivity, his life during those same months, and his reaction to the incessant attention upon his return.

Most foreigners know the state from the stream of "B" westerns filmed near Sedona, Tucson, and elsewhere, and seek out the same vistas as part of their tours when visiting. Diplomats and journalists from the Soviet Union, however, are barred from much of the state as part of a curious reciprocity between the U.S. government and the Soviet Foreign Ministry. At the end of 1983, the State Department updated its sixteen-year-old listing of places closed to Soviet visitors. In Arizona, Soviets could visit the cities of Phoenix and Tucson, but not their surrounding counties. To the west, they could enjoy Yuma and La Paz counties, but not Mohave; Yavapai and Gila counties were open, but neighboring Coconino and Pinal were off-limits; and in the south and east, Graham and Greenlee counties were approved for Soviets, but Santa Cruz, Cochise, Apache, and Navajo were forbidden.

The treatment of foreigners in Arizona, as elsewhere in the U.S.,
has not always been kind. During World War II the state, like several
others, was home for many German POWs, and also for Americans of
Japanese descent, who were held in internment camps. A Prescott
newspaper greeted some of Arizona's first Chinese settlers in 1869 with
the headline MORE CHINAMEN. "Three more Chinamen arrived here
during the week," the *Daily Arizona Miner* observed, "and have gone
to work. There are now four of them, which is quite enough." Enough
Orientals populated Arizona by 1901 that the Anglo-run Territorial
Legislature passed an anti-miscegenation law barring intermarriage

between whites and "Negro or Mongolian" partners. Not until 1962 did Arizona finally repeal the law barring interracial marriages.

Sun City and Green Valley have each attracted out-of-staters for their own singular qualities. As the country's premier retirement community, Sun City has experienced phenomenal growth since its beginnings in 1960. Green Valley has succeeded as a retirement center in part because of its uniform architectural design and because it has maintained an upper-middle-class population. Jerome and Bisbee take up the slack at the other end of Arizona's age and income bracket with their friendly store-fronts catering to a curious mix of aging hippies, youthful artists, small-town merchants, reluctant war veterans, retired miners, single parents, and venture capitalists. These two towns have, virtually by themselves, restored the words "quaint" and "nestled" to Sunday newspaper travel-writing.

Singers, too, have shown Arizona's face to the world: Glen Campbell ("By the Time I Get to Phoenix"), The Eagles ("Standin' on a corner in Winslow, Arizona..." from "Take It Easy"), Slim Critchlow ("The Crooked Trail to Holbrook"), Exit ("The Coming of the White Man"), Linda Ronstadt ("From Tucson to Tucumcari/Tehachapi to Tonopah..." from "I'm Willin' "), and Paul Revere and the Raiders ("Arizona"), but most of all, Bobby Troup's "Route 66." Troup's song, composed in 1946, was revived once again toward the end of 1984 when the last stretch of interstate highway bypassing old 66 was formally dedicated. The event took place in Williams, which, like other towns owing their existence to route 66 travelers, must devise another economic base or fade away.

The official territorial song, composed in 1901 by Elise A. Averill and Mrs. Frank Cox, was "Arizona—The Sun-Kissed Land." It may have been the first formal composition with Arizona as its theme but seems now to be a paean long forgotten.

> *O Arizona, sun-kissed land!*
> *Thy day of birth is near at hand;*
> *Upon thy mountains' rugged crest,*
> *Thy native sons still call thee blest....*

By contrast, Ferde Grofe's "Grand Canyon Suite," using no words to carry its message, has been for almost a half-century in the repertoire of symphony orchestras here and abroad.

Arizona: The Land and the People, a comprehensive source of information from an up-to-date perspective, is a distinctive addition to the long line of books about Arizona which began with the Territory's 1871 volume carrying a forty-three-word title. With its publication we alert newcomers to look closely at the land they have chosen. We ask visitors to gain some understanding of the features which attract them. And we suspect that those who have lived here awhile will also learn a few new things about their state.

Opposite: Golfer at Paradise Valley Country Club, northeast of Phoenix. TERRENCE MOORE.

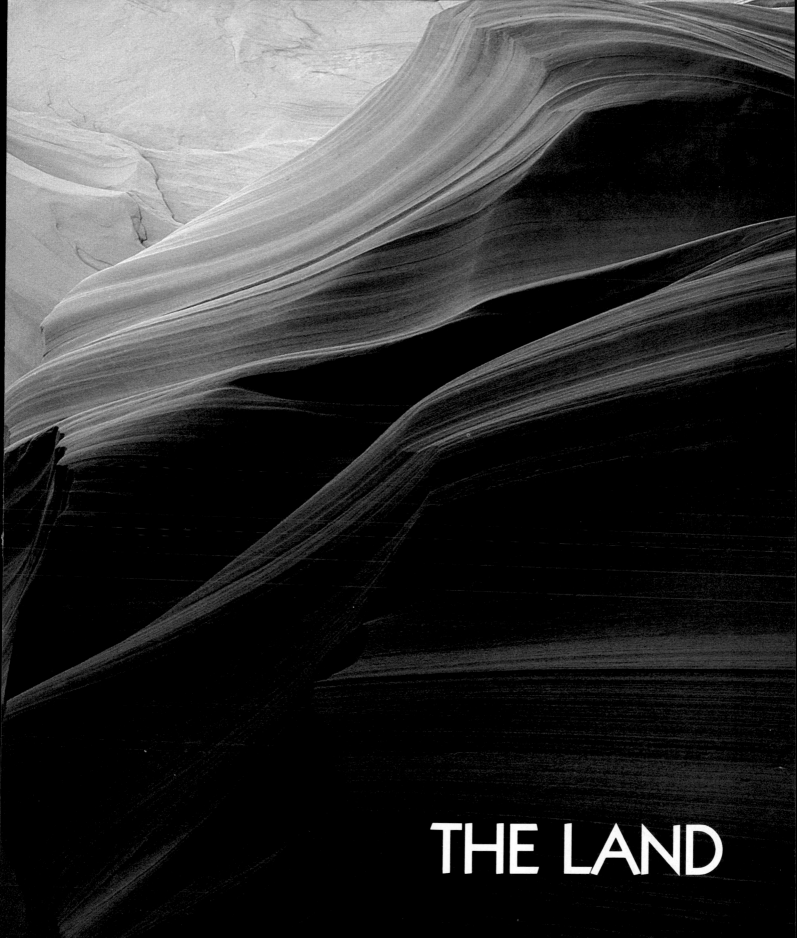

THE LAND

Part One

STEPHEN TRIMBLE

THE LAND

This is a brand-new state. Arizona joined the Union in 1912, the last territory in the "lower forty-eight" to achieve statehood. It still remains a symbol of the frontier, of the desert, and of the West—as much myth as real landscape.

The Marlboro man rides down a cascade of orange sand in Monument Valley. Postcard-red cliffs above Sedona turn up in a score of western movies, scripted as land from Texas to Montana. On Hollywood movie sets, directors arrange saguaro cacti on wooden platforms to transform the Southern California Mountains into their version of Cochise's stronghold.

In Spain, billboards advertise cigarettes called "West" with pho-tomurals of smiling truckers posed in northern Arizona. Japanese tour-ists "see America"—Disneyland, Las Vegas, and the Grand Canyon—and then go home. A *Time* magazine cover illustration for a story on Texas prominently features saguaros, though the Arizona cacti never naturally grow east of their home state.

Travelers cease insisting that Arizona must be one vast desert when they become snowbound in Flagstaff on a frigid winter's night, or drive the endless curves of U.S. 666 north from Safford through the White Mountains or the Interstate through the sunlit stands of pon-derosa pines along the Mogollon Rim.

Arizona divulges itself slowly. A summer's walk at Saguaro National Monument in midday confounds you with such intense heat and light that you cannot imagine this desert exuberant with life. Your first look into the Grand Canyon may disappoint, overwhelm, or dis-orient. The Canyon takes time: many strolls on the rim, a walk down into the gorge, a ride on the river.

In the chapters that follow, we speak over and over again of change. The deserts sweeping across the state from northwest to south-east have existed for just ten thousand years. Arizona's mountains and plateaus were formed recently in geologic time; even the Grand Can-yon has existed for only ten million years.

Understanding Arizona requires a recognition of the relative new-ness of this world and a feeling for the slow pace of geologic time. Ice

Overleaf: Jaidito Canyon, part of the Grand Canyon. MICHAEL COLLIER.

Above left: Bobcat at the Arizona-Sonora Desert Museum, Tucson. TOM BEAN.

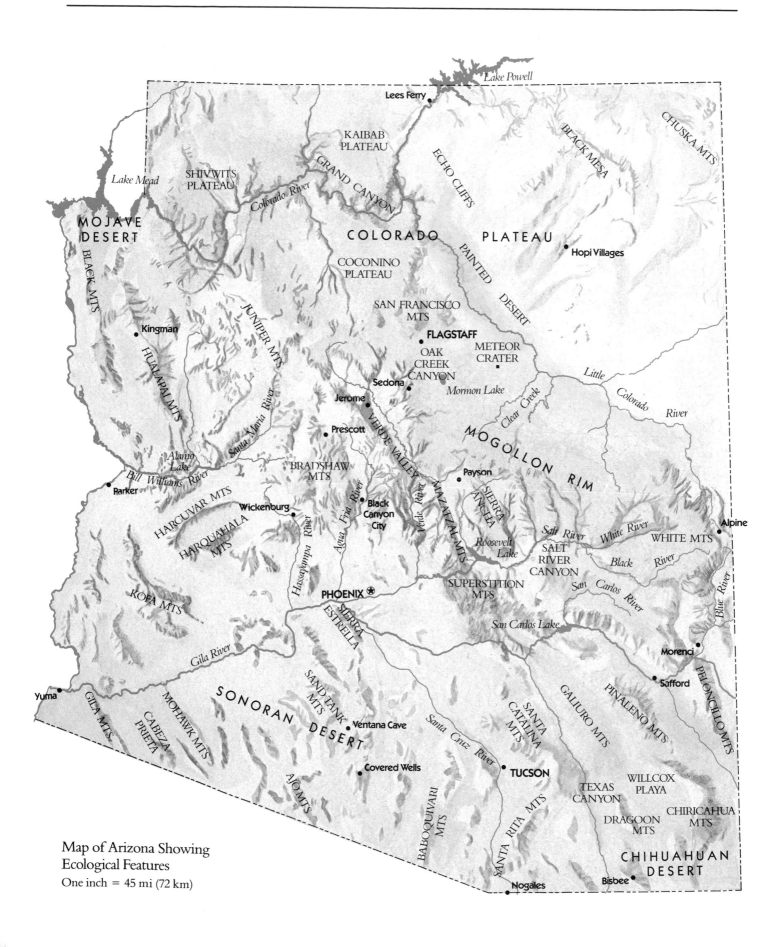

Map of Arizona Showing
Ecological Features
One inch = 45 mi (72 km)

ages, earthquakes, volcanic eruptions, uplift, and erosion—the geologic story seems cataclysmic. But the Earth works its way through these chapters slowly.

•

Desert. Mountain. Canyon. Arizona is contained in these three words. In the south and west lie the three great biological divisions of the desert: Mojave, Sonoran, and Chihuahuan, ecological provinces equivalent to the geologic province known as Basin and Range—low, hot, naked plains spread between sharp, fierce desert mountains. Northward stands the Colorado Plateau, the land of dry mesas and slickrock canyons climaxing at the Grand Canyon. A transition zone of mountains unites desert and plateau in a confusing and unique jumble that combines plants, animals, and landscapes from both north and south. Other isolated mountains stand throughout the state, islands of coolness and forest, sky islands.

Water ties together these diverse landscapes. Summer flash floods and winter ice at higher elevations carve the canyons and whittle away at the cliffs. In Basin and Range country, erosional debris buries the mountains; on the Plateau, arroyos and rivers wash away rubble and leave canyons jagged and clean. The interior mountains, more than anything, serve as watersheds; they give birth to the rivers of the desert.

Winter rains come from the Arctic in great Pacific storms that barely reach the Southwest. Clouds cover the state as these frontal systems sweep through, and rain falls light and steady, soaking the ground slowly with what the Navajos call female rain.

Summer rains come hard and sudden: male rain. Moist air moves in from the Gulf of Mexico, and less commonly from the Gulf of California. This air rises over the sun-warmed land, cools, condenses, and brings thundershowers.

Summer rains decrease to the northwest, winter rains decrease to the southeast. Yuma, Globe, Flagstaff, and Lake Mead lie near the line of half winter/half summer precipitation. Within this curve, most rain comes in winter; beyond the curve, most rain comes in summer.

Mojave Desert: winter rain, female rain. Chihuahuan Desert: summer rain, male rain. Sonoran Desert: rain in both seasons, and consequently the lushest desert vegetation of all.

Lack of water makes the deserts; scarceness combined with unpredictability. In 1905, Yuma received more than eleven inches of precipitation, in 1953 a third of an inch. Sooner or later, though, the rain comes. Arizona's Indian people know this, and their ceremonial calendars match the rhythm of seasonal storms—with dances, songs, and prayers for rain.

The rain comes. It comes from the sacred mountains: the San Francisco Peaks, Baboquivari Peak. Clouds build. Thunder rolls through canyons and across desert plains. And soon the showers follow, to carve modern Arizona into the landscape of the future, to water plants, to make life possible for animals and humans, and to complete—and begin—another cycle of Arizona seasons.

Opposite: Sycamore Canyon in the Prescott-Coconino National Forests, central Arizona. JACK W. DYKINGA.

MOUNTAIN ISLANDS

I NUVATUKYAOVI: HOME FOR KACHINA SPIRITS

In January of 1858 Edward Fitzgerald Beale with twenty men, fourteen camels, and a few mules and wagons left the Colorado River to return to New Mexico. He had completed the dangerous task of surveying, in the heart of Indian country, a wagon road from Fort Defiance to the river. Looking to the highest of the San Francisco Peaks as a guide, Beale became enchanted with the mountain:

> Our way today has been over a country of great beauty and exceedingly rich in grass and cedar timber...the old mountain is covered with snow, relieved by the dark green patches of pine, and the plain at its base, with its black forest of gigantic timber presents a beautiful sight as the sun is setting this evening.

Beale was not the first to fall under the spell of this mountain.

For a thousand years or more, northern Arizona's Hopi Indians have assigned a religious significance to the peak dominating the view southwest of Hopi country. We call it Mount Humphreys. They call the mountain "Nuvatukyaovi," home of the Kachina spirits.

The ancestral Navajo people first arrived from the north five or six hundred years ago and saw the mountain. They called it "Dook'o'ooslid," one of the boundaries of the Navajo spiritual world and a reservoir of natural life. In our own times, Arizonans who live in the shadow learn to cherish this landmark, and mountain environments in general.

Some of the state's best kept secrets can be uncovered on its mountains. Who could guess that Arizona, land of spiny plants, poisonous reptiles, intense sunshine and summer heat, water shortages, and barren canyons, would have also hundreds of thousands of acres of luxuriant pine, fir, spruce, and aspen forest? And deep within the back country of the larger mountain systems are wildflower-laden alpine meadows, mountain streams with native trout, and even a stretch of treeless, windblown tundra.

Driving major highways in Arizona, one quickly notes how much the landscape is broken by mountain ranges and jagged peaks. On the

Flora of the San Francisco Mountains, a range north of Flagstaff. Above left: Penstemon. Opposite: Aspen grove. STEPHEN TRIMBLE.

approach to Flagstaff, Mount Humphreys can be seen for many miles from any direction. The highest point in the state, it is one of five peaks that are connected by a two-mile ridge, and it stands 12,633 feet above sea level.

Just looking at the Peaks, or any other cloud-penetrating mountain tops, does not explain why these elevated land masses are sometimes called "sky islands" or "mountain islands." But consider the nature of oceanic islands and the relative isolation of their flora and fauna. Unless the plant and animal inhabitants of the island can swim or fly great distances, they are, in fact, trapped. Moreover, just as it is difficult for them to leave the island, it is difficult for newcomers to reach it. On the larger Arizona mountains, where lowland desert habitats gradually slope upward to forested environs, the forms of life are also isolated. For example, a tree squirrel from the San Francisco Peaks simply would not survive the journey across an "ocean" of desert to the pine forests of the Santa Catalina Mountains some two hundred miles

Opposite: Mount Humphreys, at 12,333 feet, the highest mountain in Arizona. STEPHEN TRIMBLE.

Right: Hikers in a meadow on Mount Graham, in the Pinaleno Mountains of southeastern Arizona. JACK W. DYKINGA.

to the south. And as it does on oceanic islands, this isolation can lead to the development of unique plant and animal assemblages.

Where the mountain range is small, and elevation from desert floor to mountain peak is not substantial, the disparity in flora and fauna is small also. But the higher a mountain rises from the desert floor and the greater the actual size of the range, the more striking and complex will be the biological differences between lowlands and uplands.

Temperature and moisture are distinctive features of mountain islands, and they account for the changing sequences of the regions' biological communities. The changes in climate from the base to the summit of a large Arizona mountain are comparable to those one expects in crossing thousands of miles of latitude on most of the continents. On a typical mountain, for every 1,000 feet of elevational rise, there is a decrease in temperature of 3° to 4° F.

As an experiment, drive a few miles south of Safford, in southeastern Arizona. You will soon come to the Pinaleno Mountains. From their base at 3,500 feet to the peak on Mount Graham at 10,713 feet—a mere ten miles of road and less than forty-five minutes of travel—you may experience a thirty-degree drop in temperature. The moisture gradient also changes dramatically from the base to the top of the Pinalenos. On the valley floor, desert plants and animals are perfectly adapted to ten inches or less of annual rainfall while the dense forests on the mountain's crest need every bit of the thirty inches usually recorded. Here as elsewhere, temperature mediates the influences of the sun's energy, rainfall, humidity, and evaporation, allowing for differences occurring in plant communities from the valley floor to the mountaintop.

ISLANDS: THEATERS OF BIOLOGICAL CHANGE

Without the study of islands, biological scientists might still be a long way from understanding the environmental pressures that lead to the creation of a species. Islands, whether they are volcanic land masses rising from the ocean floor or forested Arizona mountaintops surrounded by desert scrublands or grasslands, provide unique laboratories for clear observation of simple evolutionary phenomena. Charles Darwin, exploring oceanic archipelagos in the mid-1800s, caught the first glimpses of the process by which living organisms change, slowly and almost imperceptibly. Investigating only mainland floras and faunas, he probably would never have recognized the biological phenomena that led to his striking conclusions. He first noted the impact of biological isolation in mockingbirds on the Galapagos Islands. Each island had its own distinct color of mockingbird. He pondered the cause of this anomaly, and in an 1835 journal entry wrote his first remarks on the concept of morphological change through inherited characteristics.

> When I see these islands in sight of each other, and possessed of but a scanty stock of animals, tenanted by these birds, but slightly differing in structure and filling the same place in Nature, I must suspect they are only Varieties...if there is the slightest foundation for these remarks the Zoology of Archipelagos will be well worth examination; for such facts would undermine the stability of the species.

When Darwin wrote those words, the belief was universal that no amount of time and isolation would allow for change in the work of Creation.

We have come a long way since Darwin. On islands, deleterious or beneficial changes in the genetic makeup of organisms can pass very quickly through a species population. Island populations tend to be comparatively small so that chance can, in a few generations, result in the population-wide occurrence or loss of a mutation. Again, the insular condition insures limited immigration of new breeding members. This is what Darwin saw, first in the mockingbirds, later in other animals within the Galapagos archipelago. Although color variations in mockingbird feathers from island to island may have had little to do with survival, each island had its distinct color of bird. Even the short distances of open water between the islands appear to have restricted the birds from flying off the islands and taking mates of a different color. If some birds did fly away and interbreed, this was not sufficient cause to influence the persistence of the singular color represented on each island.

The same factors—isolation, inbreeding, and chance—have left their mark on Arizona's mountain islands, where parts of the flora and fauna exhibit differences resulting from some of the same evolutionary influences Darwin saw at work on oceanic land masses. Within each of the major mountain ranges, there are unique biological treasures worth exploring. But that is only part of the mystery. If there are very special plants and animals secluded on Arizona's mountain islands, how did they get there in the first place? For this answer, we must drift back to the landscape of many thousands of years ago.

ORIGINS OF THE ARIZONA MOUNTAIN ENVIRONMENTS

Biologists have known for a long time that the distribution of vegetation throughout the land does not occur randomly. Climate dictates the kind and amount of plant cover that will survive and flourish in a particular place. To be sure, other factors such as depth and quality of soil and availability of ground and surface water are important, but it is the seasonal pattern of temperature and precipitation which most controls regional vegetation patterns. It takes only relatively small changes in long-term global temperature patterns to cause major changes in the plant and animal varieties that live in an area.

Several thousand years ago, Arizona was a very different landscape. Most of the land was covered by woodland and forest; there were no deserts. What evidence do we have to reach these remarkable conclusions? For one, we have learned to read the strange records of the land itself: the widths of tree-rings, which tell the history of rainfall and climate; the spores of many kinds of pollen, which tell us of past plant life; and the like.

Thanks also to a group of small rodents, known as woodrats or packrats, we have a quite detailed record. Woodrat nesting areas have been occupied by successive generations of rat families for millennia. Primarily nocturnal, these rats spend their nights foraging on vegetation within several meters of the nest. Small branches, twigs, leaves, seeds, fruits, as well as colorful stones and sometimes human artifacts, are dragged into the den. Where dens have been in crevices and shallow

caves protected from precipitation for thousands of years, the nest (or midden)—an aggregation of plant material, rat urine, and feces—is often hardened into a distinct mass. Thousands of nest samples have been collected, transported to laboratories, and dated by various techniques. Then they are partially dissolved until the plant parts can be identified. By knowing the age of the sample and the kinds of plants the animals were collecting at the time, the scientist can achieve a composite interpretation of the ancient landscape.

The woodrat collections show distinctly that twenty thousand years ago the Arizona climate was cooler and wetter throughout, with most of the rainfall occurring during the winter season. There were few summer thundershowers, and midsummer temperatures were far less severe in such areas as those now called Phoenix or Gila Bend. For at least ten thousand years the climate remained virtually unchanged. Plants and animals of the forests flourished. Then, about nine or ten thousand years ago, global weather patterns changed and the Arizona climate became as we know it—characterized by relatively small amounts of winter precipitation and a distinctly warmer summer temperature range. The change was like the onset of a permanent drought.

Within three to five hundred years after the winter rains decreased and temperatures increased, the verdant covering of forests had disappeared from the lowlands, giving way to the developing deserts. Not all of the lowland forests succumbed. Woodlands adjacent to streams and rivers were able to survive, as they still do—riparian trees such as cottonwood, sycamore, box elder, and others clinging to existence on the streambanks, sheltering many kinds of wildlife, and reminding us of the spread of ancient forests.

Of course, such changes in vegetation have had profound influences on the animal communities still inhabiting Arizona's mountain islands. To illustrate this let us view the state from several thousand feet in the air and imagine two scenes: first we see the land as it appeared 10 to 20 thousand years ago. We see most of the state as mixed woodland, but along the margins of the lower valleys there are fringes of desert scrub plants, and interspersed within the woodlands, especially on south-facing slopes and well-drained soils, we will find the ancestors of many of our familiar cactus varieties. The important aspect of this first image is that woodland dominates elevations above 1,500 feet. The site of what was to become Phoenix, at a little more than 1,000 feet above sea level, is covered by scrubland or chaparral-type growth, but at higher elevations woodlands seem to be everywhere. How strange the Santa Catalina foothills near Tucson appear with dominant stands of cypress, fir, and evergreen oaks where today we see saguaros and palo-verde trees. As for most of the mountains above 6,000 feet, their slopes eventually give way to conifer forests, and on the cloud-penetrating peaks, like those of the San Francisco and White mountains, are major expanses of tundra habitats.

In our second image we see the modern distribution of Arizona's vegetational communities as they have appeared for the last eight thou-

Opposite: West Clear Creek, in the Mogollon Rim country.
DAVE FOREMAN.

sand years. Because of the more arid conditions, the zonation of the vegetation is dramatic. Today the valleys between mountains are not joined by lush woodland, except along riverbeds; the arid and summer-hot lowlands are home for cacti and other desert-adapted species. Moving upslope from the valleys to the mountains, the climate becomes cooler and more moist and the types of plants which can become dominant change accordingly. The woodlands are now restricted to elevations above 4,000 feet, the conifers are mostly on the higher mountain slopes above 6,000 feet, and the only tundra left is a 1,200-acre refuge on the very top of the San Francisco Peaks.

Back in the days when woodland habitats filled the valleys between mountain ranges, there were comparatively few natural bar-

riers to prevent forest-dwelling animals from walking or crawling from one end to the other of what is now Arizona. With climate change nine or ten thousand years ago, the plants and animals that were adapted to forest conditions were forced out of the lowlands, which became deserts. These creatures "retreated" up the mountain slopes and survived, or remained in the desert and perished.

Within the mountain islands of Arizona, where several thousands of years of isolation have given time for natural selection and genetic isolation to work their magic, we find many organisms, both plant and animal, that because of shared habitat and common ancestry were once indistinguishable. Now, in the shadow of their long separation, we can see and measure remarkable differences. Some of these organisms have changed so much that they are no longer considered the same species. This means that even if the isolating barriers are overcome, these organisms can no longer interbreed and produce viable offspring. Others are still similar enough in genetic makeup that they can interbreed and produce healthy but morphologically intermediate offspring.

LIFE ON A RESTING VOLCANO

The San Francisco Mountains are the largest and most recently formed of a series of northern Arizona volcanic ranges. Until 1.8 million years ago, the place where these mountains now sit was nothing more than a gently rolling plain. It took a little over 1.5 million years of intermittent activity for this volcano to reach its highest elevation of about 16,000 feet, some 3,000 feet higher than it is today. Now this volcano looks like a truncated cone with a base twelve miles in diameter, rising more than a mile from the plateau. During the erosional periods that caused the decomposition of the top 3,000 feet of the original cone, an interior valley was formed on the north and east side of the mountain. In this inner basin one can find ample evidence of a glacier that formed during cold moist climate more than 50,000 years ago. Once the climate began to warm, it took more than 300 years for the ice mass to melt.

One of the most breathtaking panoramas in all of Arizona can be enjoyed from on top of the San Francisco Peaks. Cross-country skis are a good way to get there between October and mid-May. From the Snow Bowl ski area, a chair-lift affords a spectacular view of the mountain island. On a clear day the one-hundred-mile vista includes scenes from the Grand Canyon, the Navajo and Hopi lands, the Painted Desert, portions of the world's most expansive ponderosa pine forest, and remnants of eons of volcanic activity. From this viewpoint more than two hundred cinder cones are visible, including one of the largest— Sunset Crater—a volcanic vent which was spewing gases and lava bombs as recently as 900 years ago.

Opposite: High grassland with Mt. Wrightson wilderness, southern Arizona in the background.
JACK W. DYKINGA.

Vegetation communities, or life zones, as they were called by biologist C. Hart Merriam, change in a regular pattern with elevation. In the closing years of the 1800s Merriam noted that plant and animal communities were distributed around the San Francisco Peaks like rings or belts, and he saw each of these belts as a special life zone, consistently characterized by a particular group of plants and animals. Although the biological elements were not limited to one zone, there was a definite ring around the mountain where certain plants and animals found optimum living conditions. For example, he saw that the Abert squirrel reached its greatest density in the ponderosa pine forest; together, the squirrel and the pine tree are members of Merriam's Transition Zone.

From the pinyon–juniper forest (or Upper Sonoran Zone) at the base of the Peaks, the vegetation changes upslope to the ponderosa pine (Transition Zone), then to the Douglas-fir (Canadian Zone), followed by the true spruce-fir forests (Hudsonian Zone), and finally the treeless tundra (Alpine Zone). Within each of the three last forest types, the quaking aspen, a tree closely related to the cottonwood and birches, inhabits old burn sites. One of the few deciduous trees able to proliferate on the old volcano, it is the aspen which gives the mountain its brilliant yellows and oranges of autumn.

At the upper edge of the spruce-fir forest, just below the timberline, are some of the oldest trees in existence. Bristlecone pines were full-grown survivors of the cold and wind when the area around Flagstaff was being blanketed by ash from the eruptions of Sunset Crater nine centuries ago. They are remarkable trees; their age and the grotesque shapes they assume near the upper limits of the timberline zone seem almost to symbolize natural power and ancient wisdom. Above the timberline is the tundra or alpine zone, a truly isolated and inhospitable terrestrial environment. This above-timberline vegetative community shows itself nowhere else in Arizona. Mount Baldy on the crest of the White Mountains to the east had tundra thousands of years ago, but with the warming climate of several millennia, the only remnant of Baldy's tundra is a patch or two of alpine grasses. Outside of Arizona the nearest tundra habitats are in the Sangre de Cristo Mountains of New Mexico and the San Juan Mountains of Colorado.

On the Peaks the tundra consists mostly of lichens and the ubiquitous yellow-flowered aven, a low-growing herbaceous member of the rose family which is common to tundra habitats all over the world. Two flowering plants that appear to be endemic to the mountain on the tundra talus slopes above 11,500 feet are the San Francisco Peaks groundsel and the Peaks buttercup. Usually not showing their blooms until the snow and ice are gone in mid-July, they live nowhere else in the world. The Peaks tundra community is impoverished in numbers of plant species in residence. In the Sangre de Cristo Mountains, for example, there are more than two hundred and forty plant species growing above the timberline. In Alaska the number is well over five hundred, but on the Peaks there are fewer than one hundred tundra

An ancient bristlecone pine.
TOM BEAN.

plants. Scientists speculate that as the climate becomes warmer and more arid, the limited tundra on the Peaks will disappear, much as it has on the White Mountains.

Thus far zoologists have found no animals unique to the area. The deer mouse and the dwarf shrew are the only warm-blooded creatures using the tundra habitat on a full-time basis. How the dwarf shrew can eke out a living in the tundra during winter is a mystery. The deer mouse can sleep the winter away, but shrews are too small to hibernate. Consequently, throughout winter, far beneath the ice and jumble of volcanic rocks, this tiny capsule of fur and nervous energy is actively foraging on sleeping grubs and bugs. The water pipit, strangely enough, finds the crest of the mountain suitable for nesting, but by the first September snows, this bird flies south.

There are, however, several larger animals whose existence has been cut short on the mountain in historic times: the wolf, grizzly bear, bighorn sheep, and Merriam's elk have all been hunted into extinction since the turn of the century. Only the elk has been reintroduced. A trainload of similar elk was brought into the Flagstaff area from Yellowstone National Park in 1924. Their populations today are sufficiently healthy to allow an annual harvest by hunters. The grizzly and wolf have no modern constituency pressing for their reintroduction. On the contrary, there is a predominant attitude among humankind that the passing of these animals is a change for the better.

SPECIAL ISLANDS IN THE SONORAN AND MOJAVE DESERTS

The highest peak in western Arizona is found just southeast of Kingman in the Hualapai Mountains. Although it is an area thought to be well within the Mojave Desert, the low country at the base of this relatively small mountain island contains an interesting potpourri of vegetation types. The area is of further interest because the mountaintop is covered with the only stand of ponderosa pine for many miles in any direction. The Hualapai Mountains are located very near the apparent "boundaries" of three large desert ecosystems: Mojave, Sonoran, and Great Basin. The vegetation on the slopes of the Hualapais serves as a prime example of how difficult it sometimes is to categorize natural systems. The rolling plains of the western side of the Hualapais are almost exclusively covered by creosotebush which blends slowly into rather dense stands of Mojave yucca on the lower slopes; these two species typify the vegetation of the Mojave Desert. On the southern and eastern flanks and bajadas, however, we find paloverde trees, an occasional saguaro, scattered cacti and shrubs—all indicators of the Sonoran Desert. Within the steep canyons of the western side of the mountain, saguaros grow in apparent contentment without paloverde. On the northern slopes are chaparral and pinyon-juniper woodlands

Opposite: Inner-basin tundra of the San Francisco Peaks. TOM BEAN.

comprised of species all typical of the Great Basin Desert of northern Arizona and southern Utah lowlands. We soon come to understand that giving the area a regional classification—Mojave, Sonoran, or Great Basin—is inappropriate.

Within this island, we would expect to find some unusual biological treasure. Indeed, the 4,500-acre pine forest hosts a creature found nowhere else in the world: the Hualapai Mountain meadow vole. This is a small, chocolate-brown, beady-eyed rodent and resident of the pine and mixed-conifer forest understory. The Hualapais reach 8,420 feet above sea level, high enough for the temperature and moisture to allow for ponderosa pine, a few Douglas-fir, aspen, and some spruce. The forest of pine and mixed conifer has persisted on the Hualapais since the area was isolated from similar forests in the Great Basin to the north and east. It has been even longer since any of the Sonoran Desert habitats to the south and east contained corridors of woodland and conifer vegetation that would have served as "bridges" for the free passage of smaller land animals. The vole has close cousins living in almost every large forest in the state, but our Hualapai resident cannot get off the mountain, nor can any of the cousins come visiting. The result has been isolation and inbreeding, the key to biological change.

The Hualapai meadow vole has been very little studied, and its future does not look too bright. Clearly it is slipping down the path to extinction. There are two principal reasons why little hope remains for its long-term survival. First, if scientists are correct when they say the climate is still warming and drying, the small pine forest on the mountain will further diminish in size. As the vole's habitat decreases, its population will decrease until that unknown point beyond which it cannot recover.

Second, even if the population should survive climatically imposed habitat depletions, it is unlikely the effects of domestic livestock grazing would leave any cover for the vole, let alone food. Meadow voles and cattle share a preference for moist, grassy meadows. It is under the grassy canopy that the meadow vole builds an intricate network of tiny trail systems. Vegetarians, the voles use the runways as foraging paths and hiding areas to escape predation. Conditions are becoming such in the Hualapai Mountains that fewer and fewer meadows are left for the voles and their covered corridors.

Traveling two hundred miles south and a little east from the Hualapais, we pass many interesting desert mountains—the Harcuvars, Harquahalas, Eagle Tails, Kofas, Palomas, and a dozen others—but our objective is the heart of the Sonoran Desert in Organ Pipe Cactus National Monument. Here we find the Ajo Mountains. An uplifted block of ancient lava approximately ten miles long and three miles wide at its extremes, the Ajos are typical of most of the smaller mountains throughout the Sonoran Desert. They are not quite high enough to support substantial forests; but in steep-walled canyons and on some northern exposures, patches of shrubs and unusual trees cling to a tenuous existence. Ajo Peak at 4,808 feet is too exposed to support much vegetation, but in the narrow and relatively cool canyons nearby there are scattered woodlands consisting of oaks, junipers, and Arizona rosewood. There is not a single dependable flowing spring in the entire range of mountains. The little water available to wildlife and humans comes from the natural tinajas or rock cisterns that await recharging from the area's scanty rainfall.

Unlikely as it seems that the terribly dry environment of this mountain range would host unique plants or animals, the Ajos support at least three endemic organisms—a snake, a flower, and an oak tree. The Ajo whipsnake and the Ajo Mountain evergreen oak can all be found within the same steep-walled canyons in the interior of the range. The flower, a member of the sunflower family, goes by the name Ajo perityle and resembles a score or more of other low-growing, yellow-flowered desert bushes. The highly specialized habitat of the perityle is a moist crack in the lava boulders. As for the whipsnake, its existence would have probably gone unnoticed but for the natural cisterns. The first collectors to encounter this rare snake found ten individuals, "two live specimens and eight carcasses which were in an advanced state of decomposition and unsalvageable"; the snakes were floating in one of the tinajas. Since that first collection, other specimens have been found in similar circumstances. If a trip to the Ajos is planned, one would be wise to take plenty of water; the quality of the tinaja water is unreliable.

SOUTHEASTERN ARIZONA'S MOUNTAIN ARCHIPELAGO

In the southeastern corner of the state, three unusual highland ranges have long been favorite areas for professional and amateur naturalists. The Chiricahua, Huachuca, and Santa Rita mountains are situated within the northwestern extreme of the Chihuahuan Desert. The diverse mixture of wildlife within the valleys, canyons, and mountaintops is unequalled elsewhere in the continental United States. Birdwatchers from all over the world flock to these mountains in hopes of observing the coppery-tailed trogon, blue-throat and white-eared hummingbirds, harlequin quail, buff-breasted and sulphur-bellied flycatchers, and hundreds of other less exotic species.

Although each of these desert ranges has distinct and unique features, their clusterings of mountain islands show more similarities than differences when compared with mountains in other regions of Arizona. The biological communities of the southeastern Arizona mountain "archipelago" have direct affinities with the Mexican highlands to the south. Many species of plants and animals reach their northernmost distributional limits in this corner of Arizona.

One of the first biologists to observe the distinctive and abrupt biotic differences between this area and other desert areas of the Southwest was Harry Swarth. Traveling east across the southern Arizona lowlands from California in the early 1900s, he was amazed at the floral and faunal changes. From the Colorado River at the western boundary of Arizona, across the lowland desert to the base of the Santa Rita Mountains, a distance of more than two hundred miles, Swarth saw little change in the vegetation of the desert. But on the east side of the Santa Ritas was a different world. The yucca-dominated grasslands of the Chihuahuan Desert were an amazing contrast to the spinescent shrubs and cacti of the Sonoran Desert. The naturalist's eye saw that the nearly thirty-mile-long mountain range formed a distinct line of separation between the biotic systems on the east and west sides of the land mass. Swarth was looking at the dividing line between the Sonoran Desert to the west and the Chihuahuan Desert to the east. In a 1927 landmark paper on animals in the Arizona deserts, he wrote that "the Santa Rita Mountains were a convenient line of demarcation, and forming as they do a colossal wall across the plains, they might easily be supposed to be a barrier in fact as they are in appearance." Here Swarth was making the important observation that both the massiveness of the range and the ecological factors related to climate prevented plant and animal life from dispersing much beyond their respective sides of the mountains. Each of these three north-south trending mountain ranges is separated by lowland valleys of desert grassland, and as one might expect, each mountain has unique biotic features.

There are probably few better examples of an endemic mammal than the ochraceous-bellied Apache fox squirrel of the Chiricahua Mountains. It is a tree squirrel, distantly related to the Abert and gray squirrels elsewhere in Arizona, and it is not unlike the eastern fox squirrel. Yet this noisy and tassel-eared inhabitant of the Chiricahua woodlands and pine forest has been separated from its northern cousins for long enough that it is a separate and distinct species. Other outstanding animals in this unique corner of the state include some with names even more colorful than the animal itself. There is the Huachuca Mountain tiger salamander, the black-headed garter snake, the barking and Tarahumara frogs, the green rat snake. And if you search long and hard enough, especially at night, you may see the coatimundi, a relative of the raccoon. This bizarre mammal looks like a cross of an anteater, a dog, and a small bear. In the past jaguars were seen more often, but like the endangered gray wolf (already extinct from these mountain islands), they may be succumbing to the necessity of sharing habitats with gun-toting predators.

Whether or not one encounters a jaguar or a coatimundi on a nighttime foray in these mountains, there should be a constant watch for really dangerous creatures: the twin-spotted, the ridge-nosed, and the rock rattlesnakes. Although these rattlers are far less poisonous and aggressive than some (the fierce Mojave rattler for instance), their bite or strike is almost as terrifying and painful. Their uniqueness should be appreciated from a distance.

Opposite: The Tucson Mountains, a chain of weathered volcanoes in the Sonoran Desert. STEPHEN TRIMBLE.

Right: A coatimundi, or chulo, in its highland habitat. BUD BRISTOW.

FIRE FIGHTING

Between May Day and Labor Day, when he's not substitute teaching, Ed Pfeifer can often be found at 8,300 feet above sea level, sitting on a stool looking out into the Apache-Sitgreaves National Forests. The Clifton District of the combined Forests, about half a million acres, runs forty-two miles north to south and twenty-five east to west. Pfeifer's view from atop the Rose Peak Lookout affords him a view deep into New Mexico's Gila Wilderness to the east, south to Dos Cabezas near Willcox, west to Four Peaks outside of Phoenix, and north to the Mogollon Rim. Pfeifer is a fire watch, one of 16 in the two million acre-plus Forests. He started a series of jobs in the forest in 1958, including director of a Youth Conservation Camp, and since his retirement from teaching high school science in Morenci twenty years later, he's spent four months each year at Rose Peak. His cabin below the tower, where he sleeps during his ten-day lookout shifts, has its radio, television, and lights powered by an experimental Department of Energy photo-voltaic solar generator. Before its installation, Rose Peak fire watches did without electricity.

Some days Pfeifer spends all his time on the twelve feet by twelve feet perch admiring birds. "I've seen ravens, crows, screechowls, and TV's—that's turkey vultures. Yesterday we had a bunch of bobtail pigeons. You see those trees over there?" he asked, motioning to the south. "We have red-tail hawks nesting there every year. The worst birds, though, are the Air Force jets. They're not supposed to fly right over us. When we complained they said they were on course, so we sent them slides with their numbers on them. Now they fly high and wide." He peered into the west, using his locater as a compass, and jotted down some figures in a notebook. "We've got a pet squirrel here named Rosey—she always comes around since we started feeding her, but she's not back yet this year."

"Maybe the hawks got her," guessed Beale Mundy, Clifton's Fire District Manager. Mundy, a New Mexico native, was making his rounds of the fire watches in the towers and the trail crews on the ground. "We have a lot of tools at our disposal," Mundy said. "Every day at one o'clock we get the fire weather forecast, which takes into account dryness, wind, temperature, and humidity. Based on that, a computer in Phoenix gives us a danger rating from one to five. A five means there are high winds and it's very dry."

The trail crew of six men and women living at Stray Horse Fire Camp works May to September, and gets six days off after eight straight work days. Many are forestry students from Northern Arizona University. "We use a wide range of equipment," Mundy said. "We can fly people over a fire in a helicopter or spray fire retardant from an old World War Two bomber." The Forest Service is experimenting with a hand-held infra-red device which can sense hidden embers and hot spots. "New technology will come into play," Mundy acknowledged, "but basically we use the same apparatus we always have—pumper units on the backs of trucks, axes, hoes, shovels—things like that.

"Sometimes we let a fire burn. The old policy was to put them all out. But now we subscribe to the theory that fire plays a more important role in the ecosystem than had originally been thought. We use fire as a tool."

Mundy started to climb down the Rose Peak tower. "I love fire fighting," he said when he reached the bottom. "It's dangerous and exciting. You have to figure how to get your people in, how to get your supplies in, how to attack, and how to get your people out. It's just like the military—without the killing."

TOM MILLER

THE SANTA CATALINA MOUNTAINS: A DESERT PYRAMID

The sharp upthrust range of the Santa Catalina Mountains is the dominant feature on the Tucson landscape. Perched like an ancient pyramid on the desert floor, the mountain range is almost triangular in shape, with its east-west base or front range extending some twenty miles from west Tucson to the Redington Pass area. The south-north axis also reaches twenty miles from the ridge of the front range to the low foothills outside the town of Oracle. Mount Lemmon, the high point, is very much in the center of the range or at the apex of the pyramid. It rises to just over 9,100 feet. The lowest elevations range from 2,500 to 3,500 feet.

The geologic formation of the Santa Catalina Mountains is far more complicated than the simple volcanic origins of some of the state's larger mountain systems. The rocks of the Catalinas are mostly granite and gneiss that were once deep in the earth's crust, either in a partly molten state and later cooled, or changed by great heat and pressure from one type of rock to another. Tectonic processes over millions of years caused the rocks to be uplifted, or to appear to be uplifted, because the valleys dropped down—geologists still debate the point. Finally, eons of subsequent erosion wore away most of the overlying rock, presenting the mountains we see today. The materials eroded from the mountain filled the basin upon which Tucson rests with a deep layer of alluvial deposits.

The vegetation of the Santa Catalina Mountains is remarkable for diversity of both species and habitats. There is evidence that the vegetational features of the Catalinas have arisen from the northern boreal forests as well as the highlands of northern and central Mexico. The greatest diversity of habitats is on the front range of the mountain where the desert base is occupied by a dense forest of saguaro, mixed cacti, and paloverde trees. With increasing elevation this typical desert vegetation intergrades into a unique and lush grassland, through a pine-oak woodland into a montane fir and pine community, and finally, near the summit, into a limited display of subalpine fir forest.

Some of the most interesting Catalina mountain plant communities occupy a climatic zone similar to the ecological unit Merriam called the Upper Sonoran, at the base of the San Francisco Peaks. Throughout the Great Basin habitats the Upper Sonoran zone is dominated by pinyon and juniper trees, with fewer than a half-dozen other tree species ever contributing to the forest diversity. Sharply contrasted with the monotonous character of the equivalent zone elsewhere, the Upper Sonoran of the Santa Catalinas is a profusion of species, colors, life forms, and unusual relics of ages past. Moving upslope from the saguaro-paloverde of the lower foothills, the first of the Upper Sonoran units is the desert grassland. This habitat is usually best remembered by the casual hiker for its splendid ocotillo with miniature scarlet trumpets for flowers, and the not-so-splendid sotol, or shin-dagger. The ankle-to-shin-high plant is simply a dangerous rosette of poison-tipped bay-onets in disguise. Without high-topped boots and thick, long pants, any excursion through this desert grassland can quickly become an agonizing ordeal.

Above the grassland is the chaparral, made up of densely impen-etrable shrub thickets of perhaps more than twenty species, all of sim-ilar height. Upslope, the chaparral yields to the woodlands with a profusion of evergreen oaks, Mexican pinyon, alligator and one-seed juniper, Arizona cypress, Apache and Chihuahua pines, and an occa-sional Arizona rosewood. The hour's drive from Tucson to Mount Lemmon provides a fascinating view of these successive vegetation types. It is especially rewarding in the summer when the temperature contrast between desert and mountain is so dramatic.

One of the most interesting and rare plants found within moist

Two views in the Santa Catalina Mountains, north of Tucson. Left: Bridalveil Falls. Opposite: A stand of oaks in the Cañada del·Oro.
JACK W. DYKINGA.

and shaded areas of the chaparral in the Catalina and Baboquivari mountains is the Davis manihot. Officially recognized as endangered by the U. S. Fish and Wildlife Service, this plant seems out of place in the Sonoran Desert mountains. From its tropical relatives in Brazil are derived cerea rubber and tapioca.

The manihot is just one example of unique floral and faunal elements in the Santa Catalinas which owe their individuality to the relatively isolated mountain island character of the range. The Arizona cypress tree, also found in limited numbers in other mountain ranges throughout the state, is well represented on cool, north-facing drainages of the Catalinas. This unique species is a relic of a forest type that covered huge expanses of North America several million years ago. Long before the last major climatic shift of 9,000 years ago began to dry up the woodlands, the cypress had begun its decline. Although there are still pockets of habitat suitable for the cypress in many moun-

tainous areas of western North America, all are clearly diminishing. One of the larger remaining forests of this tree is on the north slopes of Bear Canyon in the Catalina Mountains.

The beardtongue or penstemon, whose flowers are blood-red tubes of nectar for hummingbirds, is a species illustrating the mountain island principle of limited distribution. It was found and described in 1915 by Forrest Shreve, pioneer ecologist, in Bear Canyon forest. The plant, now named an endangered species, alerts us to the fragility of its tiny habitat in Bear Canyon.

BIGHORN SHEEP

Populations of animals restricted to small areas can also often face tough living conditions over the long term. Such is the case with the small herd of desert bighorn sheep living within the Pusch Ridge Wilderness Area, a 57,000-acre preserve within the Coronado National Forest at the western scarp of the Catalina Mountains. A wilderness area was established by an act of Congress in 1978 explicitly to protect the area's declining desert bighorn sheep population.

Throughout the mountains of the Southwest, bighorn herds have been on the decline for many years, and the population within the Catalinas is no exception. Once thought to be the largest and healthiest herd in the state (220 animals in 1930), the Catalina herd had dwindled by 1983 to fewer than sixty animals. A variety of factors has led to the decline in regional bighorn populations and, as in the case of the Catalinas, most of these factors relate to the expanding human populations in the valleys below the bighorn haunts.

In years past, the Pusch Ridge bighorn sheep herd had a far greater range than at present. Today the entire herd is limited to ten to fifteen square miles of country on the western slope of the mountains in the immediate vicinity of Pusch Ridge and Alamo Canyon. Prior to the expansive human settlement of the region, the bighorn ranged freely throughout the local mountain archipelago. Breeding rams would typically extend their searches for available ewes from the Catalinas to the Rincon, Santa Rita, Tucson, and Silver Bell mountains. Each of these mountain systems once had its own resident bighorn population; now sheep sightings in this part of Arizona outside the Pusch Ridge area are exceedingly rare. Busy highway corridors and residential areas restrict the movement of the bighorn into other ranges. Housing and recreational needs of the human population continue to encroach on the last bighorn refuge. Moreover, many of the areas within the Catalinas that have been abandoned by the sheep in historical times have become unsuitable habitat for the animals because of dense growth of chaparral, and in the absence of natural fires, the grassland areas preferred by the bighorn have become overgrown and are of no food value to the sheep.

Opposite: Finger Rock, in the Santa Catalina Mountains, after a winter storm. JACK W. DYKINGA.

A particular problem is the large number of hikers exploring the sheep's habitat at the time of year when the ewes are giving birth. Pima Canyon, on the east side of Pusch Ridge, is the most popular hiking area on the entire mountain. In 1981 more than twenty-five thousand people penetrated the back country of Pima Canyon. Unfortunately, the best season for hikers is February through April, during the critical lambing period. The hikers' unleashed dogs could very well be an important factor contributing to the sheep's decline. If a dog chases or in any way disturbs a ewe with a new baby, the youngster is immediately abandoned. Keeping dogs either leashed or out of the area during lambing periods would be a positive first step in forestalling further decline in the herd. Researchers are now exploring the possibility of other protective measures for the bighorn and its habitat, such as a possible moratorium on the annual hunt which still takes a single ram from the herd. There is also interest in controlled burning to restore grazing habitat, and positive responses from local land developers in sharing the responsibility for bighorn needs.

Opposite: Desert bighorn rams at the Arizona-Sonora Desert Museum, west of Tucson. TOM BEAN.

Right: Maple leaves in autumn color, Santa Catalina Mountains. JACK W. DYKINGA.

We have only sampled the mountain islands found within Arizona's geographical boundaries. Within most of the other large ranges—the Peloncillos, Mohawks, Superstitions, Mazatzals, Sierra Anchas, Lukachukais, and Chuskas—special biological features persist. In remote areas of the northwestern part of the state, it is still possible to climb pinnacles where few humans have ever set foot. Some of these awe-inspiring, steep-cliffed sky islands, in and to the north of the Grand Canyon, will always beckon the serious naturalist. We can only wonder at the undiscovered and undescribed species and unique life forms that await these explorers. Much of the rugged land of the Arizona back country has yet to be fully investigated. Most of the larger plants and animals are surely known, but still there are smaller forms—the aquatic and terrestrial insects, the primitive plants, the world of fungi and microorganisms. We can hope and believe that there will always be mysteries in the mountain islands where isolation and inbreeding define the cycle of living and dying, and where the new appear as the old depart.

THE COLORADO PLATEAU

Arizona should have been named Colorado. No other state drains exclusively to the Colorado River. And it is the river that gives its name to northern Arizona's rocky sweep of canyons and mesas climaxing at the Grand Canyon.

Pioneer geologist Clarence Dutton described this land in 1880 as "the extreme of desolation, the blankest solitude, a superlative desert." It remains all of these—a place for solitude, a place of extremes and superlatives.

The Colorado Plateau is a major continental division, on a par with the Rocky Mountains and the Great Plains. It covers the Four Corners states in the shape of a heart turned sideways. The point of the heart lies in western Arizona where the Colorado River leaves the Grand Canyon. The upper lobe swings northward to Dinosaur National Monument on the Utah-Colorado border. And the lower lobe reaches almost to Albuquerque, New Mexico. The cleavage dips westward in Colorado around the San Juan Mountains near Mesa Verde—properly sacred country for the axis of a heart.

Plants define some regions of Arizona—the saguaro and cre-osotebush and Joshua trees of the Sonoran and Mojave deserts, for example. But rocks define the Colorado Plateau. Indeed, when John Wesley Powell and his cohorts set about mapping and naming this region in the 1870s and 1880s, for namesakes they chose the river and flat-lying rocks, "Colorado" and "Plateau."

The Colorado River and its tributaries have dissected a great stack of nearly horizontal sedimentary rocks here, creating a series of alternating mesas and canyons, maddening to anyone bent on line-of-compass travel. Plateaus higher than their neighbors give the land its first-order ups and downs. Upwarps and monoclines briefly upset the flat lie of the formations. Here and there, volcanic mountains stand as islands, sheltering fir trees and mountain wildlife, even alpine tundra.

But most of the plateau is high, sparsely-vegetated, flat and rocky. It divides neatly into six sections, one of which—the Uinta Basin—lies far north of Arizona in Utah and Colorado. A second, the volcanic Datil Section, sneaks into Arizona from New Mexico only at the White Mountains. The other four all meet at Lees Ferry.

Above left: Piñon nuts.
STEPHEN TRIMBLE.

Opposite: Lees Ferry, in Glen Canyon National Recreation Area. TOM BEAN.

LEES FERRY

Northern Arizona has its natural and spiritual beginning at Lees Ferry on the Colorado River.

Though the Colorado enters the state some thirty miles upstream, it does not become an Arizona river until Lees Ferry. Here, the High Plateaus and the Canyon Lands, the two "mostly-Utah" sections of the Plateau end. And the two "mostly-Arizona" sections, Navajo Country and the Grand Canyon, begin.

John D. Lee, legendary Mormon pioneer, first began operating the ferry here in 1871, using one of John Wesley Powell's abandoned boats. Until 1929, when Navajo Bridge over Marble Canyon opened, the ferry was the only wagon and auto route across the Colorado from Utah to the Grand Wash Cliffs nearly three hundred miles westward. From the time of the Spanish, as Frank Waters put it in *The Colorado*, the crossing was "42nd and Broadway" for the Colorado River basin.

Geographically, just as much goes on here.

Above Lees Ferry lie the last 15.5 miles of Glen Canyon—southernmost of the Canyon Lands. "Last" here means both "termination" and "sole survivor." For beyond these few miles of remaining canyon

lies Glen Canyon Dam, which floods Glen Canyon upstream for 180 miles. Glen was the loveliest of the slickrock canyons, the only major gorge on the Colorado without rapids, and protector of the most remarkable cathedral-like side canyons. Lake Powell covers all of Glen Canyon now except for the last few curves of river between the dam and Lees Ferry.

The Grand Canyon officially begins below Lees Ferry. A change in rock formations punctuates the boundary precisely. Rocks of Navajo Country and Canyon Lands, including the unmistakable golden Navajo Sandstone, end along the river at Lees Ferry. Older rocks of the Grand Canyon replace them, beginning with the Kaibab Limestone.

Opposite: Padre Bay, Lake Powell.
JAMES TALLON.

Right: The Vermilion Cliffs, running along Arizona's boundary with Utah.
TOM WEISKOTTEN.

REMARKABLE ART

The San Francisco volcanic field lies on the western edge of the Painted Desert in the Colorado River Basin. Among its 273 identifiable craters is Roden Crater, named for a man who owned the land before the turn of the century. When he first saw it from the air in 1974, artist Jim Turrell thought its red and black cinder coloring "looked like a two-tone '55 Chevy." He had spent most of a year piloting a small plane over the Rockies and the Pacific coast from Canada to Mexico, looking for a natural landform to mold into a project combining dimensions of light, space, and sky. Some forty miles north of Flagstaff, just off the Navajo Indian Reservation, he found it.

Turrell's international reputation made him an unlikely candidate for life in Coconino County. A native of Los Angeles, Turrell has exhibited at major museums throughout the United States and Europe. His art, however, bypasses conventional mediums and dwells on perception. He deals in the illusion of light, and makes light of illusion. By placing movable walls and wall-sized frames in strategic spots around a large room, Turrell has shown that light plays tricks with the eye and the brain, compelling the viewer to reexamine at once his own vision. This fascination with distance and light has led to his most ambitious project yet: to carve out portions of the interior of the 600-foot-tall crater so that sun, star, and moonlight enter a series of chambers in the interior of the half-million-year-old dormant volcano. The chambers and the opening which allows light to enter them are designed with utmost precision so that optimum advantage can be taken of the light of the celestial bodies as they arc through the heavens. After walking into the volcano through a fumerole—a side vent—you will find yourself entering a succession of open rooms ending with a gently rising tunnel, slightly longer than the length of three football fields, which opens into one last chamber inside the crater bowl. The incline of the tunnel compels you to look to its opening inside the crater from a perspective which swoops your vision skyward.

What had seemed to be an opening at the tunnel's end turns out to be merely an opening in the ceiling of that last chamber, and the sky appears as a thin, flat, translucent skin. Twelve marble stairs lead from the chamber into the crater bowl itself, where you will emerge inside "as if you are walking into the sky," Turrell says. "You will see space filled with light. The physical tangible qualities of light will be present."

This devotion to manipulating natural light consumes and amuses Turrell. "My work deals with light itself," he told an interviewer. "It's not the bearer of the revelation—it *is* the revelation."

Turrell's grandiose project is carried out in stages, when equipment—such as an army-surplus "mole," a machine used to burrow through the volcano's wall—and money—many foundations have contributed toward the expected $5.7 million price tag—are available. Project blueprints themselves are intriguing, and Turrell has already exhibited sketches and schematic diagrams in museums. He maintains an almost daily written and photographic diary of the Roden Crater project's development. The Griffith Observatory in Los Angeles and the U.S. Naval Observatory in Flagstaff have helped with astronomical calculations necessary to determine when light will enter the tunnel and at what angle. It is the blend of the most modern sciences with ancient sky worship—and years of physical labor—which give Turrell the aura of a twenty-first-century renaissance man. He cites Old Sarum in England and the Jai Singh non-telescopic observatory in India as historical precedents for his creation.

When completed—Turrell estimates the beginning of the 1990s—the project will be opened to the public for visits, with strict limitations on the number of people on the site at one time. Although some 240,000 cubic yards of dirt will be moved to create Turrell's art, from the outside the volcano will appear virtually untouched.

TOM MILLER

JAMES TURRELL

With this simple change in rock layers come transformations in scenery, topography, color, fossils, erosional character, and even the plants capable of growth.

River runners begin their trip through the Grand Canyon at Lees Ferry. They ride on what one of Powell's boatmen called "the back of the Dragon," watching the waters of the Colorado cut down into older and older rocks, until they reach some of the oldest rocks exposed in North America. The Grand Canyon Section takes in not only the great chasm but the plateaus which edge its rims on the north and south as well. Still higher plateaus step northward into Utah in the "Grand Staircase," climaxing at Bryce and Zion national parks.

The Paria River flows out through the last of the High Plateaus to meet the Colorado at Lees Ferry. It passes through an enormous red wall, the Vermilion Cliffs, first step in the Grand Staircase. Here political boundaries, prone to slice through lakes and mountain ranges, ignoring natural divisions, almost correspond with real landscapes. The natural boundary of Arizona follows the Vermilion Cliffs, which retreat a few miles into Utah for most of their length.

East of Lees Ferry the physical boundary between Arizona and Utah also curves a few miles north of the straight line on the highway map. The southern boundary of the Canyon Lands Section follows the Colorado River into Utah, heading eastward up the San Juan River. The dividing line between the Canyon Lands and Navajo Country to the south is hazy. Deep canyons give way southward to more shallow ones. Abrupt mesas give way to broad plains and easier travel.

At Lees Ferry the Navajo Country begins dramatically with one of the major bends in plateau rocks, the Echo Cliffs Monocline. Facing head-on into the equally spectacular Vermilion Cliffs, the Echo Cliffs feel architectural, a continuous escarpment that disappears around an imaginary corner to the southeast. They begin a great arc that forms a backdrop for the Painted Desert, an arc finished by mesas along the Little Colorado River. Within this arc lies Navajo Country, stretching far eastward into New Mexico and Colorado.

First to describe the country around Lees Ferry, Fray Silvestre Vélez de Escalante passed through with his companions on October 26, 1776. Retreating from an attempt to reach California overland from Santa Fe, the Spaniards were struggling eastward toward home. Escalante summed up the network of cliffs and canyons: "It has an agreeably confused appearance."

Remember this agreeably confusing view from Lees Ferry, for we will return here before we leave the Arizona plateau. Face downstream with the Colorado River, swirling along in cold green currents fresh from the bottom of Lake Powell, trapped in its gorge and headed for the depths of the Grand Canyon. Behind lie the Canyon Lands of Utah, ending at Glen Canyon. To your right the High Plateaus stairstep northward. Off to the left, hidden by the Echo Cliffs, lies Navajo Country—Petrified Forest, Monument Valley, Canyon de Chelly, and the little-known land in between.

NAVAJO COUNTRY

In *Death Comes for the Archbishop*, Willa Cather's Father Latour leaves the Little Colorado for the 400-mile ride back to Santa Fe. Her description of Navajo Country through which he journeyed remains unsurpassed.

> ...there was so much sky, more than at sea, more than anywhere else in the world. The plain was there, under one's feet, but what one saw when one looked about was that brilliant blue world of stinging air and moving cloud.... Elsewhere the sky is the roof of the world; but here the earth was the floor of the sky.

To understand such a place requires attention. Simple, yet subtle; open, yet packed with stacks of geological data; even in its more spectacular stretches, like the Painted Desert, the land never rises high enough to dominate the "world of stinging air and moving cloud." It is no accident that the Navajo set Mother Earth and Father Sky side by side.

In summer, thunderclouds sail across the vibrant blue, casting moving pools of black shadow on red earth. Receding curtains of rain form a wall you drive toward but never seem to reach, a mirage of mountains edging the plain. In winter, snowbanks sparkle like piles of rhinestones in the dazzle of early morning until the sun cuts through clear air, melting the icy jewels, leaving only soggy earth.

To feel the lay of this land, plant yourself in its center, atop the great flat summit of Black Mesa. Southward, washes drain past the ancient Hopi villages through the Hopi Buttes to the Painted Desert and Little Colorado Valley. Clockwise from southwest to northeast the earth drops onto other broad mesas: the Moenkopi, Kaibito, Rainbow, and Shonto plateaus and Tsegi Mesas.

On the north edge of Navajo Country, deep canyons lead down through plateaus to the Colorado and San Juan rivers. These canyons carve a maze around the mysterious sacred dome of Navajo Mountain on the Utah line. They make it one of the most difficult-to-reach places on the Colorado Plateau—the perfect setting for both good guys and bad guys to hide out, in cliffhanging novels from Zane Grey to Tony Hillerman.

Eastward, Chinle Wash and the Pueblo Colorado Valley form a continuous lowland separating Black Mesa from the Defiance Plateau/ Chuska-Lukachukai-Carrizo mountain highlands. This latter series of high landmarks along the Arizona border isolates New Mexico's part of Navajo Country, the San Juan Basin—another case in which Arizona's natural landscape closely matches it political boundaries.

This is the rough shape of the land. How it got that way, what it is made from, and what each of its rock layers has to tell us about time will suffice to keep generations of geologists engrossed.

Rocks from the Age of Dinosaurs cover the surface of all of

Opposite: Paria Canyon, named after the Paiute words meaning "place where the elk drink."
JACK W. DYKINGA.

Navajo Country. Because canyons have not deeply carved into this land, and faults have not broken it into numerous blocks, rock formations remain at the same level over enormous areas. Only a few exceptions interrupt this tableland of "middle-aged" rocks.

The exceptions are big ones, though. From Black Mesa southeastward to St. Johns lie vast lake deposits, the Bidahochi Formation of Pliocene age—just 4 to 8 million years old, much younger than any of the surrounding rocks. Under Black Mesa, old rocks dip deep below the earth's surface in a great basin. Rocks can stack deeper here than elsewhere in the Navajo Country, and they therefore expose younger rocks at the surface. Black Mesa thus stands as an island of Cretaceous rocks (youngest of the Mesozoic periods) in a sea of older layers.

The opposite has occurred in two other places, where upwarps have brought older rocks to the surface. Erosion has breached their summits, exposing layers from the preceding Paleozoic Era. The De Chelly Sandstone is the most conspicuous of these, visible in the Defiance Upwarp at Canyon de Chelly itself, and in the spires of Monument Valley in the Monument Upwarp.

"De Chelly" is a good name for these great canyons and spires. Spaniards coined the words in trying to pronounce in Castilian the Navajo *tsegi*—rock canyon. No single word carries more of the essence of the Colorado Plateau.

The names of rock layers may seem foreign at first, but their sequence rings out like a chant. Each has its distinctive personality, each a unique relationship to its neighbors.

Start at the bottom, where the Mesozoic layers begin. Moenkopi, Chinle, Glen Canyon Group (Wingate, Moenave, Kayenta, Navajo), San Rafael Group, Morrison. Then the Cretaceous layers of Black Mesa: Dakota, Mancos, and the Mesa Verde Group. These names—and the rocks they represent—document 165 million years of earth history, from 230 to 65 million years ago.

The journey through the Age of Dinosaurs begins with the red siltstone of the Moenkopi, its ripple marks, formed by currents in shallow sunlit waters washing over ancient mudflats of Moenkopi streams and ocean shoals. Tracks made by a primitive reptile called *Chirotherium* can be spotted most easily in the masonry fireplace of the old lodge at Cameron Trading Post!

Above the Moenkopi lies the Chinle Formation, one of northern Arizona's real treasures. The lowest layer in the Chinle contains riches in the form of numerous pockets of uranium. Younger Chinle rock erodes in colorful badlands that form scenic treasures—today's Painted Desert and Petrified Forest. Throughout, the Chinle yields fossils about 200 million years old, from the concentration of kaleidoscopic rock logs at Petrified Forest National Park to many vertebrate bones, including the earliest dinosaurs known on the Colorado Plateau.

This landscape of scarlet and gray-blue Chinle badlands destroys preconceptions about just how fast time passes. The summer sun sizzles your composure. Waiting for the cool of evening, time creeps by.

Fragments from an incomprehensibly ancient world erode from the Chinle hills to complicate your understanding of present and past.

Agatized trees litter the ground, most carried here by ancient rivers big enough to treat 200-foot logs like twigs. Less obvious are bits of bone from the Chinle animals: oval plates from armored reptiles; heavy bones from the lumbering, mammal-like reptile *Placerias*; long-snouted, toothy skulls of crocodile-like phytosaurs; and the light bones of the graceful dinosaur *Coelophysis*. Already, dinosaurs were sophisticated animals. *Coelophysis* was an agile six-foot predator that hunted quick-as-a-bird through the forests, and may indeed have been warm-blooded.

The Chinle becomes an old, instantly recognizable friend. Near Cameron, Petrified Forest, St. Johns, and its namesake town of Chinle, unmistakable Chinle Formation badlands turn up in colorful, sculptural whimsy. The next set of formations upward—the Glen Canyon Group—bridges the Triassic and Jurassic; these layers build landscapes just as forthright as the Chinle and quickly become just as recognizable.

Most of the Glen Canyon Group (the Wingate, Moenave, and Navajo sandstones) record times when desert sand seas covered northern Arizona—poor environments for fossilization. Today, these imposing cross-bedded sandstones mark the landscape with archetype "slickrock." The dusky red Wingate erodes in sheer columnar cliffs, the tan Navajo in monumental domes of bare stone. Navajo Sandstone is a key layer in deciphering the roadside stack of plateau rocks. Watch for it at the summit of the Echo Cliffs, in the "shark's-teeth" of Comb Ridge near Kayenta, and in smooth whalebacks along lower Chinle Wash.

Flash floods headed north out of Arizona toward Glen Canyon carve Navajo Sandstone into magical "slots." At the bottoms of these canyons in the Rainbow Plateau the searing desert sun finally mellows. It penetrates between narrow, fluted walls to the cool, lowermost recesses. Here, distilled through reflections of orange stone and lavender desert varnish, the light is unique.

The Kayenta Formation of the Glen Canyon Group breaks up the sequence of fossil-poor desert deposits. Again, we have a chance to trace life. Back from the rim of the Painted Desert on the Moenkopi Plateau, ledges of stream-deposited Kayenta have yielded one of the earliest plant-eating dinosaurs yet discovered. Museum of Northern Arizona paleontologists screening dirt from likely sites in the Kayenta have discovered tiny teeth from the earliest-known mammals in the western hemisphere.

The five formations of the San Rafael Group top the broad surfaces of the Kaibito and Moenkopi plateaus. Slicing into the latter, southeast of Tuba City (a village named for a Hopi headman, not a sousaphone), Coal Mine Canyon's San Rafael yellows and reds form a landscape of cliffs, spires, and badlands to rival any of the more famous plateau canyons.

The uppermost of northern Arizona's Jurassic layers is the Morrison, which gives us one of our primary images of the past, the time

of the giant dinosaurs. The Morrison landscape some 150 million years ago included lumbering sauropods like *Brontosaurus, Stegosaurus* with a twin row of plates along its back, and great predators like *Allosaurus.* Though the best Morrison fossils come from elsewhere, including the little Colorado town of Morrison which gives the formation its name, large dinosaur bones also have come to light in Arizona.

Pick up the chant again with the Cretaceous rocks of Black Mesa. The soft gray shales of the Mancos record the last time the ocean covered the plateau. Using the sequence of fossil clams, oysters, and squid-like ammonites, paleontologists can date the lower, older Mancos beds to within 100,000 years—incredibly precise measurements for events of 90 million years ago!

The Mesa Verde Group caps Black Mesa. Deposited on the edge of the retreating Mancos sea, these swamp deposits contain coal. The Navajo and Hopi tribes have leased rights to this coal, and great draglines now scoop it from Mesa Verde beds at the rate of twelve million

Above: Canyon de Chelly (pronounced "Shay"), long a home to Navajo herders. STEPHEN TRIMBLE.

Opposite: The Chinle Hills, in the Painted Desert, seen from the air. COLLIER/CONDIT.

tons each year. A railroad and slurry pipeline carry it to Page, where the Navajo Power Plant turns Black Mesa coal into electricity.

South of Black Mesa, dark volcanic necks and mesas capped by lava flows form the Hopi Buttes, blunt landmarks visible north of Interstate 40 near Winslow and Holbrook. Nearly two hundred small volcanoes erupted here in Pliocene time, when Lake Bidahochi covered the area. The volcanic remnants now rest on Bidahochi Formation plains. These black prominences seem stern, even ominous, rising above what novelist Thomas Wolfe called, in *A Western Journal*, the "demented reds" of the Painted Desert.

Molten rock rising through the flat sedimentary rocks of Arizona's plateau landscapes has created a giant spiderweb of cooled lava that ties together far-flung mesas and mountains. Even the most impressive volcanic monuments of the Navajo Country, such as 1,000-foot Agathla in Monument Valley, are dwarfed by the evidence of eruptions to the south, across the Little Colorado.

Above: A dinosaur track in the sandstone of the Colorado Plateau.
MICHAEL COLLIER.

Left: Ponderosa pine cone. TOM BEAN.

Opposite: A pinyon jay.
STEPHEN TRIMBLE.

THE LITTLE COLORADO

The Little Colorado River begins near Springerville, on the lee side of the Mogollon Rim, where the Colorado Plateau ends above central Arizona chaparral country. In its journey to the Grand Canyon, it collects water from points as distant as Black Mesa above Kayenta and the San Francisco Peaks at Flagstaff.

The river symbolizes the paradox of water on the plateau. It is a major tributary of the Colorado and shaper of a gorge of its own in its lower reaches. Yet the Little Colorado remains dry for most of its length most of the year.

Water comes to this land unpredictably and in meager rations. Some ecologists include part of the Colorado Plateau in the North American deserts, either as a southern extension of the Great Basin Desert, or a separate desert in its own right, the "Painted Desert." Others call the plateau "steppe," letting its primary title remain physiographic. Either way, this is dry country.

Plants grow here where available moisture allows survival. With increasing elevation, moisture increases, allowing desert shrubs to give way to grassland to woodland to forest. These bands of vegetation—from Mojave Desert at the bottom of Grand Canyon to San Francisco

Peaks tundra—gave C. Hart Merriam a perfect demonstration of life zones in 1889.

Above 7,000 feet, ponderosa pine forest begins, on island mountains, the highest mesas, and in a continuous stand along the Mogollon Rim for more than two hundred miles from Williams to the White Mountains. On the White, Chuska, and San Francisco mountains, and on the Kaibab Plateau, ponderosas yield upward to subalpine forest. Below the ponderosas, pinyon-juniper woodland, grassland, and desert shrubs dot the land in a pattern controlled by water availability and underlying rock formation.

The wall of the Mogollon Rim itself stands just 100 feet high in its beginnings north of Prescott. Between Payson and Show Low it rears 2,000 feet over the Tonto Basin, averaging about 8,000 feet above sea level. Formed by erosion at least 15 million years ago, regional uplift and faulting later increased its relief.

A fine view of the Rim opens before you on the drive north from Phoenix on Interstate 17. On the steep grade that drops into the Verde Valley, you look across to the Rim, with Sedona's Red Rock Country carved from its foundations. Its summit is eerily flat—the textbook definition of the Colorado Plateau made visible. On the plateau behind the Rim rest the San Francisco Peaks in elegant silhouette. All of northern Arizona seems to fall away from the Peaks; their sacredness to Hopi and Navajo is easily understood.

The interstate climbs gradually up the Rim on a natural ramp, for a great basalt flow cascaded down toward the Verde here. Younger volcanics sit atop the Rim at its eastern end in Arizona, forming the White Mountains. This huge concentration of flows and cinder cones climaxes at 11,590-foot Mount Baldy, where volcanic rocks have piled 4,000 feet thick.

Volcanic rocks also stretch from Seligman to east of Flagstaff. Flows get younger with each mile eastward. The great mountains rising from these coalescing rivers of basalt also range in age from older, westernmost Bill Williams Mountain (4 million years), to Sitgreaves Mountain (2.5 million years), Kendrick Peak (less than 2 million), and the San Francisco Peaks (which erupted from 2.8 million to 200,000 years ago).

These higher mountains formed from sheets of thick lava layered with volcanic ash, gradually building "stratovolcanos" much like Mount St. Helens. And like the latter, the San Francisco Peaks volcano transformed itself in a great eruption some 500,000 years ago. The classic 15,000-foot "Fujiyama of Arizona" collapsed, its east side blown out. Ice Age glaciers subsequently steepened the semicircle of remnant summits, to leave Humphreys Peak at 12,633 feet the highest point in Arizona.

Four hundred cinder cones surround the San Francisco Peaks; Sunset Crater erupted fewer than a thousand years ago. The area is clearly active still, and one day a new cinder cone may form in someone's backyard in the eastern suburbs of Flagstaff!

Ponderosa pine and lupine on Mt. Lemmon near Tucson.
JACK W. DYKINGA.

These volcanic fields—the Whites and the Seligman-to-Flagstaff flows—link the two ends of continuous ponderosa pine forest and make the Mogollon Rim even more conspicuous. Moving north from the Rim means leaving black basalt and cinders for red sandstone and purple shale, dropping down from ponderosas, and reentering the deserts and woodlands.

Start at the Mogollon Rim and follow the Little Colorado or one of its tributary creeks. Along the Rim grow the open forests of ponderosa pine, described by Willa Cather in *The Song of the Lark*: "...the great pines stand at a considerable distance from each other. Each tree grows alone, murmurs alone, thinks alone. They do not intrude upon each other."

Frequent light fires kept the ponderosa forest open before pioneers began to suppress fires and log the biggest old-growth trees. Today, ponderosas yield the Southwest's most important commercial timber, while Gambel oaks interspersed between them fuel woodstoves through long Flagstaff winters.

Northern Arizona receives half its annual precipitation from winter storm fronts and half from summer "monsoon" thundershowers. Higher plateaus and mountains receive most of this moisture in both seasons. In winter the Mogollon Rim casts a "rain shadow" northward, accentuating the aridity of the central Little Colorado Valley. Summer afternoon thundershowers depend on convection currents which intensify over the mountains. Thus rainfall drops off sharply with each mile outward from a peak or mesa.

In Fort Valley (about 7,300 feet in altitude), at the foot of the San Francisco Peaks, almost 23 inches of moisture fall yearly. A few miles farther out from the Peaks at Flagstaff, the total drops off to 19 inches, and by the time you reach Walnut Canyon National Monument—just 700 feet lower than Fort Valley—precipitation has fallen to 17.5 inches and ponderosas are giving way to pinyon and juniper. Fifty miles east of the Peaks, Winslow (about 4,900 feet) makes do with just over 7 inches annually.

On mesas behind the Mogollon Rim—and on higher plateaus of the Navajo Country—pinyon and juniper grow in soil too dry for ponderosas and too rocky for grassland. These trees are the true masters of the plateau landscape. They often grow from cracks in bare rock, which provides them with an extra measure of moisture when rains come and runoff funnels down their cracks to thirsty roots.

One astounding story about these elfin trees revolves around pinyon jays. These members of the crow family move through pinyon groves in raucous flocks, decimating the cone crop and caching pinyon nuts in ground litter in their traditional nesting areas.

Pinyon jays store vast numbers of seeds in the fall, living off them in the spring nesting season, when other food is scarce. The pine, in turn, relies on the jays for reproduction, since its heavy wingless seeds have evolved to attract jays, not to be dispersed on the wind. Jays never harvest all their caches, and those forgotten sprout and replenish the jay's "orchards" of pinyon pines as well as the gene pool of the trees.

Other jays also harvest and cache pinyon seeds. A flock of 150 Clark's nutcrackers near Flagstaff stored a ton of pinyon nuts during a single fall harvest. Nutcrackers have a special pouch under their tongues for transporting seeds and can carry up to ninety-five nuts on each trip, flying as far as thirteen miles to the cache site. As Ronald Lanner puts it in *The Piñon Pine*: ".... piñons were invented by jays. The jays still hold the patent—and continue to collect most of the royalties."

Below the wooded mesas, Great Plains grasses, such as blue grama, mix with Great Basin species such as galleta to cover the vast plains of the "floor of the sky." Most short-grass prairie receives from

Opposite: Buck mule deer at the North Rim of the Grand Canyon. TOM BEAN.

10 to 15 inches of annual precipitation. Northern Arizona grasslands fall at the low end of this range or below it, making them very fragile indeed.

These are bunchgrasses, not sod-formers like the tall prairie grasses that once covered the Midwest. Overgrazing and disturbance have drastically decreased the area of grassland on the plateau, and desert shrubs have taken over much old prairie, particularly in sandy soils. Junipers, too, move into grassland on thin rocky soils when grasses weaken.

Valleys and plains of the plateau see a delicate interplay between grassland and desert, water and drought, grazing and fire. Shadscale and saltbush deserts fill not only the lower basin of the Little Colorado but lower Chinle Wash. These plants tolerate long, cold winters and rainfall of only from 5 to 8 inches yearly. They took over just 5,000 to 12,000 years ago, as the cool Ice Age climate disappeared in a warm and dry period.

By the time Spanish and American explorers began to write about this country, livestock introduced to Indians by the former had grazed the plateau for centuries. Even so, cattle and sheep ranchers who came to Arizona in the late 1800s found plateau grasslands still lush.

In the late 1880s, the number of cattle and sheep on Little Colorado ranges reached a maximum of 1.5 million head. Then the summer rains failed. Drought continued from 1891 to 1894, and stock ate the range bare. When rains returned, erosion wreaked havoc with the denuded plains. Deep-rooted shrubs invaded former grassland.

Changing fire regimes now favor root-sprouting shrubs and Eurasian cheatgrass. Today, native prairie grasses have to struggle for water and space with tough shrubs like snakeweed.

The Little Colorado itself once ran along a broad, densely grassed floodplain, with groves of cottonwoods and many beaver dams. Floods spread up to a mile wide over this lush bottomland. But when Mormon farmers came to the Little Colorado in the 1870s, they cleared this rich land and dammed the river for irrigation water.

Suddenly, remaining floodplain vegetation was cut off from the perennial flow of the river. Beaver were trapped out or gave up and moved on. Dams washed out in spring runoff and summer monsoons, sending violent floods downstream, gullying the channel. As undrained standing water on the old floodplain evaporated, salts built up. Today, only such salt-tolerant plants as greasewood and saltgrass grow where once marshes and prairie grass flourished. Stark dead cottonwoods look like illustrations for *A Night on Bald Mountain*.

Some tributaries still support rich riparian woodlands. Streams draining south off the Mogollon Rim are well known—Oak Creek, Beaver Creek, Sycamore Canyon. But such canyons as Chevelon Creek and East Clear Creek running north to the Little Colorado also protect ribbons of cottonwoods, box elder, Arizona walnut, and velvet ash.

Like the vegetation, wildlife has suffered from the arrival of humans on the plateau. Pronghorn, once widespread in the grassland, are rare. On the Navajo Reservation, mule deer are scarce, even with restocking. Desert bighorn now survive only along the Colorado River in Grand Canyon, and wolves and grizzlies are extinct.

When Aldo Leopold worked as a forest ranger in the White Mountains in the early 1900s, he saw the last grizzly brought down from Escudilla Mountain, changing forever the feel of the land: "Escudilla still hangs on the horizon, but when you see it you no longer think of bear. It's only a mountain now." As he watched the green fire die in the eyes of a wolf he killed, he began "thinking like a mountain," eventually developing the conservation ethic of *A Sand County Almanac*.

The Little Colorado still flows, despite these problems, down from the Rim, through the farming towns pioneered by Mormons, past Meteor Crater. The river cascades over Grand Falls, detouring around the lava flow that dammed it, finally, trickling between the steep walls of its gorge to meet the Colorado River in Grand Canyon.

GRAND CANYON

It gave writer Haniel Long "cosmic vertigo." J. B. Priestley wrote, "It is not a show place, a beauty spot, but a revelation." In 1892, tourist Gertrude Stevens said, "I fainted when I saw this awful looking cañon. I never wanted a drink so bad in my life."

I once watched a woman at Mather Point trying to make sense of her first view of the Canyon. She took a Polaroid picture, then stood looking first at the Canyon, and then at her photograph, and again back into the depths of the real thing, bemused. Which was the real Grand Canyon?

The Canyon is simply too big to comprehend quickly, even in person. From the air, its 277-mile course across northern Arizona does not fit comfortably in a single view. A red scar through the green of flat enclosing plateaus, it remains separate from its surroundings, a place all to itself.

Within the Canyon, walls of warm stone shelter and enclose you. From the rim, you peer into the Canyon as into the underworld. It makes you just as uncomfortable as would the real thing.

What is this place that so challenges our imaginations? The river leads to the answer. At its deepest point in this grandest of canyons, the Colorado runs 6,200 feet beneath the rim of the Kaibab Plateau. It carves four separate inner gorges within the greater Canyon: Marble Canyon, and Upper, Middle, and Lower Granite gorges.

Return to Lees Ferry once more. As the river runs past the mouth of the Paria and on down into Paleozoic rocks in Marble Canyon, it carves south for many miles along the eastern foot of the Kaibab Plateau. The East Kaibab Monocline, one of the great Colorado Plateau folds, determines its course here. The monocline formed as the Rocky Mountains began to rise beginning about 65 million years ago. The river probably has passed through Marble Canyon for at least 30 million years. Appropriate to this old section of the Canyon, the Hopi *sipapu*, or the place where people emerged into this world, lies here.

About sixty miles below Lees Ferry, the Little Colorado joins the master stream. A few miles farther the river turns westward and plunges *through* the Kaibab Upwarp (the Paiutes' "mountain lying down")—a very unlikely thing for a river to do. Water indeed flows downhill, and for a century—since John Wesley Powell first ran the river in 1869—geologists have not ceased to argue about the scenario that propels the river through the 9,000-foot-high Kaibab Plateau and keeps it flowing downhill.

Every attempt to explain the Grand Canyon must take into account several facts. The ancestral river has flowed through Marble Canyon for a long time. But at the other end of Grand Canyon, the sequence of rock formations indicates that the river could not have flowed in Lower Granite Gorge through the Grand Wash Cliffs until about six million years ago. The problem: to integrate these two facts—an old Marble Canyon and a young Lower Granite Gorge separated by the Kaibab Upwarp. To allow enough time for erosion of the Canyon. And still to keep water flowing downhill.

One theory has the river establishing its present course in central Grand Canyon before erosion left the Kaibab Upwarp standing high above the surrounding desert. We know the ancestral river departed the area by a different route. But where did it go? It could not drain south until four to five million years ago because the Gulf of California did not exist until then. It may have flowed northward into closed basins, although no evidence has turned up in Utah to prove or disprove this idea. And we have to allow a reasonable period after its diversion through the Grand Wash Cliffs to account for the depth of the western Canyon, already carved to within fifty feet of its present depth as long ago as two million years.

An alternate version has the Kaibab Plateau blocking the river's path, sending the ancestral Colorado from Marble Canyon *up* the present Little Colorado channel, draining southeast, perhaps into Lake Bidahochi. Meanwhile, a river on the west side of the Kaibab began to cut headward into the great upwarp, finally breaking through and capturing the flow of the southeastward-flowing river. Later the Little Colorado developed, taking over the abandoned channel of the ancestral Colorado but flowing in the reverse direction from volcanic highlands created far to the south on the Mogollon Rim. The problem: no proof exists of the ancestral Colorado's path southeastward.

We do not yet know why the Colorado cut through these high plateaus. But it did. And in doing so, it has created a canyon more than a mile deep, thirteen miles wide in places, with an exposure of rocks like no other.

The Kaibab Plateau rims the Canyon on the north at its deepest and widest point, across from (and 1,500 feet higher than) the South Rim on the lip of the Coconino Plateau. Westward, other plateaus form the rim of Grand Canyon, the Kanab, Uinkaret, and Shivwits plateaus on the north and the Hualapai on the south.

Great faults rough out these huge chunks of landscape, the westernmost—and greatest—separating the Colorado Plateau from the Mojave Desert basin and ranges. This fault forms the Grand Wash Cliffs, where the Colorado River leaves the Grand Canyon. North of the river and its canyon lies the Arizona Strip, an isolated land of sagebrush and volcanic mountains known for its villages of Mormon polygamists, Southern Paiutes, long dirt roads to Kanab Canyon and Toroweap Point, and writer Edward Abbey's imaginary residence at Wolf Hole, Arizona.

Twenty-one sedimentary formations build the walls of Grand Canyon, resting on a foundation of metamorphic Vishnu Schist shot through with Zoroaster Granite. These rocks document the story of the earth from 1.7 billion years ago to the end of the Paleozoic—235 million years ago—barely yesterday on the geologic time scale. The

Opposite: The Grand Canyon from the air. COLLIER/CONDIT.

ancient Precambrian rocks exposed in the inner gorge bare the roots of mountain ranges worn away to plains near the time the first algae began to create an oxygen-rich atmosphere.

Thinking in terms of a billion years is well nigh impossible for most of us. The rocks of the Navajo Country take us back to the uppermost layer of the Grand Canyon—only five percent of the way back to the beginning of the earth. From these Kaibab Limestone rims to the ancient Precambrian inner gorge lies another third of Earth history.

The gaps alone span staggering pieces of time. Between the metamorphism of the Vishnu Schist and deposition of the next layer up—part of the late Precambrian Grand Canyon Supergroup—450 million years passed. This missing record is nearly twice as long as the Mesozoic and Cenozoic eras combined. At the top of the Supergroup, another period of erosion makes for 250 million years' worth of missing layers—the "Great Unconformity" which marks the top of the inner gorge.

Above lies the familiar sequence of Grand Canyon layers, including the Tonto Platform eroded from the Bright Angel Shale, the great

Above: The South Kaibab Trail, which winds from the rim of the Grand Canyon to the Colorado River.
JACK W. DYKINGA.

Opposite: Columbine.
MICHAEL COLLIER.

cliffs of the Redwall Limestone (not really red, but ivory, stained rufous by the Supai Group above, and major barrier to Inner Canyon hikers), and the creamy, cross-bedded Coconino Sandstone.

These and the rest of the Canyon rocks trace life from its beginnings through the first land plants and animals. Through trilobites, squid, fish, amphibians, and reptiles. But the story ends there: the Kaibab Limestone was deposited before dinosaurs evolved, before birds preened in the morning sun, and before mammals began to scurry through Mesozoic forests.

Rocks, time, and the river. These have made the Grand Canyon. But the river does not carve the Canyon singlehandedly. It rasps down through the stack of formations like a ripsaw, carving a groove no wider than its course. Tributary streams take responsibility for keeping pace, widening the Canyon, isolating buttes and building temples. When water comes, it accomplishes virtually all of the erosion on the plateau.

Water also determines the plant distribution of the Canyon, from pine forests of the rims to blackbrush shrubs of the Tonto Platform to the Mojave Desert of the inner gorge. At seeps, where water springs forth perennially, verdant hanging gardens seem lusher because of their isolation in the desert. It takes only one patch of yellow columbines, a few monkeyflowers dropping red blossoms into still pools, the echoing ratchet of a single calling male treefrog, to change the mood of a side canyon from parched to sylvan. Havasu Creek—home to the Havasupai Indians—is the ultimate of such paradises, with its travertine-festooned waterfalls and tangles of wild grape.

These days, water takes on a new meaning in the Canyon. As Philip Fradkin puts it in *A River No More: The Colorado River and the*

BICYCLE TOUR

Any sane person traveling the 400 miles from Grand Canyon Village to Nogales would head down to Williams, cut over to Flagstaff and south to the border through Phoenix and Tucson. Total driving time, allowing for food, gas, and rest stops: nine hours. But long-distance cyclists belie the definition of sanity. They spend a week longer on the road, and take a more cumbersome, harsher, and ultimately more rewarding route. That was the idea originated by Jay Rochlin and Rich Corbett, members of the Greater Arizona Bicycling Association, who dreamed up The Grand Canyon to Mexico, Almost Across Arizona, Bicycle Tour. Two other GABA members, Lori and Ed Stiles, spent their 1980 vacation developing the route on highway shoulders with as little traffic and as much scenery as possible. The first weekend of every October since then, an ever-growing number of cycling enthusiasts has pushed off from Grand Canyon Village, and pedaled into Nogales eight days later. So many people have joined the annual tour, in fact, that they now leave in groups of no more than 150 at a time. Participants come from throughout the United States and Europe.

The first 120 miles, to Flagstaff, follow the Grand Canyon's lower lip and head over to Cameron, then south to Flagstaff via a stunning detour along the U. S. Park Service road to Wupatki and Sunset Crater national monuments. The 14 miles between Wupatki—stark red sandstone Indian ruins—and Sunset Crater—which last erupted in A.D. 1066—take cyclists on an incline of almost 1,500 feet. "That's my favorite stretch of the whole tour," Ed Stiles says, "going uphill all the way with Indian ruins on all sides of you."

The next few days' push to Globe, by way of Payson, takes the tour out of the Colorado Plateau past Mormon Lake and the Mogollon Rim, to Tonto Natural Bridge and down across Roosevelt Dam, and finally up and over to Globe. The Stileses say these 185 miles include "a long, steep descent, a lung-wrenching climb, 14 miles of dirt road and a narrow, one-lane catwalk across the largest masonry dam in the world."

During the final few days of cycling, which cover the same distance as the Flagstaff-to-Globe stretch, the fleet of touring bikes coasts 3,000 feet downhill over twenty miles from El Capitan Pass into copper mining country, weaves uphill through the western end of the Santa Catalina range, cuts a crosstown swath through Tucson, and wheels on to Nogales.

The satisfaction that the tour bestows on its participants, besides its physical and spiritual highs, includes

ED STILES

making friends along the way: fellow cyclists, pleased merchants, friendly motorists, sympathetic campground managers, and café owners. In Nogales, Mexico, it seems, the whole town shows up to greet the weary and triumphant pedalers and escort them through the streets as heroes. The mayor and local cyclists turn out to lead the new arrivals past friendly crowds, down the major thoroughfare, and to a city park for music and dancing.

The tour guidebook, written by the Stileses, offers packing suggestions ("if you can't eat it, fix your bike with it, wear it or sleep in it, it's not worth taking"), friendly advice ("watch for the cattleguard just before you get to Strawberry, near milepost 271" on highway 87), practical tips ("a hardshell helmet could save your life in a high-speed crash on one of the steep mountain descents"), and cautionary warnings (Oracle's town park "is not a very good campsite... because it is often used late into the night for drinking parties."). Arizona's "mountains and canyons, deserts and alpine forests," they write, is "the kind of country that begs for the hum of high-pressure tires on the open road."

TOM MILLER

Below: Havasu Falls, Grand Canyon.
STEPHEN TRIMBLE.

West, "... the history of Arizona in the present century could be viewed as a continuing effort to keep cool." The booming cities of southern Arizona need water and power. And they need more power on hot days than cool ones, more at midday than at night.

Today the Colorado River in Grand Canyon runs by computer in response to these needs. Its flow varies daily to generate power on convenient schedules at Glen Canyon Dam. Lake Mead affects the last thirty miles of Grand Canyon by drowning it under reservoir water and silt. But in the twenty years since its construction, Glen Canyon Dam has transformed the ecology of all 240 miles of remaining river in the Canyon.

Before the dam, the Colorado roared in spring runoff, averaging almost 90,000 cubic feet per second (cfs) in its annual maximum, and occasionally surpassing 300,000 cfs. In winter the river trickled along at 4,000 cfs, once dropping to 700 cfs. Its water temperature varied from

near freezing in winter to over 80° F in the western Canyon in summer. A unique set of fishes evolved in this wildly fluctuating environment; other Inner Canyon organisms adapted to the river environment over thousands of years.

The dam changed all this. From deep beneath the surface of Lake Powell, clear, green water leaves the dam at 45° year-round. It warms only six degrees even in summer on its downstream plunge to Lake Mead. The programmed water release normally varies between about 2,000 cfs and 29,000 cfs. Several native fish species have become extinct or exceedingly rare since these changes: Colorado River squawfish; razorback sucker; and the roundtail, humpback, and bony-tail chubs. Introduced rainbow trout and carp now dominate, making Glen Canyon between the dam and Lees Ferry a phenomenal place for sport fishing—at the expense of native species.

Without the enormous summer floods, some beaches (crucial camps for river runners) are eroding away, with minimal new sediment coming in to replenish them. The great boulders washed down side canyons in flash floods, on the other hand, pile in the river and stay put, unmoved by the puny, controlled flow released by the dam. Crystal Creek poured debris into the Colorado after a single storm on December 8, 1966, turning a minor rapid into a rock garden with a legendary boat-eating "hole."

With less variation in water level, new lush riverbank vegetation has developed: willows, tamarisk, and seep willows providing rich resources for a host of vertebrate and invertebrate animals. The old high-water mark strip of mesquite, catclaw, and apache plume still survives on upper terraces.

Animals and plants have not yet accommodated to the new computerized ecology of the river. In very wet years, when the dam must open its floodgates, high water sweeps away riverbank communities, almost like the old days. In 1983, for instance, the river ran at 92,000 cfs once again. We simply do not know what permanent effects Glen Canyon Dam will have on Grand Canyon ecology; for a final answer, we may have to wait until Lake Powell silts up in a few centuries.

This is not the first time drastic changes have swept over the Canyon. A few decades ago, humans bent on protecting deer and livestock from predators killed hundreds of cougars, bobcats, coyotes, and wolves on the Kaibab Plateau. The deer herd grew from 4,000 in 1906 to between 30,000 and 100,000 in 1924—at least in part because of its release from heavy predation. Overgrazing led to mass starvation, and with the permanent loss of predators, hunters outside the national park must approximate the natural balance today.

An earlier revolution in the Grand Canyon took place about 10,000 years ago. During the cool Ice Age climate 15,000 years ago, many trees and other high-elevation plants extended their range down to the inner gorge. They mixed with desert plants to form communities unknown today, complete with such long-extinct animals as Shasta ground sloths and Harrington's mountain goats. As the climate

Glen Canyon Dam.
MICHAEL COLLIER.

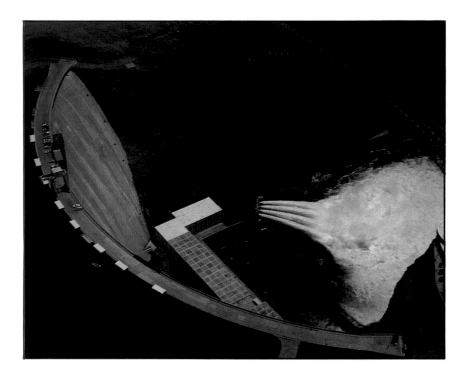

warmed, trees moved upward with the limits of adequate moisture—some as much as 1,000 meters—until modern plant communities developed.

The Grand Canyon—and the plateau—still offers scientists endless riches. Its geology lies exposed, answers to earth puzzles there for the taking. Its biology remains poorly known because of the enormous difficulty of field work. Its Indian tribes—Hopi, Havasupai, Hualapai, Navajo—live in as traditional a way as any, a last chance for us to understand alternate ways of living close to the North American land.

As Wallace Stegner makes clear in *Beyond the Hundredth Meridian*, the Colorado Plateau has changed little since John Wesley Powell "unlocked the last great unknown region in the country and made it his own.... In that region so simple and so empty of people, scientific knowledge lay on the surface like the moss agates and jasper geodes of some of its valleys, ready to be scooped up in the hand."

In the end, small images may stay in our memories longer than large concepts, even a concept as overwhelming as time in the Grand Canyon. Spring-green willow against walls of pink granite and veined black schist. Downscale flute-arpeggios of singing canyon wrens. The black silhouette of a raven soaring across the smile of sky visible from the bottom of a side canyon. Or an Inner Canyon waterfall after a storm. White foam on Redwall, Temple Butte, and Muav limestone runs down the arms of a V on the cliff, joining in a last funnel, and dropping in free fall into the river in a soft patter of water over the rumble of thunder. The wisp of white foam—not enough sediment on the bare rocks above to color it—disappears like a dream. Here for a moment, then gone. Leaving the walls of the Canyon dry once more.

THE MOJAVE DESERT

The Mojave Desert is the innermost sanctum of North America's arid lands. It is the smallest of North America's deserts and extends from the southwestern corner of the Colorado Plateau to the San Bernardino Mountains in California. Arizona, on the desert's eastern border, claims only a small portion of the Mojave, from the lowlands north of Lake Mead down past Topock. The Mojave is a transitional desert, grading into the Great Basin Desert near Tonopah, Nevada, and into the Sonoran and lower Colorado River deserts south of Needles, California. Its transitional nature is particularly apparent in Arizona, where Mojave vegetation includes big sagebrush in the north, and saltbush and creosotebush in the south.

Our name for this desert comes from a Mojave Indian word, "hamakhava," which means "three mountains" and refers to the Needles, south of Topock, peaks named by Joseph Ives in 1857. In 1942 Forrest Shreve described the Mojave as a high, temperate desert, occurring up to 5,000 feet, although most of it lies between 2,000 and 4,400 feet in elevation. For the most part it is a broad wasteland floored by dry desert lakes and valleys, and interrupted by low ranges of mountains.

While interior drainage characterizes much of the central and western Mojave Desert, this is not the case in Arizona. Red Lake, south of Lake Mead, is the largest of only a few closed basins in western Arizona, and all of the other large Mojave valleys in the state eventually drain into the Colorado River. Low mountain ranges divide these valleys, and several of the ranges—the Black, Cerbat, Hualapai, and others—rise to over 6,000 feet in elevation. Hualapai Peak, on the extreme eastern edge of the Mojave, reaches more than 8,400 feet.

Only two small rivers arise in the entire Mojave Desert. The Amargosa and the Mojave rivers flow into Nevada and California, respectively, and terminate in desert sinks. The Colorado River drains the Mojave's eastern borderlands, but acquires little water from the surrounding terrain. Its most significant tributaries in this part of Arizona are Burro and Trout creeks, and Big Sandy Wash, all arms of the

Above left: Datura. STEPHEN TRIMBLE.
Opposite: The Colorado River near Needles. COLLIER/CONDIT.

Bill Williams River. Cottonwood and Grand washes drain into Lake Mead from the Arizona Strip, and Detrital and Hualapai washes enter from the south. These normally dry arroyos sometimes flood with spectacular fury following heavy summer rains.

The journals and letters of the early Mojave explorers and the writings of Mojave County historian Roman Malach provide keen insight into the history of this desert country. The native tribes inhabiting the area include the Shoshonean Chemehuevis in the California Mojave, the Mojave and Hualapai Indians in Arizona, and the Southern Paiute Indians to the north. Hunters and gatherers, these tribes practiced some limited agriculture. The Mojave Indians were met by Coronado's conquistadores in the sixteenth century.

Exploration, trapping, and mining attracted American interests in the region during the first half of the nineteenth century. Early expeditions into the area were led by Jedediah Smith, James Ohio Pattie, John C. Fremont, Edward Beale, Lorenzo Sitgreaves, and Joseph Christmas Ives. With camels and diplomacy, Beale sought a route to California in 1857. He treated the native tribes with the respect of a gentleman among his peers, as had most of the other early explorers. But later prospectors and settlers were less civil and treated the Indians harshly, provoking attacks and recriminations which later led to war.

The mid-nineteenth century found the Mojave a rough and ready frontier. Stern-wheel paddleboats churned upstream against the Colorado River's muddy torrent belching out plumes of black smoke. In 1857 Joseph Ives and Charles Johnson raced to find the head of navigation on the river. Ives went on to explore the South Rim of the Grand Canyon, and Johnson established a major shipping industry on the stretch of river below the present site of Hoover Dam.

The Civil War and the Indian wars brought the cavalry to the eastern Mojave. Lieutenant J. R. Hardenbergh led Company D to a bleak outpost at the mouth of El Dorado Canyon on the California side of the river in 1867; his soldiers defended the fort against flies, boredom, and the relentless summer sun. They soon turned to prospecting. Men of character, such as John Moss and William Hardy, built and lost mining fortunes and empires in the Mojave. Joseph Pratt Allyn, the first associate judge for the territory of Arizona, left one of the more colorful narratives of life in La Paz and along the Colorado River in the mid-1860s before suffering from political slander and ill health. La Paz, the principal shipping port for mineral ore on the lower Colorado River, was briefly considered as a site for the territorial capital. Today nothing remains of that bustling nineteenth-century city; it has been reclaimed by the desert's silence.

In time the Indians were defeated and restricted to reservations. The Mormon Church never established its much-desired route to the sea from Callville, Nevada, to the Gulf of California. Exploration of this land was motivated largely by the search for valuable ores. Prospectors, encouraged by stories of mineral wealth, searched every inch of

Opposite: Marsh on the Colorado River. COLLIER/CONDIT.

the low mountains for gold, silver, lead, tungsten, zinc, and uranium. A few struck it rich (and mining continues to be one of the eastern Mojave's main industries), but most early prospectors died in poverty and ignominy, leaving few records of their deeds or presence.

Tales of greed, failure, and deceit run through the Mojave's history, a hundred to every one of heroism and humanity. The stories are like veins of silver and lead, running up to the surface and petering out in the present. The Mojave is harsh land, baked by the sun, a land where human survival was a matter of foresight, experience, and endurance. The dire extremes of the land and climate brought out the worst and sometimes the best in its inhabitants.

Just north of Topock, a jungle of plant life crowds into a narrow belt along the river. The Colorado is broad and marshy in this reach, its floodplain surmounted by old river terraces. Cattails, bulrushes, and

other streamside plants provide a lush habitat for rails, yellowthroats, yellow-headed blackbirds, waterfowl, and many other bird species. Water alone is responsible for the striking contrast between the riverside plant community and that of the surrounding desert, which is only slightly removed from the river's floodplain.

In this area, salt cedar, a weedy, sun-loving shrub, has been crowded out by its tree-forming relative, the anthel. Both were introduced into this country from the Middle East prior to the turn of the century, the former for erosion control and the latter for shade. But salt cedar, producing its windblown seeds in great abundance, has invaded nearly every drainage in the Southwest. At Topock Marsh, where populations of both species coincide, the anthel, a tree which rarely survives in the wild, shades out its noxious, more successful congener, salt cedar.

The road to Oatman from Topock Marsh is rutted and slow. Poorwills alight on it in the evening to warm their feet on the pavement. Their eyes flash red in the headlights before they fly up—a flash of white wing bars and they're gone.

There is a time at dusk when the late summer's desert wind changes direction. An upslope, southwesterly breeze occurs during the day. At night cooler mountaintop air settles, creating a slight downslope breeze. The breeze blows across the long bajadas that stretch down to the Colorado River from the Aquarius Mountains. This part of the Mojave is not a land much carved by the river. It is a rough and tumbled terrain faulted into low mountains, raw in the harsh heart of the Mojave Desert.

At twilight beyond the dusk only a faint coral glow remains on the horizon and the desert begins to come to life. The quiet, rasping chirps of *Bootettix* grasshoppers ricochet from the creosotebush as they do during the day, but the crickets join in. In the wash, screech owls wake up for the night's hunting and try out their voices. A lone elf owl, far from its preferred saguaros, adds his maniacal little cackle. Somewhere off to the west, coyotes fill a corner of the desert with a mad, high-pitched jazz improvisation.

Slowly, as twilight turns entirely to night and the desert is lit only by starlight, the little bumping notes of screech owls echo from all directions. The constellations stand out clearly: Pegasus just up on the eastern horizon; Cygnus, above, headed south, for even in early September the season for migration has begun; and Scorpio's grand arc fills the southern sky over the Needles.

At sunrise the September sun backlights the creosotebush and its understory of gray-green bursage. A cactus wren gargles in the distance. Low-growing, sparse desert plaintain, now burnt out and golden yellow, waves in the slight morning breeze. Spiky and blackened *Chorizanthe*, a tiny buckwheat, sticks up out of the desert pavement. Blue paloverde trees border the drainages, and an occasional ocotillo spindles skyward at the horizon, but little other life can be seen across the desert floor of tiny cobbles and scattered volcanic rocks.

MOJAVE GEOLOGY

Ephemeral human beings perceive the desert as a harsh, unchanging land. But in geologic terms the Mojave has only recently acquired its desert character. For most of the past 4.6 billion years the region has been a submarine continental margin and shelf. Half a billion years ago Paleozoic seas began to deposit vast sheets of limestone and dolomite, and erosional debris from the North American continent also settled on the ocean floor. Irreconcilable tectonic stresses developed in the earth's mantle as North America slowly migrated northward, colliding with other continents and rotating clockwise. These stresses crumpled and faulted western North America into numerous mountain ranges. The Antler Orogeny (a mountain-building event) left a substantial range of mountains in central Nevada 350 million years ago, but for the most part these mountains have eroded away. More recent orogenies created the Rocky Mountains and the Sierra Nevada Range. The most recent orogenic event has sundered the intermountain West, creating the Basin and Range geologic province in which the Great Basin, Mojave, and Sonoran deserts now lie.

Between 60 and 18 million years ago the eastern Mojave Desert area was higher than the neighboring Colorado Plateau. The southwestern margin of the Plateau lay near sea level, receiving erosional outwash from the northern Mojave. Beginning 17 million years ago, Basin and Range tectonism produced block-faulted mountain ranges with intervening basins in the Mojave region. In time these trenches became saline lakes and left thick deposits, such as the Muddy Creek Formation in the Lake Mead area.

Of great importance to the region has been the integration of the Colorado River drainage. Invasion of the sea into the lower Colorado River basin began less than 12 million years ago with the initial opening of the Gulf of California by the San Andreas fault system.

PAST AND PRESENT CLIMATES

During the early Tertiary Period about 60 million years ago, the American West was tropical lowland occupied by extensive savannas and broad-leaved evergreen trees. A drying trend began during the mid-Eocene Epoch, about 45 million years ago, gradually increasing in severity to the middle of the Pliocene Epoch (about 4 million years ago), when desert conditions were most pronounced in the West. North America's desert species are thought to have undergone much of their evolutionary adaptation at that time. The last glacial advance, the Wisconsin Ice Age, reached its zenith 22,000 years ago and then retreated, fully disappearing by 12,000 years ago.

The effects of this last ice age on the Mojave Desert and the Southwest have been studied intensively through paleontological and tree-ring techniques, and by using the plant remains preserved in pack-rat nests and in cave deposits of ground sloth dung. The Wisconsin ice sheet itself extended only as far south as the Canadian border in western North America, but glaciers formed in the Sierra Nevadas, the Rocky Mountains, and on a few peaks in Nevada, Utah, and Arizona. The accumulation of ice at high elevations was probably accompanied by a cooler, possibly dryer climate. Large animals wandered the region: mammoths, camels, bison, horses, ground sloths, cave bears, saber-toothed cats, and dire wolves, as well as other, smaller vertebrates. *Teratornis merriami*, a vulturine bird with a wingspan of more than twelve feet, and California condors floated the Mojave skies and roosted in high cliff-face caves.

With the retreat of the glaciers, a warm, wet period began. During this Pluvial period some species of highland plants, such as juniper

Opposite: Joshua Tree forest, with the Grand Wash Cliffs of the Arizona Strip in the background.
STEPHEN TRIMBLE.

trees, moved into the Mojave Desert. As the climate changed, the large animals suddenly disappeared, possibly hunted to extinction by the early humans who began to occupy the region. The severe drying trend of about 9,000 years ago turned climatic conditions more desert-like and caused a retreat of the upland plant species to higher elevations. The region has been gradually and irregularly drying out since that earlier, more lush period.

Today the climate of the Mojave is the hottest and driest of the American deserts. Due in part to a rain-shadow effect (the Mojave is blocked off from moist Pacific air by mountains), the severe climate of this desert is also the result of a subsiding dry-air pattern characteristic of the zone from 20° to 30° latitude north and south of the equator. Death Valley, in central eastern California, falls within the Mojave's borders. Temperatures in Arizona's corner of the Mojave Desert reach to 125° F during the summer months at elevations below 1,000 feet.

Overall the Mojave is a winter-precipitation desert, but along its eastern margin in Arizona, summer rains contribute considerably to the total annual precipitation. Summer thunderstorms produce unbelievable deluges of rain in short order. Flash floods damage roadways and property and occasionally result in loss of life. Annual precipitation varies from 6.5 inches below elevations of 1,000 feet to 12.5 inches at 4,000 feet elevation, and to more than 20 inches in the highest mountains. Evaporation, characteristically high in all deserts, consumes nearly eight feet of water annually from the surfaces of Mojave reservoirs. The Mojave has winters that can be unexpectedly cold, with snow and below-freezing temperatures at even the lowest elevations. Although it is the smallest of North America's four deserts, the Mojave more than makes up for this with climatic ferocity.

LIFE IN THE MOJAVE DESERT

Patterns of vegetation and animal life, as well as topography, geology, and climate, distinguish the Mojave from the other three North American deserts. The most conspicuous Mojave plant is the Joshua tree, a scarecrow-like tree of moderate elevations which provides little in the way of shade or wood. Succulents are not as well represented in the Mojave as they are in Arizona's other deserts. For example, the cacti are not as diverse or abundant, probably because of cold winters, low summer rainfall, and extreme temperatures. The most common cacti are teddy bear cholla and other prickly pear cacti; barrel cacti are less abundant. About one quarter of the Mojave's plant life is endemic.

Travelers in the Mojave can distinguish several distinct habitat types, based primarily on topographic relief and proximity to water. There are valley floors, riverside and streamside habitats, gently sloping bajadas, and the steeper slopes of the mountain piedmonts. Above

Left: Jackrabbit. ROBERT CAMPBELL.
Opposite: Chuckwalla.
C. ALLAN MORGAN.

4,400 feet elevation, the characteristic desert vegetation yields to pinyon-juniper woodlands. Higher still, pine forests dominate the landscape.

The desert guards its spirit and its life with patience and passion, with callousness, effrontery, and toxin. It surrounds its innermost secrets with a roughness and an alien peculiarity that is always surprising. We see this in all of its creatures, from plants armed to the teeth to beetles and skunks that jump into headstands before letting loose their noxious musks. Except for some of the wildflowers, everything in the desert sticks, strikes, stinks, hisses, or scuttles off in a huff.

In the face of the Mojave's extreme heat and dryness, desert plants and animals have few options for survival. They must either confront or retreat from the stresses imposed by their harsh environment. A few Mojave organisms simply accept desert heat and desiccation. Phreatophytes are streamside plants whose roots reach into the water table. Desert phreatophytes such as the anthel, mesquite, and cottonwood trees simply transpire more water on hot, dry days. It has been estimated that on a warm day these plants lose water equivalent to the weight of their foliage every hour. Creosotebush and house finches are Mojave Desert organisms that can tolerate severe water loss. Birds in

general maintain high internal temperatures (104° to 108° F), and they do not overheat until ambient temperatures rise above their body temperature. Desert iguanas, jackrabbits, and ground squirrels let their body temperatures rise above normal, but usually just for a short period of time. This strategy is called "heat loading."

Heat evasion takes place on an hourly or daily time scale and is accomplished by many desert animals and some plants. Lizards regulate their body temperature by sunning or sitting in the shade. The speedy desert iguana rests in the morning sun on its burrow until its body temperature reaches 38° C and then moves off for the day's activities. A number of delicate wildflowers such as the evening primrose and sacred datura protect themselves from desiccation by blooming at night and are pollinated by night-flying moths. Nearly all Mojave mammals are nocturnal, a behavioral adaptation which allows them to conserve water. One exception is the black-tailed jackrabbit, which, in theory, should lose five percent of its body weight (as water) per hour on a hot day, but by controlling water loss behaviorally it loses only one percent per hour. Many mammals and even the gopher tortoise evade water loss by retreating to humid burrows during the heat of the day.

To avoid desert conditions some species, such as the round-tailed

Above: Skunk. L. L. RUE III.
Left: Round–tailed ground squirrel.
W. W. GOODPASTER.

ground squirrel, go into estivation, the summertime equivalent of hibernation. Other species become active only during the milder periods of the year. A host of wildflowers, such as desert marigolds and sego lillies, blanket the desert floor in early spring and finish their life cycles before the summer heat sets in. An exceptional example of heat avoidance is seen in the giant red velvet mite. These large mites measure a quarter of an inch in length and dwell in humid, silk-lined tunnels in sand dunes. Once a year, for a few hours, they emerge, feast on termites, mate, and then re-dig a burrow in which they spend the rest of the year. This frenzy of activity takes place only after a good soaking rain between December and February.

Coping with extreme heat and too little water has required such extreme evolutionary development that many desert organisms literally cannot tolerate more moderate conditions. For example, Mojave creosotebush cannot stand more than 7.5 inches of winter precipitation but requires a minimum of about 3 inches of precipitation to survive. Birds and mammals dissipate excess body heat by panting. *Urohydrosis* is a polite term for the way turkey vultures cool themselves—by urinating on their legs. Conservation of body water in Mojave kangaroo rats is achieved by production of urine three times as concentrated as human urine. Chuckwalla lizards, strict vegetarians in a world where plant life is often salty, secrete excess salt from special glands. Mojave plants such as creosotebush have reduced water loss by developing waxy leaf cuticles (coatings) or, in the case of cacti, with hairs and spines which can keep their surfaces cooler.

Nearly seventy percent of the Mojave Desert is covered by creosotebush (*Larrea tridentata*), an olive-green, resinous shrub and a plant with every bit as peculiar and unique a natural history as any life form in the desert. There are five species in the genus *Larrea*, with all but *L. tridentata* restricted to South America. Apparently our creosotebush jumped continent three million years ago when South America collided with North America. The plant quickly and vigorously colonized all of western Mexico and the American Southwest, and has come to dominate the low, hot desert bajadas here.

Creosotebush blooms in the early spring and sometimes in the late summer. Its spindly, diffuse branches catch the light desert wind, giving the plant an airy appearance, and after a desert shower its resins infuse the air with a crisp, musky aroma. Each plant catches wind-blown sand and eventually appears to be raised on a small mound of earth. Seedlings are rarely found except along roadways, where increased water runoff promotes their survival. These young plants appear healthier and are darker green in color. Southwestern Indians used creosotebush as a poultice for wounds and as an emetic.

The most impressive feature about the creosotebush is the age that some of the plants attain. Frank Vasek of the University of California at Riverside has been counting the growth rings on creosote root-masses in the central and western Mojave Desert and radiocarbon-dating the cores of these plants. He believes that creosotebush may attain an age in

The Tom Reed Mine, Oatman, 1952.
ANSEL ADAMS.

excess of 11,000 years, making them the oldest living things on earth. Even the resilient 4,500-year-old bristlecone pine is a youngster by comparison.

Still, for all of its remarkable attributes, the creosotebush desert seems barren and lifeless by day. Driving by a seemingly endless, shallow sea of creosotebush in the mindlessness of the desert heat, one can almost forget that the plant exists. *Bootettix* grasshoppers, a few lizards, and small, fuzzy white velvet ants are about all one sees by day. The velvet ants, which parasitize groundnesting bees, apparently mimic the hairy white fruit of the creosotebush itself. For all this apparent sterility, one inevitably finds a suspiciously large number of rodent burrows around the base of these plants. Kangaroo rats and pocket mice burrow into the soil beneath them, and because of their ability to metabolize water from seeds, these rodents never need free environmental water. Creosotebush also hosts a large diversity of reptiles and insects, but nearly all of the species associated with it are nocturnal and are only seen, if at all, making a last mad dash across the highways at night, or as roadkills in the morning before the ravens show up.

Near Oatman, one sees brittlebush, teddybear cholla, and Mojave yucca. Brittlebush, among the hardiest of the low desert plants, puts out a bouquet of yellow, daisy-like flowers in March and April, and in good years turns the Mojave's piedmont and alluvial fans to gold. Most of the desert year, however, it stands, stubbornly resisting the heat, its grey-green, finely haired leaves shimmering in the desert sun. The plant is well adapted to desert conditions; but if the summer rains fail, its beautiful foliage gradually withers and drops to the ground, and the plant appears dead. These exceptional plants produce a toxin which leaches from fallen leaves and prevents other species of plants from germinating beneath the brittlebush's low canopy, where they might preempt light, water, and soil nutrients.

The Mojave yucca is a sturdy relative of the Joshua tree. It forms a short, stout trunk and points a nest of sword-like leaves skyward. To say this species is "well-defended" is a gross understatement, and one can only wonder what Cenozoic beasts so preferred Mojave yucca pods that the plant was forced to these extremes of self-defense.

In the shade of creosotebushes and yuccas, zebra-tailed lizards can be found. The zebra-tailed lizard is a diurnal insectivore which wags its black-and-white-striped tail and thermoregulates by sunning or shading beneath creosotebush and bursage. One of the fastest North American lizards, it has been clocked at speeds of nearly twenty miles per hour. It feeds on insects, including the golden fruit flies that plague desert visitors.

The Joshua tree, named by early Mormons, is the largest and most characteristic plant endemic to the Mojave Desert and perhaps best expresses the unique spirit of the region. It is in the genus *Yucca* and has been given the Latin species designation of *brevifolia* for its short,

KNOW YOUR DESERT

Before going into the desert, a major Arizona industry warns its new employees, "always inform a relative or neighbor exactly where you are going and when you will return." This cheerful advice should give visitors and residents alike some idea of desert travel conditions on foot and in the car. When Forrest Shreve spent time in the same desert, he traveled on feet—a horse's, a mule's, or his own.

Chandler Heights. TERRENCE MOORE.

Shreve, a Maryland native who moved to Arizona in 1908 at age thirty, headed up teams of scientists who laid the groundwork for studies of the desert and the mountain islands anchored in their midst. "To know the desert," he wrote, "involves an acquaintance with all its aspects, and all its physical features, as well as all of the animals and plants that have learned how to find in it a congenial place to live. The most significant lesson that the desert dweller can learn," he continued, "is to regard himself not as an exile from some better place, but as a man at home in an environment to which his life can be adjusted without physical or intellectual loss." Today, Shreve's findings are crucial to understanding Arizona's 113,417 square miles.

A great deal of the state lies in what naturalist Gary Nabhan calls "the snorin' desert." Between sudden moisture and dry heat hangs a precarious balance, which we call life. What stands out about the land throughout the state is that it depends upon a fixed amount of water to maintain itself. When that water suddenly increases or undergoes a drastic reduction, the life it supports changes as well. The most startling example of this is the fissure, a crack in the surface caused by too much groundwater being pumped from underground aquifers. Fissures, which have been recorded at four hundred feet deep and nine miles long, used to appear only in rural areas when irrigation was the water's main use. But urban and suburban demands for water have changed that, and by the mid-1980s more than a hundred recorded fissures had slashed through the state—some through housing developments or crossing highways. The biggest fear is that fissures may intersect with the Central Arizona Project's concrete canal and aqueduct network, thereby damaging the very effort undertaken to replenish water from the sinking underground water table. Is Arizona's land trying to tell its people something?

TOM MILLER

Above: Creosote bush. Right: Mojave
rattlesnake. C. ALLAN MORGAN.

dagger-like leaves. It forms a branching tree thirty to forty feet high and bears stalks of big, succulent, creamy white flowers in the spring. These flowers produce a musty odor and bloom for a single night.

The successful establishment of a Joshua tree seedling is a rare event. Joshua trees have somewhat circumvented the problems associated with germination in a hostile environment by sending out running shoots that sprout up some distance away from the parent tree. The yucca skipper takes advantage of this root-sprouting strategy. It is somehow able to distinguish the preferred runner-sprouted Joshua trees from seedling trees, and lays eggs on them. The larvae hatch, drop to the ground, and burrow into the running roots to feed on the dense tissue there.

An essential problem with our understanding of the evolution of a species such as the Joshua tree is our lack of appreciation of time. We tend to regard present species as having evolved in conditions similar to what we experience in our brief lives. But many present-day Mojave species survived drastic climatic changes in the late Pleistocene, having evolved much earlier and under more rigorous conditions. We tend to ignore the fact that the plants and animals of our American deserts

Left: Yucca in bloom.
TERRENCE MOORE.

Opposite: Gila Monster.
ROBERT CAMPBELL.

evolved alongside the important megafaunal grazers, browsers, and carnivores which have only recently died out. The influence these animals, especially the herbivores, exerted on our modern plants may be reflected today in strange patterns of plant growth and distribution.

Joshua trees, for example, do not often occur in valleys which seem suitable for them. Mammoths and giant ground sloths almost certainly relished Joshua tree pods. A fair amount of ground sloth dung containing Joshua tree remains has been found. The seeds of this strange tree are hard and black and probably passed safely through the guts of these great beasts, as juniper and mesquite seeds do through cattle today. Certainly coyotes, rodents, and birds may now disperse some of these seeds, but germination is a rare event, and tens of thousands or even millions of seeds need to be produced and scattered before even a single tree will germinate successfully.

Yet germinate they do, and around them in the Joshua tree forest of the Mojave Desert teems an abundance of life. Clumsy Gila monsters, mildly venomous black and orange lizards, feed on birds eggs and young rodents. Red-tailed hawks nest in Joshua trees and prey on rabbits, ground squirrels, and snakes. Found almost solely beneath fallen Joshua trees, the reclusive desert night lizard feeds on termites in the rotting logs. Rattlesnakes, jackrabbits, coyotes, cactus wrens, scorpions, and ravens—the diversity of life in the Joshua tree forest is astonishing.

The real spirit of this desert world is in the sun-baked ground and in the strange plants and creatures that hail from it. The mystery may be too large and simple for any of us to ever fully appreciate, especially in the Mojave, where Nature plays her cards close to the vest, like the gambler she is.

THE SONORAN DESERT

Eighty miles due south of Phoenix, or eighty miles west from Tucson, the traveler comes to Window Valley.

Arriving from the Papago Indian village of Santa Rosa on the east, the valley at first seems unspectacular—miles and miles of creosotebush flats, the monotony broken only by gray ironwoods hulking along dry washes. Then, continuing west toward the Castle Mountains, volcanic landforms begin their enchantment; jagged peaks, turrets, cliffs, natural arches and caves, all changing shape as the narrow road twists and turns. The Sonoran Desert plants that spread across the foothills are as bizarre in their own way as the landforms: ocotillo, like a thorny spray caught in midair; the giant saguaro cactus, arms up to the sun; and jumping cholla cactus, with golden-edged branches reaching out at every angle imaginable.

On a hill at the southern edge of the Castles is a natural arch called Window Mountain. To reach the arch requires an hour's hike from the road, but the view to the south is worth it. It's the place the Indians call *Nakaijigel*, or "Pierced Ear." Looking southward as the dry winds whip up through the opening in the rock, an expanse of desert appears that is as dramatic as any within the Basin and Range province. To the southwest, the rugged Ajo range forms the dividing line between Organ Pipe Cactus National Monument and the Papago Indian Reservation. Between the arch and the Ajos, creosote and white bursage provide a scant scrub cover to the fine-textured, limy soils of the arid plains, exemplifying the Lower Colorado subdivision of the Sonoran Desert. Due south, one of the world's densest saguaro cactus forests stretches across the bajadas below the Quijotoa Mountains. During the peak heat of summer few Papago families still camp on the bajada slope and harvest the nourishing red fruit of these tall columnar cacti. Above Covered Wells in the Quijotoas, Arizona Upland vegetation—foothills paloverdes, saguaros, jojoba bushes, and pincushion cacti—forms a more diverse cover in terms of plant stature, shape, and texture. To the southeast lies the sacred mountain of the Papago, Baboquivari Peak, and its neighbor, Kitt Peak. The latter is home to some of the world's

Above left: Burrowing owl.
TOM WEISKOTTEN.

Opposite: Saguaros at sunset.
ROBERT CAMPBELL.

most sophisticated telescopes. Grassland and woodland plants here replace plants of the desert as elevation and rainfall increase.

From Window Mountain, the Sonoran Desert can be seen extending far into Mexico. Indeed, it is worth remembering that only a third of the Sonoran Desert's 120,000-square-mile area falls within Arizona's boundaries. Most of this cactus-and-scrub-dominated desert lies in the Mexican state of Sonora, with Mexico's Baja California and southern California, across the Colorado River in the U.S., rounding it out.

VENTANA: WINDOWS TO THE DESERT WORLD

Just as the natural arch provides a window to the great geographic expanse of the desert, a cave nearby is a window through which one can look at the rich history of the region. Called Ventana Cave in the writings of the great archaeologist Emil Haury, this rock shelter has had debris left on its floor by human visitors over more than 10,000 years. Combined with the plant debris gathered up by packrats and left in smaller dry caves elsewhere in the Castles, these historic remains give us a sense of changes that have occurred in desert life since the end of the Ice Age.

Until about 11,000 years ago, when woodland plants were found in the vicinity of Ventana Cave, winter rain fell more plentifully than it does in Window Valley today. Pinyon pines, junipers, and Mormon tea thrived in this cooler, wetter regime. So did plants that are not known in the area today, even at somewhat higher elevations—big sage, barberry, and scrub live oak. Such desert plants as brittlebush and barrel cactus were mixed in with these woodland species. They have persisted to this day.

Large animals that later became extinct in North American deserts—tapirs, sloths, and horses—found sufficient food in the area. Their bones (along with later remnants of kangaroo rats, desert tortoises, porcupines, and other animals that have persisted in the region) have been unearthed from strata in the caves dating earlier than 11,000 years ago. Paleo-Indians made their first "recorded" appearance at Ventana around 9200 B.C., judging from the date assigned to a scraper and hammerstone found in the rock shelter. Charcoal and hunting artifacts from roughly the same period have been found in loose association with horse and tapir bones at Ventana.

Between 10,000 and 8,000 years ago during the summer warming trend at the end of the Ice Age, true desert dwellers such as catclaw, hackberry, brittlebush, mesquite, and barrel cactus began to function more prominently in the community. We know little about human reactions to these changes in the Ventana area, because of a hiatus in the human record between 10,500 and 4,500 years ago.

About 8,000 years ago, a climate with warm, wet summers

Opposite: The ever-thirsty mesquite, and morning glories.
JACK W. DYKINGA.

encouraged desert plants such as brittlebush and catclaw, while juniper and oak soon dropped out of the picture altogether. The period from 8,000 to 4,000 years ago, known as the Middle Holocene, was warm throughout much of the world. It was then that the dramatic summer storm patterns of the Sonoran Desert were apparently established. Thus the Sonoran Desert's most distinctive characteristic relative to other American deserts—its pattern of one short summer rainy season and one modest winter rainy season per year—is a relatively recent phenomenon.

At the beginning of this period, mesquite became more obvious in the caches of packrats, and possibly in the cave vicinity in general. Perhaps the use of the dozen or so bedrock mortars—deep holes ground into the surface of a boulder in the upper cave—began at this

Above: Hedgehog cactus in bloom.
TOM WEISKOTTEN.

Left: Mexican poppies.
ROBERT CAMPBELL.

time. Bedrock mortars are still used to grind mesquite pods into palatable flour by a few Papago women. Earlier in history, they aided desert Indians in processing this desert legume, their most important wild food. Other important native food plants, such as prickly pear, purslane, and pigweed amaranths, appeared locally during this period. The latter two may have increased with human disturbance and are common trail, field, or floodplain weeds today.

Archaeologist Frank Bayham has observed a change that was evident at least 4500 years ago in the use of the cave. Bayham has documented a change in the relative quantities of the bones of various kinds of wildlife left by hunters using the Window Valley. Jackrabbit bones were the most common early in this period, but the overall range of wildlife used was diverse. Later, mostly the bones of mule deer were left, though some bighorn and pronghorn bones were deposited also. Bayham believes that during this stretch of time the cave was used less and less as a base for nomadic people who carried on their daily activities in the vicinity. Gradually, people settled in larger agricultural communities out on the major floodplains. They came to the cave less frequently, using it as a temporary camp for hunting or gathering. This pattern of cave use persisted until at least 600 years ago.

Sometime within the last 4,000 years, many other characters assumed their role in the life of the Sonoran Desert. These include woody perennials such as foothills paloverde, which dispersed northward from the west coast of Mexico where they had persisted during cooler periods. When the prehistoric desert culture now known as the Hohokam began to leave its mark on the Window Valley community, the Sonoran Desert looked much as it did when the Spanish conquistadores arrived centuries later.

By the time Christianity started changing the Old World, agricultural civilization had already been established in southern Arizona. Plant remains buried in Ventana Cave have never been too precisely dated, but they include bottlegourds, cushaw squash, and sixty-day flour corn varieties that Papago farmers in nearby Santa Rosa still cultivate. Another plant, devil's claw, which the Papago now grow as a basketry fiber, does not appear to have been domesticated by the time some Hohokam visitor cast its dried fruit inside the cave.

Today, periodic visitors to this cave continue to leave their marks. Prairie falcons roost on the cliffs above and scream at anyone who enters. Bats and swallows defecate in its upper reaches. Papago women leave footprints on the short but steep trail to the spring where their ancestors had scooped up water during their saguaro-gathering camps. At the mouth of the cave, they can still feel the warmth of this "solar collector" that keeps flowers around it blooming long after they have been frosted or have dried up on the desert plains below. These wildflowers are pollinated by honey bees, introductions from the Old World, which have found a home near a seep dripping down from the spring. Archaeologists and artists come to ponder over the ochre and white petroglyphs of sun and mountain shapes painted across the rock

PHOENIX: DESERT METROPOLIS

In the spring of 1867, John Y. T. Smith, a company commander at Ft. Yuma during the Civil War, established a hay camp along the north side of the Salt River. Hoping to provide alfalfa to the nearby military installation at Camp McDowell, he built some crude living quarters, constructed a road to the camp, and proceeded to harvest the hay. Finding the living difficult and the economic rewards marginal, Smith soon abandoned his enterprise to become the ferryman at McDowell Crossing. His modest holdings and improvements, however, have been considered the first in what is now the Phoenix metropolitan area.

Shortly after Smith left the area, John W. Swilling, along with a few other Anglo settlers from the small mining camp of Wickenburg, moved fifty miles southeast into the Salt River Valley. Taking up where Smith left off, Swilling, an aggressive and canny promoter, homesteaded land on the north side of the river, cleared out ancient Hohokam irrigation ditches, built new ones, negotiated contracts with nearby army installations, and began to develop the agricultural area. In order to encourage settlement, Swilling and his backers established a townsite near the center of the valley and accepted the name "Phoenix," suggesting that a new and flourishing civilization would spring up from the ashes of the old. Indeed, most considered the name a marked improvement over "Pumpkinville," one of the settlement's earlier designations.

From its founding, Phoenix possessed a booster spirit among its people. One early promoter of the townsite noted, "When the railroad steams through our country, the Salt River Valley will be the garden spot of the Pacific Slope and Phoenix the most important inland town." Phoenix, a late arrival on the southwestern urban frontier, would become the most populous city between Dallas and Los Angeles.

During the remainder of the nineteenth century, Phoenix maintained steady but unspectacular growth. It became a service center to the hinterland and emerged as the most fertile and productive agricultural area in the territory. In 1881 its 1,700 residents incorporated as a city. In July 1887 a spur of the Southern Pacific Railroad reached Phoenix, connecting the community to the outside world. Two years later, territorial leaders moved the territorial capital from Prescott to Phoenix. This combination of political and economic factors pleased local promoters and lured outside investors. By the turn of the century, more than 5,500 people resided in Phoenix.

Problems, however, accompanied growth and progress. In 1891 Phoenicians witnessed the awesome destructive power of the unharnessed Salt River. In February, what was called "the biggest flood the Salt had ever known" erased years of human effort in the valley. A decade-long

drought followed the disastrous flood. By 1897, one of the worst years of the drought, water barely trickled in the Salt River, crops failed, water shortages for livestock and domestic uses became acute, and the local economy ground to a halt.

Fortunately for Phoenix and Salt River Valley residents, the vagaries of flood and drought took place against the backdrop of the national irrigation movement of the 1890s. With the passage of the National Reclamation Act of 1902, federal reclamation became a reality, and local leaders responded with the formation of the Salt River Valley Water Users Association the following year. This organization dedicated itself to resolving water rights disputes and to lobbying for a federal reclamation project. The forerunner of today's Salt River Project proved successful in attracting one of the first federal irrigation and storage projects, and by February 1911 the largest masonry block dam in the world, Theodore Roosevelt Dam, and its accompanying structures, provided Phoenix and the valley with a stable water supply, assuring the continued growth of the agricultural economy. Phoenix looked, and continues to look, to the federal government as a benefactor.

With a guaranteed water supply, astute local entrepreneurs and outside investors, aggressively promoted the valley and speculated on its future by diversifying the economy. Agriculture, especially cotton and alfalfa, nevertheless remained the primary economic activity in the valley. The young city affirmed its growing reputation as a resort mecca and haven for health seekers during the decades that followed. Hotels and guest ranches, such as the Westward Ho, the Wigwam, and the Arizona Biltmore, facilitated the development of one of the area's most important sources of income, tourism. The tourist industry was further stimulated by increasing automobile and railroad traffic and in 1927 the beginning of regular airline service to Phoenix. The "Garden Spot of the Southwest" was brought closer than ever to the rest of the nation.

Meanwhile, a local business elite emerged, perhaps best characterized by Dwight Heard, a wealthy Chicago businessman who moved to Phoenix to regain his failing health. Heard sought to stimulate the cultural life of his adopted home and worked to establish libraries, theaters, museums, and other trappings of urban refinement. Not all Phoenicians, however, prospered during this period. Minorities—Mexicans, Mexican Americans, Native Americans, and Blacks—resided in poor neighborhoods on the south side of the city, with little opportunity for social or economic advancement. By 1930 Phoenix resembled other developing urban areas around the country, for it possessed both the amenities and problems of twentieth-century urban civilization.

Despite the problems of economic stagnation and unemployment during the Great Depression, the city continued to grow. Increasingly mobile, Americans were attracted to the Valley of the Sun, where new resorts like the Camelback Inn lured those tourists who could afford such luxury. In addition, New Deal policies, especially in the areas of banking and construction, fueled residential and commercial expansion. Finally, the development and widespread adoption of air conditioning enabled the state's largest city to conquer, to some degree, the oppressive summer heat.

World War II triggered an economic boom and population explosion. In four years the war wrought changes that otherwise might have taken a generation. The U.S. military brought money and manpower into the valley, and by 1942 three army camps and six airbases ringed the metropolitan area. Defense industries such as AiResearch and Goodyear created thousands of jobs and contributed millions of dollars to the local economy.

Between 1945 and 1960, more than three hundred new manufacturing and industrial enterprises moved into the city. The majority of these new industries were light and clean, involved in science and technology, used little water, and were relatively pollution-free. By 1955 manufacturing became the number one source of income in Phoenix, while agriculture dropped to second place and tourism to third. By 1960 the thousands of skilled, white-collar employees, working in air-conditioned comfort at Motorola, Sperry-Rand, or Kaiser Aircraft and Electronics typified this most recent population influx. On weekends they could be seen dining out, fishing or water-skiing, or taking in a movie at the Palms Theater on Central Avenue.

The nearly 2,500 people who settled in the city each month during the 1950s came from all over America, but especially California, Texas, and Illinois. Phoenix attained a growth rate of three hundred per cent, the highest rate of growth among the fifty largest metropolitan areas in the nation. By 1960, half of the state's population lived in the Phoenix metropolitan area.

Since the 1960s, expansion has continued. A new business elite has emerged, best exemplified by the "Phoenix 40," a group of self-appointed business leaders dedicated to the continued growth of the business sector of the community. People, automobiles, shopping centers, fast-food franchises, and housing developments have claimed once-fertile agricultural acreage. The urban Valley of the Sun has all the symbols of advanced American civilization: universities, museums, theater, professional sports teams, as well as smog, crime, and slums. Certainly the car-bombing murder of Don Bolles in 1976 and recurrent revelation of land fraud illustrate the other side of the valley's growth. As Phoenix moves toward the twenty-first century with the psychological assurance that forthcoming Central Arizona Project water will sustain economic and urban expansion, the optimism characteristic of the new civilization in the Salt River Valley doubtlessly will remain.

JACK L. AUGUST, JR.

face above the cave. They ask "Why?" or "How long?" whenever they notice a piece of history left in this nook above Window Valley. Yet they leave, as all other humans have in the past. They leave the place to the owls of the night, which Papago elders believe to be the spirits of their gone ones. The owls wait until no one remains, then ask, "Who? Who? Who?," as the moonlight reaches into the cave.

Foothills Palo Verde in bloom.
SUZI MOORE.

SONORA: NATURAL RANGES AND POLITICAL BOUNDARIES

Speaking of southern Arizona and adjacent Mexico as he knew them in the 1760s, Padre Ignaz Pfeffercorn observed that:

> Sonora is an altogether blessed country. Its hills and valleys shine with gold and silver mines.... The fertility of the soil incites wonder. It produces incomparably all plants, trees and growing things which require rich soil and warm air.... On the hills, as well as on the plains, there are the most excellent pastures, where grow in superabundance the choicest grass and all kinds of healthful herbs. Because of this Sonora has the most desirable conditions and conveniences for a considerable livestock industry and has, for some thirty odd years, nourished a multitude of animals on its fine pastures the whole year round.

Yet this same area was called a place of "sterile lands" by Padre Luis Velarde in 1716, and termed a "hopeless desert" by William Emory in 1857 and the same by D. D. Gaillard in 1894. Visitors obviously ran hot and cold on the region, alternately believing it to be a great wasteland, or a wilderness waiting for some crafty hand to make it burst into economic bloom.

What defines this region, and why do people have such strong reactions to it, negative and positive? The earliest European visitors such as Pfeffercorn defined the region culturally, on the basis of the area in which they could travel using guides who could comprehend some of the related languages spoken nearby. From the land of the Yaqui, northward to the region of the River Pima on the Gila and Santa Cruz, certain guides could speak the range of Uto-Aztecan languages found there, although Apache and Yuman languages were another issue altogether. Delimited by the Sierra Madres on the east, the Colorado River on the west, and the Mogollon Rim, some one hundred miles beyond Phoenix, on the north, this area also makes up more than ninety percent of the range of the saguaro cactus, a fact not lost on later naturalists who tried to define the Sonoran Desert as a biogeographic province. With the Gadsden Purchase of land from Mexico in 1853, the U.S. acquired part of the acreage formerly known as Sonora.

Still, this has not stopped people from thinking of the area as one (now binational) region with regard to its history and certain climatic and ecological phenomena. Forrest Shreve was one such stalwart defender of the coherence of bioregions. He observed that "in studying vegetation it is more satisfactory to cover a natural area than a political one, since the boundaries of states and provinces are so often straight and independent of natural features of the sort that limit the range of types of vegetation."

Shreve believed that regardless of other geographic definitions (such as the Basin and Range geological province) under which this

Opposite: Teddy bear cholla, Organ Pipe National Monument.
JACK W. DYKINGA.

region could be subsumed, the Sonoran Desert was a distinct biological entity. Among the many plants characteristic of the Sonoran Desert, there are a number that are found exclusively within the region. Fewer animals, however, are restricted to this desert alone. Among the animals limited to the Sonoran and Mohave deserts are Bailey's pocket mouse, round-tailed ground squirrels, and the desert kangaroo rat, as well as the desert tortoise, chuckwalla, sidewinder, desert iguana, and rosy boa.

Yet there are other animals, some of them common to most hot dry regions of the western U.S. and Mexico, that are such a part of this

Opposite: Coyote, the sacred trickster.
BUD BRISTOW.

Right: The heat of the desert lulls a
peccary. JAMES TALLON.

living community that the Sonoran Desert would be something
altogether different without them. It is hard to imagine waking up in
this desert without hearing the squawks of a gang of cactus wrens from
saguaro to saguaro. Or the whistles and flurry of wingbeats of a covey
of Gambel's quail. And what about the busy tapping of Gila wood-
peckers, and their dipping in and out of saguaros where they nest?
What would a winter wash scene be without phainopeplas hovering
over the mistletoe in the canopies of mesquite? And where would our
own desert humor be without roadrunners?

    With the presence of these animals, desert places are too lively to
be written off as mere scenery or static backdrops in front of which
man plays out his hand of tricks. The vegetation itself is more than just
a still-life stage prop, for the great variety of Sonoran Desert life forms
is never apparent all at once. In a sense, its seasonal changes are as

striking as those between a colorful autumn and a naked winter in New England.

Perhaps the season of extremes in the Sonoran Desert is not so much the winter as it is the late spring and early summer. After the spring wildflowers bloom, but before the summer storms begin, a hot period as long as two months in duration causes evaporation of any moisture left in the upper soil strata. Hardly any rainfall falls in May or early June, and when it does, it is seldom enough to make the washes flow. Some small animals, such as the Harris antelope ground squirrel, withdraw from activity during this time of year. In drought periods, the desert agave, or century plant, will not open its stomatal pores to implement photosynthesis at all; this strategy reduces water loss from the succulent leaf tissues. Ocotillos bloom early in this period, for that is when the hummingbirds that pollinate them migrate through Arizona, but they may lose all their leaves and contract their stems to cut back on water loss and heat loading. Standing in the open sun, a human feels the dry heat reach deep. This is what you could call being in "the dead of summer."

By mid-July, a single sudden storm of one to two inches of rain changes the desert world overnight. Spadefoot toads hear the rumble of thunder, feel the downpour drench the soil they are buried in, and come croaking up out of the ground to go and mate in recently filled water holes. Coyote gourds—some of which can endure more than a year of drought as a root without any vegetative growth—suddenly send out several feet of vines with hand-like leaves, crawling into trees and leaving apple-sized gourds behind. Summer ephemerals, or weedy wildflowers that can mature in less than two months' time, quickly carpet the desert floor. Their growth is rank. Their leaves move to follow the sun, as their roots plunge down to take advantage of as large a reservoir of soil moisture as they can reach. If rains are enough, some trees that bore fruit and some birds that hatched eggs in the spring will reproduce for a second time.

Thus trees that were little more than skeletons have resprouted leaves, and they have dozens of annual plants covered with insects crowding at their feet. Ephemerals, root perennials, cacti, succulents, and rain-responsive leafy trees and shrubs intermix in a structural diversity that looks like a circus freak show compared to late May's ghost-town feeling.

Many of these plants again go dormant by late October. Animals like the spadefoot are already back in the ground. Marsh hawks are gliding low as the cooler weather begins in November. But if rains come late in the fall, a gradual green hue will leak out to stain the desert ground, slowly growing into a more prominent mat of many colors. Although these winter ephemerals may not bloom until late February or March, they are the flowers that will paint the desert into a dazzling diversity of tints and tones that last sometimes two weeks, or in good years, two months. Many of these winter ephemerals are low-growing rosettes that hug the earth most of their brief lifetime, then send up

The Sonoran Desert is home to many birds. Opposite, clockwise from top left: Cactus wren C. ALLAN MORGAN; Gambel's quail ROBERT CAMPBELL; Gila woodpecker JAMES TALLON; and roadrunner C. ALLAN MORGAN.

shoots of flowers as the winter begins to warm to spring. Perennial herbs and shrubs flower at this time, too. Sometimes it looks as if volcanic hillsides have been caught on fire by brittlebush, their yellows are so intense.

Birds that nest in late spring in the Midwest nest here much earlier. Sparrows from the Great Plains sometimes arrive in November to use late-season grasses and winter-seed plants like woolly plantain. They usually begin to leave again by early March.

Ecologists have often asked themselves why the Sonoran Desert has such a variety of life forms existing together. Hasn't one kind of plant evolved a strategy so well adapted to the desert that it can dominate others under all conditions? The mountain forests have monocultures of ponderosa pine; the saline flats near Willcox Playa have miles upon miles of saltgrass; why has no single life form won out on a Sonoran bajada?

The answer may be that so much unpredictability and variation exists year to year in the Sonoran Desert that no one life form can outcompete others all the time. During extended droughts, the slow-growing, conservative cacti and succulents can endure stress that kills trees and keeps annuals from germinating. In the wet summers, certain rapidly photosynthesizing plants called C4 species can produce the most mass under high temperatures, with great efficiency of water use. But they are often frost-sensitive or do poorly during cooler, winter temperatures. The ground-hugging winter ephemerals do best then, but they must go dormant as seeds during the time of greatest heat. Even saguaro cacti, the most indicative plants of the Sonoran Desert, never cover the ground and control the whole biological community the way pines or prairie grasses do. Perhaps only in creosote or saltbush flats can you find the single-species pattern of dominance, but it is actually more characteristic of other North American deserts. In the final analysis, it is not so much the saguaro itself but the mix of plants in which saguaros are included that makes the Sonoran Desert so distinctive an entity.

A LITTLE WATER CAN GO A LONG WAY

Carl Lumholtz had just come in from the Camino del Diablo, or Devil's Road, between Yuma and Sonoita. Tough traveling, even with guides, even when it is not the hottest part of the year. He rested for a moment at an oasis that the Papago and their forerunners had drawn upon for centuries. The contrast between the Gran Desierto of lava and sand and Quitobaquito, the last irrigated patch of greenery before Yuma, hit him between the eyes:

The little stream of crystal clear spring water at Quitovaquita is

Opposite: Organ pipe cactus.
JACK W. DYKINGA.

PAPAGO CHICKEN SCRATCH

One comfortable fall day five musicians from central Arizona recorded some tunes at Chaton Studios in Paradise Valley, near Scottsdale. Their music, however, was less suited to a wealthy Phoenix suburb than to gritty bars, occasional church dances, and all-night outdoor gatherings. The group records for Canyon Records, a Phoenix company which deals exclusively in Indian music, and on that particular day, Joe Miguel & The Blood Brothers, a Papago Indian band, completed their second album of *waila* music, better known as chicken scratch music. Chicken scratch resembles an orchestrated Eastern European polka with Turkey-in-the-Straw pacing, a strong bass line, some *oom-pah oom*pah, and is heavily Mexican in influence. The name is said to come from the unusual six-beat step to which

SUZANNE STARR

the music is danced, resembling a chicken scratching the ground, and—when danced outdoors—sounding like it, too.

"The difference between Papago chicken scratch and Mexican *norteña* music," explained band leader and alto saxophone player Joe Miguel, "is that our music is faster. Also, the beat is slightly off-tempo." His band included brother Layne Miguel, whose battered *bajo sexto* —similar to a twelve-string guitar—still carried more than half of its strings; Richard Garcia, an accordion player from Casa Grande; José Velasco, Jr., a Phoenix drum-

mer; and electric bassist Ronnie Joaquin. Garcia's fingers sprinted up and down his B-flat Hohner. Velasco's taped drumsticks rushed out a syncopated rhythm. Joe and Layne wove a circular melody line. Joaquin's bass gave hurried cadence to the musical free-for-all.

"Joe Miguel & The Blood Brothers, Volume 2" came out as a cassette tape, not an album. Canyon Records hasn't released an actual album in a long time, according to founder Ray Boley, whose first record in the early 1950s featured Edward Natay, a Navajo singer. Since then Boley has recorded, on location and in studios, more than 500 albums, eight-tracks, and cassettes of Indians from Canada to Mexico. His recordings sell in the trading posts and main villages on and near reservations, and by mail-order to anthropologists, folklore buffs, and other followers of eclectic music. "The Indian Studies Program at the University of Zurich," Boley noted, "has a standing order for one of everything we release." In 1976 a Papago chicken scratch band traveled to Washington, D.C., to perform at the Smithsonian Institution's Bicentennial Festival of American Folklife.

"We recorded our first chicken scratch band in the early 1970s," Boley said. "I'd been hearing people talk about chicken scratch, but I didn't know what it was. Someone invited me to a chicken scratch dance on the Papago reservation, so I went with my Sony and two microphones and set them in front of the speakers." The result was the first of many chicken scratch albums.

Sales of chicken scratch tapes are limited, and, like any type of entertainment, depend on the economy. "We sell to the poorest segment of American society," an assistant to Boley offered. "When the copper mines are suffering, we do too. They won't buy tapes if they can't buy milk."

Canyon Records ordered a run of 750 copies of the new Joe Miguel tape to sell in its Phoenix shop and through the normal Papago outlets. Five months later, after steady sales, 400 more were ordered.

Was Joe Miguel disappointed that his music came out on tape instead of a record? "I don't know anyone who buys records anymore," he said, "unless you have a record player in your pick-up." The Blood Brothers laughed.

TOM MILLER

Above: Dos Playas, Cabeza Prieta, southwestern Arizona.
DAVE FOREMAN.

smaller than a brook, but it seemed much alive as it hurried on in its effort to keep the dam full. As I had been long unaccustomed to seeing running water, and for twenty days had drunk it more or less brackish, the tiny brook seemed almost unreal and was enchanting in its effect. It was also a delight to indulge in my first real wash for nine days.

Today, seventy-five years later, thousands of people drive by Quitobaquito on Mexico's borderland Highway 2 without even noticing it. The oasis pond itself covers less than an acre. In Arizona there are sewage ponds, golf-course water traps, surf-machine recreational ponds, and water towers that hold more liquid volume than this little place. But for centuries, Quitobaquito was significant enough that two major trails crossed at this vortex. You can see shell from the Sea of Cortez and turquoise, obsidian, pottery, and glass from the west coast set down in little mounds that travelers left behind.

For similar reasons, Ventana Cave attracted human visitors for millennia with just a minor seep dripping into the dust back in the shadows. Frank Bayham reminds us that such a small water source was like a mini-oasis, the Arabic root of "oasis" being "oueh," to dwell,

and "saa," to drink. Hardly any of the archaeological reconstruction done there would have been possible if that seep had not existed; people would have had little reason to spend time in a place devoid of water. In contrast, some urban drinking fountains probably have a greater daily flow than the little fault does at Ventana.

In deserts, little energy can flow and few nutrients can cycle without water. Moving from Tucson to Yuma, the potential evaporation increases from four feet per year to a little over two yards. Rainfall decreases from about twelve inches a year to less than four on the average. Combining these two factors crucial to the desert's water balance, the potential loss of water from the desert exceeds rainfall loss by four times at Tucson and by as much as eighteen times in Yuma County. Simply speaking, since plants cannot survive on deficit spending the way governments do, they must either concentrate water from other sources or throw in the towel.

Thus, much of the desert's productivity is concentrated along washes where rainfall running off a larger area is concentrated. When a downpour occurs, it is like a trigger that shoots energy into the desert community to renew it. Not only energy, but nutrients as well, since much of the release and conversion of elements essential to plant growth occurs soon after rains and their floods. In the 1890s geologist–ethnographer W. J. McGee arrived on the edge of a wash north of Nogales just after a flash flood had rolled through it for a half hour:

> The after-effects of the flood were not conspicuous, though significant. The most striking effect was the accumulation of flotsam, chiefly twigs and branches.... A less striking effect was the accumulation of a nearly continuous film of sediment...usually an inch in thickness, though sometimes it lines depressions to several inches.

McGee later added that this unevaporated residue from storm floods serves in "soaking the soil and fertilizing it...just as the valley of the Nile is fertilized." Subsequent desert studies have shown that floodplain sites receiving such water and nutrients are sometimes twenty-five times more productive than less favorable sites nearby. By the time small ephemeral tributaries coalesce into intermittent rivers like the Santa Cruz, the volume of both the energy-charged water and its suspended materials is enormous. About the same time McGee described the flashflood on a little arroyo, J. M. Berger, government farmer at San Xavier Indian Reservation, was pondering its cumulative impact as the inundation reached the Tucson area:

> ...the floods are continually causing damage to irrigating ditches and to roads and bridges, and in many locations also prevent the planting of a so-called second crop; but otherwise these floods do much good, as the considerable amount of sediment they bring is considered to be, and, as a matter of fact, is, a great fertilizer, and land so overflowed does not need any artificial fertilizing.

Opposite: Saguaro cactus, 1938.
EDWARD WESTON.

Flood movement of soil is, of course, a normal geological process, even when the magnitude of materials is increased due to man's poor management of the land. But erosion and deposition are not the only geological processes that have shaped Sonoran Desert landforms. Geologists believe that all of southern Arizona was once a high plateau. Through a series of earthquakes, it began arranging itself twelve to fifteen million years ago into the mountain ranges and valleys we see today. Other landforms were at times imposed upon this situation. For example, the Sentinel Plain and Pinacate lava flows in southwestern Arizona are less than six million years old. Other landforms, such as the Yuma sand dunes, are more recent, due to the westward blowing of particles left by the meandering of the Colorado River. Lava-derived desert pavement and dunes can be seen juxtaposed with old silty plains in the Cabeza Prieta Wildlife Refuge. Here you can observe how plants respond to three very distinctive substrates, each with its own moisture-holding capacity and nutrient load.

While the Cabeza Prieta is a good place to ponder plant competition for water, one need not go further than the suburbs of Tucson or Phoenix to get a sense of how the availability of water shapes the places people are willing to locate. Today a person in Phoenix uses an average of almost 300 gallons of water a day for domestic and recreational purposes. Tucsonans average 160 gallons daily, while Papagos on the San Xavier Reservation average 50 gallons a day. As urban areas grow in deserts, there are inevitably struggles over the allocation of water resources. Groundwater depletion, due primarily to pumping for agricultural production, has caused the subsidence of the ground surface in certain areas. It has also brought about arguments: over who should get how much groundwater and why. Even the use of partially treated sewage waters has become a topic of controversy, as some parties want this resource used on public parks and golf courses, and others want it mixed with better quality water to facilitate its application in irrigated agricultural production.

Whatever the outcome of such conflicts, however more sophisticated our management of water resources becomes in future years, we must remember that rainfall, floods, and droughts will always leave us with a somewhat unpredictable situation from year to year. A field ravished by a three-foot-deep flood one year may be limited in its water use the next by a drought. Bumper crops of wildflowers may follow several years of unspectacular shows. However much we may be able to buffer ourselves from this variability in terms of urban supplies, it will nevertheless meet us in the desert again whenever we go out to jog, hunt, gather, or meditate away from peopled places.

The vast area of the Sonoran Desert continues to be unpeopled, perhaps to a greater extent than most areas of the country. Modern Arizona residents regularly have the chance to contrast their own resource use with that of plants and animals, and even with that of indigenous cultures and their strategies of desert survival evolved over thousands of years. For many of them, a little water goes a long way.

Opposite: Palm Canyon, in Kofa National Wildlife Refuge.
JACK W. DYKINGA.

THE CHIHUAHUAN DESERT

T he rocky maze of Texas Canyon is the gateway to the Chihuahuan Desert. Fifty miles east of Tucson, the Interstate climbs away from the San Pedro River and across eroded, gravelly slopes sparsely covered with thorny mesquite and occasional tufts of bunchgrass and bur-roweed. The road gets steeper; suddenly huge rounded shapes loom on all sides; pale domes of granite surround the highway.

Pulling off the highway at the Dragoon road and walking away from the pavement, the traveler will find twisted trails between rock outcrops, heading first one way and then another. Some routes are hidden by overgrowth of oak trees. Coral-bean shrubs grow from rock crevices, their three-lobed leaves turning yellow in the late summer and contrasting with the strings of bright scarlet beans hanging on the open pods. It is easy to be caught and scratched by the curved thorns of the low wait-a-minute bushes, and to step on a rattlesnake curled in a protected niche is an ominous possibility.

Scarcely more than a hundred years ago, entering Texas Canyon meant risking attack by Apaches. The Overland Mail driver had no time for scenery but rolled on through the threatening, secret ravines, hurrying out into the open Sulphur Springs Valley and the safety of Fort Bowie.

In southwestern Arizona, the Chihuahuan Desert is at its north-westernmost extremity. Three-fourths of the desert is in Mexico, and approximately one-half of that is in the state of Chihuahua, from which the desert gets its name. The desert occupies the high central plateau of Mexico and is in a tremendous basin defined on three sides by impos-ing mountain ranges. To the east is the Sierra Madre Oriental in the states of Nuevo León and Tamaulipas. To the south the transverse ranges of the Sierra Madre del Sur cut across southern Zacatecas and San Luis Potosí. On the west the crest of the Sierra Madre Occidental follows the border between Chihuahua and Durango and the coastal states of Sonora and Sinaloa. The desert extends north until it finally disappears into the plains grassland of the United States.

Because of its mountain barriers, much of the Chihuahuan basin

Above left: Coral bean.
C. ALLAN MORGAN.

Opposite: Cochise Head, a major peak in the Chiricahua Mountains of southeastern Arizona.
DAVE FOREMAN.

country does not drain to the ocean, but into closed basins of varying size. The only major route of external drainage is the Rio Grande and its tributaries, the largest of which is the Río Conchos of Chihuahua. As a result of this lack of external drainage and consequent areas of erosional lowland, the area has a fairly uniform base elevation of just over 3,500 feet. Throughout its range the Chihuahuan Desert generally is between 3,000 and 5,000 feet in elevation, dropping to around 2,000 feet along the Rio Grande. The Sonoran Desert, by contrast, ranges from sea level to 3,000 feet.

The basin landscape, lacking big rivers with permanent water and broad floodplains, could not support permanent settlement but did

Black grama grass.
U.S. SOIL CONSERVATION.

provide a livelihood for nomadic bands of Apaches and their predecessors, the Sumas and Jocomes. To the northwest and west the fertile floodplains of the Gila River and its tributaries were occupied by Pimas and Papagos. To the south the verdant, narrow canyons of the Río Bavispe were farmed by Opatas. The Conchos occupied foothill valleys of the Sierra Madre near the present town of Casas Grandes, Chihuahua. But the dry open plains of the Chihuahuan Desert were no-man's-land, uninhabited except for occasional bands of Apaches traveling from one mountain retreat to another.

One such camp at the south end of the Peloncillo Mountains was described by John Bourke, a cavalryman in the command of General George Crook, in *On the Border with Crook*:

> The whole ravine was romantically beautiful: shading the rippling water were smooth, white-trunked, long, and slender sycamores, dark and gnarly ash, rough-barked cottonwoods, pliant willows, briery buckthorn, and much of the more tropical vegetation...

Crook met there with Geronimo and other Apache leaders in March 1886 to discuss the Indians' surrender. As a result of their negotiations, most of the Apache band accompanied Crook back to Fort Bowie. Even though, after the meeting, Geronimo and a few others disappeared into the Sierra Madre for some weeks, the Apache threat to settlers in southeastern Arizona was gone. With it went a way of life peculiarly adapted to the desert.

THE VIEW FROM BARFOOT

Imagine an early February day. Low clouds are covering the Tucson basin, and a gentle rain is sprinkling the edge of the Sonoran Desert. The storm goes on for miles east of Tucson. Past Benson, on the climb into Texas Canyon at the north end of the Dragoon Mountains, the gentle rain changes to snow. East across the broad San Simon Valley and into New Mexico, a light mantle of snow covers the plains from horizon to horizon, extending all the way to Las Cruces.

In the vicinity of the Dragoons, the traveler crossing the eastern edge of the subtropical Sonoran Desert enters a region of intermingling grassland and scrub that marks the beginning of the Chihuahuan Desert region. The snow blanket gleams for miles with an occasional spindly acacia or yucca rosette poking its way through. In the Tucson basin and in low valleys to the west the rain nourishes a thriving growth of young ephemeral plants, while in the high plains of the Chihuahuan Desert, freezing temperatures inhibit winter growth. There, for many species, growth will not begin until summer when rains coincide with warm temperatures.

Barfoot Lookout on the crest of the Chiricahua Mountains is a good place for watching the weather of southeastern Arizona. Following Highway 181 south from Willcox for thirty minutes and turning east up Pinery Canyon, the grassland gives way to oak woodland, and finally, near the crest, to pine forest. The crest road leads to Barfoot Park, and from there it's a short but steep trail to the lookout. The view is spectacular—dark wooded slopes falling away to the paler browns and yellows of the valley floor. On any day with sunshine, the mountain spiny lizards are active on nearby rocky slopes.

On an early summer morning the sky is brilliantly clear and still, but by midmorning little white clouds can be seen hovering over all the mountains on the horizon, including Chiricahua Peak close to the south. Within a few hours the wispy patches have billowed into tall cumulus clouds casting dark shadows. By midafternoon the clouds have climbed high enough to be caught by the upper air currents moving west and are carried away from the mountains to trace a path of rain across the desert. Sometimes the rain begins falling only to evaporate before reaching the ground.

In winter the storms move in from the west. Instead of forming here and there and growing from nothing to a violent tempest in a few hours, these storms arrive full grown. Visible first as a long white smudge across the western horizon, a winter storm expands to a threatening gray wall and finally engulfs the mountain in a dense rainy mist that may close in for days, sending the spiny lizards down into the rock crevices until the sun comes out.

The average annual rainfall on the desert plain is eight to ten inches. More falls on the mountains. At the western edge of the desert, about half of the yearly precipitation is in the summer and half in the winter, but as one moves east, a larger and larger proportion falls in the summer. Deep in the desert, winter rain is almost unknown.

The view northwest from Barfoot is dominated by Willcox Playa, the only Chihuahuan interior drainage basin in Arizona. The playa lies in a basin of semi-desert grassland between the Dragoon and Chiricahua mountains that hints at the extensive basins to the south and east in Chihuahua and beyond.

Because the runoff from rainfall accumulates in the playa rather than leaving the watershed through streams and rivers, more water is available there than would be expected from the normal rainfall in the region. In some basins this results in permanent water, but in most it simply means standing water is available for a greater part of the year.

The playas thus provide a desert habitat that really is not desert at all. Depending on the length of time water is present, the vegetation may be a marsh of sedges and aquatic herbs, or dense stands of grass—especially sacaton and tobosa. At increasing distance from the playa bottom, moisture decreases and along with it vegetation cover—from thick stands of grasses and other non-desert-adapted plants to open stands of true desertscrub. These patterns are evident around the margin of Willcox Playa where thickets of alkali sacaton and giant sacaton give way to drought-resistant tobosa grass. Finally, in the drier soil,

Opposite: Lookout Point, in the heart of the Chiricahuas. TOM BEAN.

SAVE OUR STORE

he number of mini-marts in Arizona seems to grow geometrically. Occasionally neighbors will resist the arrival of a convenience store when it upsets the aesthetics or traffic pattern in their community, but almost always to no avail. That's why the effort to save Moore's Grocery on Tombstone Canyon in Bisbee proved so remarkable. Run by Alonzo "Lonnie" Moore since 1962, the store had its origins in 1914 when his parents opened a small market just down the street. Like everything else in this one-industry town, Moore's rose and fell on the health of the copper industry and the men who worked in its mines. During strikes, which seemed to come with every contract, Moore and more than a dozen other grocers in town extended credit to hungry families, secure in the knowledge that when the mine shaft whistle blew again, they'd be repaid.

Lonnie returned to help his folks run the grocery after graduating from college with a degree in electrical engineering at the beginning of World War Two. One by one the small independent grocery stores in Bisbee closed—most of them in the early 1970s when Phelps Dodge phased out operations begun before the turn of the century. Moore's and a couple of others hung on tenaciously. As Bisbee's population shifted, so did Moore's customers. Wry humor, neighborhood gossip, corny signs,

TOM VAUGHAN

home delivery, and room to chat made Moore's a part of everyday life for many. All it lacked was a pot-bellied stove.

Those final years of extending credit took their toll. Thousands of dollars in charge accounts went unpaid. Business, no matter how friendly, couldn't keep utility bills paid. Customers noticed Lonnie's heart wasn't in it any more, and sometimes he didn't bother to open for days at a time. Bette, his wife, was seen around the store less and less frequently. The network of good neighbors and nodding acquaintances which regularly found itself at Moore's was delighted, then, when they read an open letter from fellow customers Brian and Larison Lockart: "We recognize that in order to put Moore's back in business, putting inventory back on the shelves is only part of the solution. We want to give Moore's a new look and a positive feeling." And so in the fall of 1983 dozens of customers and friends from all parts of town showed up to patch the roof, scrub down the shelves, walls, and floors inside, and give the outside a complete facelift. Electricians rewired, carpenters solidified the shelves, painters beautified the front, and others donated their skills and equipment as well. Everyone, it appeared, pitched in. To many, it seemed to be what an old-fashioned barnraising must have felt like generations earlier. The Lockharts called it "an appeal to optimism."

The spiffy façade and spotless interior was matched by a most unusual fund-raising campaign: contributors could deposit money into a special account, and withdraw it later in ten-dollar increments as groceries. About 130 people responded, depositing more than $6,000 in the "Save Our Store" account, almost all of which went to restocking the shelves. Moved by the outpouring, Moore redoubled his efforts. He moved his piano to the store's front, and feigned annoyance whenever a customer interrupted his playing.

Stories like this deserve a happy ending, but this one has a twist. Business was fine for a few months, then leveled off. By summer the grocery was again failing, and this time Lonnie closed it for good. He hadn't looked so relieved in years, friends admitted afterwards. Former customers saw him bat a tennis ball around against the wall at St. Patrick's play yard and heard him continue with his music. He still kept up his Sunday morning walks at the Mule Mountain Divide, joined by those far younger and less fit. Everyone noticed an extra spring to his step.

TOM MILLER

grasses thin out and shrubs such as mesquite and white-thorn acacia dominate the surrounding hills.

There is a catch to living on the wet basin floor. In many such older playas the lower center portion of the basin is devoid of any growth. This is the result of centuries of accumulation of dissolved salts along with soil particles that are washed into the playa. When the playa soil gets wet, the ground turns into a salty soup that literally sucks the water out of the roots of plants. Only a few of the most salt-tolerant species—saltgrass, pickleweed, saltbush, and seepweed—extend out onto salty flats.

Beyond the playa edge the vegetation is a pattern of grassland intermixed with desertscrub common to all the Chihuahuan region and not restricted to the wetter playa bottoms. Throughout much of the region climatic conditions are at the balance point between desertscrub and grassland: too dry for well-developed grassland, wet enough that the desert is invaded by many grassland species. The Sonoran Desert around Tucson actually receives more rain but supports relatively few grass species; rainfall in the Chihuahuan Desert is more effective because it lies at higher, cooler elevations.

Because the climate is close to the transition between desert and grassland, fairly small variations in other environmental variables (soil, for example) may make the difference between the presence of desertscrub or grassland at any particular site. Coarse gravelly or sandy soil can let water penetrate rapidly away from the surface. In hot weather the soil surface layers may dry out in a few days. Finer-textured soil will hold more water near the surface. This difference in water-holding ability may make the difference in the survival of some shallow-rooted grasses. In the Chihuahuan Desert landscape a variety of soils with many different textures, ranging from rocky and gravelly fans around rock outcrops and hills to sandy plains and clayey valley bottoms, results in a mosaic of vegetation including both grassland and desertscrub.

The San Bernardino Valley, in the extreme southeast corner of Arizona between the Chiricahua and Peloncillo mountains, illustrates this variety. About ten miles east of Douglas, following the same route that Crook rode on his way to meet Geronimo, one crosses the low southern ridge of the Parilla Mountains and begins dropping into the San Bernardino Valley. The long sloping bajada from the ridge to Black Draw is dissected with numerous small gullies. For miles the slope is dominated by shrubs, including the red stems of white-thorn acacia, creosotebush, tarbush, spiny little-leaf sumac, spreading ocotillo, and mariola. The stands of shrubs stretch low and unbroken, except for a few straggling ocotillo, with bare gravelly soil between. Grasses are almost absent from the entire bajada.

Continuing east, the road crosses the wash a short way above the old Slaughter Ranch at San Bernardino Spring and climbs the east side of the valley. The country is dominated by tobosa and other less abun-

dant grasses, including sand dropseed and plains bristlegrass, with scattered mesquite. A brief look tells the story: the soil here is sandier than on the other side of the valley and lacks the abundant gravel and cobbles. Although it receives almost the same rainfall, the loamy soil on this gentler slope holds its water closer to the surface and supports a higher cover of grass.

THE LIMESTONE MYSTERY AND THE PACKRAT'S ANSWER

On the north end of the Santa Rita Mountains the dense pine-oak woodland of higher elevations gives way to open grassy slopes with scattered Emory oak and Mexican blue oak. For several miles north of the Greaterville Road the rolling slopes alternate between open grass on the south-facing slopes and mixed stands of oak and juniper on those facing north. In the vicinity of the abandoned mining camp of Rosemont, two or three miles east of the knife-like backbone of the mountains, one hillside stands out from the rest; it is covered with a thick growth of sandpaper-bush, white-thorn acacia, ocotillo, and tarbush. These species dominate the northwestern Chihuahuan Desert, but none can be found for miles to the east. Stands like this are scattered widely; the largest are found on the Whetstone Mountains and the Tombstone Hills. Looking down, we see that the rocks underfoot contain small marine fossils, crinoids and other sea creatures. The rock is limestone, as it is in the Whetstones and the Tombstones. The soil that weathers from these rocks is high in carbonates, and the Chihuahuan plants flourish on it. As one looks across the distance between the sandpaper-bushes on the Santa Ritas and those on the far-off Whetstones, the question comes to mind: how did these plants get here?

Along the upper stretches of the San Pedro River, almost to the town of Naco on the Mexican border, the river cuts into old alluvium. Erosion has exposed the petrified bones of mammoths. Paleontologists have unearthed the remains of giant ground sloths. These animals and others roamed the Chihuahuan Desert region during the Pleistocene, from about 2 million years until 10 to 20 thousand years ago. What is known about the habitat and diet of these animals suggests that they did not live in desertscrub such as grows today along the San Pedro River.

To the east in Willcox Playa, researchers have drilled holes deep into the lake-bed sediments, seeking better understanding of these ancient biotic communities. In the past the playa was filled with water throughout the year, not mostly dry as it is now. By examining the plant pollen preserved in the sediments, the identity of the plants living around the lake in times past can be determined. Pollen found in clay

Opposite: The Chihuahuan Desert.
JACK W. DYKINGA.

Opposite: Willcox Playa.
JAMES TALLON.

Below: Chihuahuan hook-nosed
snake. WAYNE VAN DEVENDER.

under Willcox Playa shows a profile of late Pleistocene plant life ending about 20,000 years ago. Many of the plants were the same as those now living in the area, but the abundant quantity of pine pollen in Willcox Playa sediment equals that collected in a mountain meadow surrounded by pine forest.

Farther east, just over the state line in New Mexico, lie the Little Hatchet Mountains, in which a small cave contains an accumulation of almost six feet of material that includes bones of many animal species. Based on radiocarbon dating, the age of the deposit is estimated to be upwards of 13,000 years. Many animals living in the area today, such as horned lizards, spadefoot toads, and rattlesnakes, are represented in the cave deposit. But the bones of tiger salamanders and voles (meadow mice) are also common in the cave, as are the bones of a fish, the Colorado chub. All of them today inhabit areas of greater moisture; none is found in the vicinity of the cave.

These pieces of evidence—extinct large herbivores, pine pollen in the lake bed, and bones of animals from a wetter climate—reinforce the belief that the landscape and climate of the Chihuahuan Desert have changed in the not-too-distant past. Analysis of pollen, seeds, leaf-and stem litter, bones, and mummified remains from packrat middens in

the Southwest support the idea that the Chihuahuan and Sonoran deserts may have attained their present boundaries in Arizona as recently as 5,000 years ago. In the warming and drying trend that followed, plants and animals that adapted to moister, cooler environments were forced to withdraw.

Over time, as the climate changed in response to repeated Pleistocene glaciations, the desert appears to have advanced and receded many times across what is today the transition zone between desertscrub and grassland and woodland. As the distribution of individual plants advanced and retreated, a few were left behind in sites suitable for their growth. Shrubs found on the limestone in the Santa Rita Mountains and elsewhere in southeastern Arizona became relics as grassland and woodland moved in around them.

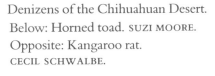

Denizens of the Chihuahuan Desert. Below: Horned toad. SUZI MOORE. Opposite: Kangaroo rat. CECIL SCHWALBE.

Related to the shifting desert margin is the story of the all-female whiptail lizards as told by zoologist Charles H. Lowe and his students at the University of Arizona. During years of collection and study, no male specimens of certain whiptails were ever captured. It turned out that this was no accident, for there are no males in these species. The female lays clutches of eggs that hatch into young lizards genetically identical to her—all without benefit of fertilization by a male. This reproduction by a single sex is called parthenogenesis. Five of the eight species of whiptail lizards in Arizona have been found to be unisexual.

These single-sex species thriving in disturbed habitats have been called "weed" species. When colonizing a new habitat, a single, parthenogenetic female lizard has a tremendous advantage over members of a sexual species that must find mates. She can move in, lay eggs, and start a new population without waiting for a male. One of these unisexual species, the desert grassland whiptail, inhabits the transition between grassland and northern Chihuahuan Desert in Arizona, New Mexico, west Texas, and northern Mexico. In this region the repeated advance and retreat of different plant communities opens up new habitats for the self-sufficient female.

THE SHIFTING SANDS
OF JORNADA DEL MUERTO

In 1942 Forrest Shreve described the major desert areas of North America. The map he drew showed the northwestern boundary of the Chihuahuan Desert to be just west of the Rio Grande in southern New Mexico, one hundred miles from the Arizona state line. Yet today, as the result of work by several investigators, it is generally accepted that the Chihuahuan Desert occupies a fairly large part of Arizona. How can one resolve this apparent contradiction involving hundreds of square miles?

During the last fifty years, at least a dozen maps showing different boundaries of the Chihuahuan Desert have been drawn by different cartographers. Several indicate that the desert does not extend into Arizona, while others show a connection through the plains of southwestern New Mexico. The total area of the Chihuahuan Desert on some maps is nearly double that on others.

The source of this confusion is in part the criteria used to define the desert. Some consider one or several climatic indicators, while others use a strictly biological definition. The simplest climatic delineation considers only average annual rainfall. More elaborate climate classification systems have been developed that define arid regions on the basis of annual rainfall and annual temperature, or on annual rainfall and potential annual evaporation. Both of these methods give similar results because evaporation is closely related to temperature. These two approaches also have more meaning biologically because they reflect the amount of water actually available to plants and animals.

A more direct "floristic" approach has been taken by some, who define the desert to be wherever desert plant species are found growing. An example is the use of creosotebush as an indicator of desert boundaries.

The floristic approach was used by Shreve to define the Sonoran Desert. He relied to a large extent on the distribution of saguaro cactus to delineate the northern boundaries. His early work has stood the test of time with little change because the distribution of saguaro is controlled by the occurrence of freezing temperatures.

Many plants of the Sonoran Desert originate from tropical regions and have a sensitivity to cold similar to that of the saguaro. The result is that the similar distribution of these subtropical species gives the Sonoran Desert an apparent cohesiveness lacking in the Chihuahuan Desert.

Traveling east from Tucson in the early fall, one sees repeating vegetation patterns extending from Fort Bowie, on the west side of the San Simon Valley, all the way to Las Cruces. The patterns broken here and there by scattered mountain ranges are otherwise dominated by rolling sandy plains and flat clay playas. The playas are bare or covered with stands of tobosa and sacaton. The miles of rolling plains are highlighted with the bright yellow flowers of scattered patches of snakeweed. In some areas the plains are dotted with sand hills capped with green hummocks of mesquite. These plains are often categorized today as Chihuahuan Desert. But is it certain they looked like this when Shreve first crossed them in the 1930s? Recent evidence suggests that they did not.

In 1932 a one-square-mile livestock exclosure was constructed to study the effects of livestock-grazing on the natural vegetation of the Jornada del Muerto, thirty miles north of Las Cruces, New Mexico. In 1935 vegetation was measured along permanent transects, and these measurements were repeated in the 1950s and again in 1980. In 1935 the vegetation both inside and outside the exclosure was dominated by black grama grass with almost no mesquite. By 1955, however, mesquite was clearly on the increase outside the exclosure, and black grama was declining. In 1980 the exclosure was a small island of grass, surrounded by country in which black grama was almost completely absent and mesquite was dominant. In addition, on what had been a more or less level plain, sand hummocks or coppice dunes like those along the route from Fort Bowie to Las Cruces had formed around the mesquite.

A similar pattern of change is reported for extensive areas of southeastern Arizona and southwestern New Mexico. Changes are better documented at the Jornada Range than at most other locations, where they occurred as much as fifty years earlier. The general pattern of loss of grass cover along with increase in shrub cover seems to have characterized many dry grassland areas adjoining both the Sonoran and Chihuahuan deserts.

The dramatic nature and geographic extent of such changes are surprisingly little understood. Several factors appear to have contributed to the shift from grassland to scrubland. From 1950 to 1955 the northwestern region of the Chihuahuan Desert experienced what some have considered the worst drought in three to four centuries. That period coincided with the most rapid period of change on the Jornada Range, suggesting that climate played a major role. However, a few fenced areas protected from grazing at the Jornada Range still have thick stands of black grama, indicating that livestock also had an effect. Additionally, modern fire-control practices favor shrub establishment. Historically, the grasslands were burned at frequent intervals by lightning-caused fires. These fires killed shrubs but generally did no harm to grasses, whose growing tissues are protected at ground level. With the suppression of grass fires, shrubs could get a foothold among the grasses, competing for water with these species and eventually displacing them.

Whatever the causes of ecological change in the recent past, the effects are far-reaching. Forrest Shreve might well not recognize the plains that he mapped as grassland in 1942. In addition to the most obvious replacement of grasses by shrubs, less apparent shifts in animal populations have almost certainly taken place. Some animals adapted to

a grassland environment are probably now on the retreat, and other desert species will be taking their places.

The sand hill country is maligned by many as unproductive, deteriorated grassland, but it has a beauty and variety of its own. The best way to see the sand hills is to sleep out in the dunes following a summer thundershower. First thing in the morning the sun catches glistening dewdrops on the mesquite leaves, and the moist air feels soft against the skin. The freshly packed sand has been erased of all tracks and is in a smooth, undisturbed condition for the day's activity. As the soil warms, lizards and beetles and other sand-dwellers begin to stir and add their tracks to the new day's record.

The small dramas of the dunes can be traced in the freshly watered sand. The tracks of lizards follow the edges of the mesquite hummocks, then dash across the open sand to another hill. The polished trail of a whipsnake scouts among the dunes, suggesting how predators lie in wait for careless lizards to get too far from protecting shrubs. Quick movement catches peripheral vision, but as one turns, nothing is

Opposite: Sandhill cranes.
JAMES TALLON.

visible but a scattering of caliche fragments exposed by the wind and shining brightly on the surface of the sand. A closer look reveals that one of those pebbles is a Chihuahuan horned lizard, or round-tailed horned lizard, a small, almost patternless animal scarcely larger than a quarter. The color of these lizards can range from almost white to gray, light brown, or even orange, depending on the color of the soil. In the dunes, instead of matching the soil, these lizards are nearly white, mimicking the small white caliche pebbles exposed on the sand surface. This creature lacks the spiny frill and distinctive pattern of other horned lizards and seems to disappear among the small rocks when it freezes motionless on open ground.

The Texas horned lizard is a close relative of the Chihuahuan horned lizard. It also can live on the dunes, but is primarily a grassland species ranging south from eastern Kansas into Mexico and through eastern and southern New Mexico into southeastern Arizona. Depending also on coloration for protection, this larger lizard (about the size of the palm of your hand) usually has various shades of brown with a distinctive yellow central stripe between paired yellow circles and crescents—a pattern reminiscent of dried, curling grass leaves on the soil surface. This larger species is actually imitating a patch of dry grassland.

Paired tracks can be seen where the kangaroo rats hopped across the open sand, stopping here and there to dig for seeds. The rats strong hind legs give them speed and agility for traversing open areas and large cheek pouches in which they can store great quantities of seeds collected during foraging trips across the sand. One species, the banner-tailed kangaroo rat, lives in grasslands adjacent to the Chihuahuan Desert, as well as in true desertscrub. It differs from other kangaroo rats by building large mounds that it keeps free of grass by constant digging, and in which it often caches quantities of seeds.

Building mounds is evidently a practice that permits the rats to inhabit dense grassland. Disturbance of the soil encourages the growth of a variety of plants on which they feed, and the open ground gives them maximum use of their jumping ability to escape predators. But with disappearing grassland, their specialized behavior may become a handicap. In areas where stands of grama grassland are dotted with active mounds, adjacent expanses of mesquite coppice dunes support very few banner-tails, suggesting that, as grassland changes to mesquite dunes, banner-tailed kangaroo rat populations may be declining.

The lessons repeatedly learned from the history of the Chihuahuan Desert and its plants and animals are unpredictability and constant change. Each year brings surprises, even to oldtimers. In 1983 many parts of southeastern Arizona received the heaviest rains yet recorded. What changes did these foretell? Will different plants find conditions just right for production of seed and replace the previous dominants? Will those seeds be the right food for animals whose populations will expand into a new habitat? Above all desert-dwellers must accept the need to change, and adapt to their singular environment.

THE ELUSIVE INTERIOR

When the Great Flood came, Changing Woman sealed herself in a giant abalone shell. She took water and food, so she could survive during the weeks of swirling floodwaters.

Time and again she knocked on the shell, but always she heard the dull echo that meant she still was being carried on the waters. Finally, her knock produced the hollow sound that told her the world had dried out and she had come to rest.

Changing Woman stepped from her shell in the Red Rock Country where Sedona is today. She was the only person that survived the flood. She was Ests'unnadlehi, *the first Apache.*

As told by Philip Cassadore,
San Carlos Apache Medicine Man

UNDER THE TONTO RIM

Tumble every Arizona environment together in a hopper and out comes the mélange of the interior. British writer J.B. Priestley encountered this land where "the mountains have married the desert" one day in 1939. He had stopped in Sedona for lunch, halfway between his dude ranch on the desert at Wickenburg and the Grand Canyon. In *Midnight on the Desert* he wrote of this "strangely beautiful" day:

> At one moment you are among the firs and the ice-cold waterfalls, and the next moment you are looking down again on sand and cactus.... And yet this place was not a little bit of everything neatly assembled, but was itself and unique.

Arizona does not divide orderly into plateau and desert. Where the forested plateaus "marry the desert," they give birth to a third major Arizona landscape. In a great central arc, a jumble of mountain ranges separates the high mesas of the Colorado Plateau to the north from the low, hot, mountain-studded plains of the Mojave, Sonoran, and Chihuahuan deserts.

Left: Sycamore in fall colors.
JACK W. DYKINGA.
Opposite: Earth paint, part of Apache girls' puberty ceremony.
RICO LEFFANTA.

The biggest landowners in this rugged country are the Western Apaches. Anthropologists say the Apaches probably did not reach this land until sometime after Spaniards Antonio de Espejo and Marcos Farfán de los Godos visited the Verde Valley in the late 1500s. When Francisco Vásquez de Coronado marched through the White Mountain country in 1540, he saw no Indians living between the desert and the plateau. However, the Apaches believe they have been here since the beginning, since Changing Woman stepped from an abalone shell in the Red Rock Country.

Either way, the Apaches controlled a piece of east-central Arizona too challenging for other tribes. Only the Yavapais and Hualapais farther west shared the resources of this country, where riches existed but were not obvious. When new arrivals began to explore central Arizona in the mid 1800s, they called it Apachería.

The rugged Arizona interior seems an appropriate sanctuary for the Apache, strong and elusive country for a strong and elusive people. Most Western Apaches live on the Fort Apache and San Carlos reservations, huge pieces of land only remnants of their original historic ter-

Below: Mexican Hay Lake, White Mountains. STEPHEN TRIMBLE.

Opposite: Black Jack Canyon, Greenlee County. EDWARD J. PFEIFER.

ritory. To the south lived the Chiricahua Apaches, now completely displaced from their homeland. Eastward, Apaches dominated most of New Mexico and adjoining states. Northward, their relations, the Navajos, controlled the plateau country between the Pueblo villages.

The Apaches lived so close to the land that they virtually blended with it. Captain John G. Bourke rode with General George Crook in his campaigns against the Apache in the 1870s and 1880s, and in his classic, *On the Border With Crook*, he described a parley with warriors "in their own haunts" on the divide between the White and Black rivers. "The knot-holes in the cedars seemed to turn into gleaming black eyes; the floating black tresses of dead yucca became the snaky locks of fierce outlaws, whose lances glistened behind the shoots of mescal and amole."

Prehistoric Indian people who lived in the interior had the same elusive quality as the Apaches. Sinagua, Salado, Hakataya, and Mogollon cultures held the mountains, their names much less familiar today than the Anasazi to the north and the Hohokam to the south.

At least a few geographic boundaries remain absolute. At one such

place in northwestern Arizona, the Grand Wash Cliffs separate the plateau from the basin and range deserts. And for some three hundred miles across central Arizona, the Mogollon Rim forms the southern boundary of the Colorado Plateau.

Bordering the Verde Valley at Sedona, above the Tonto Basin between Payson and Christopher Creek, and (only slightly less imposing) across the northern edge of the Fort Apache Reservation, the Mogollon Rim is incontrovertibly distinct. North lies the plateau. But what lies to the south?

"Desert" is one answer to this question. Go all the way south to Phoenix, where you *know* you are in desert. Heading north on Interstate 17 beyond Black Canyon City, you can easily tell when you enter a new landscape. Saguaros disappear; summer heat moderates. Looking north from Wickenburg, Florence Junction, or Safford, you clearly can see where the Sonoran Desert laps the feet of mountains—big mountains.

Between these two recognizable boundaries—the Mogollon Rim and the desert—lies Arizona's elusive interior. Here lies compressed all of Arizona's variety in glorious chaos. Broken land dissected by many rivers leads down from the Rim to the deserts.

Creosotebush marks valleys as desert while only a few miles away grow ponderosa pines. In between, evergreen shrubs and oaks grow in distinctive chaparral and encinal, yet the interior does not fit into iron-clad outlines of plant communities. Arizona ecologist Charles Lowe simply footnotes an essay on chaparral by saying "there is considerable confusion as to what constitutes chaparral in Arizona."

Geologists, too, have trouble placing precise boundaries on this central mountain belt, or even settling on a single name for the region. The name Apachería almost means "unexplored." Other alternatives: the interior, the central mountains, the uplands; the Transition Zone; the Gila Mountain province; the Mexican Highlands.

The Apaches clearly knew this land better than anyone. And they still do.

Changing Woman heard a voice from the other world, the medicine man's world. It told her to go to the east, to the edge of the mesa at dawn and kneel to let Sun shine his rays inside of her. She did this three times, but the sun did not penetrate her.

The voice told her to go back a fourth time. She did, and the breath of Sun shone inside of her. Soon she realized she was pregnant. Her child, the son of the Sun, grew up to become the Apache hero Naiyenezgani, Slayer of Monsters.

As a young man, Slayer of Monsters journeyed to the home of his father. After proving himself by completing the many difficult tests set him by Sun, he returned to the Earth and shared with his people the gifts of his father, the gifts of the Sun—horses, proper clothing, the bow and arrow.

Opposite: The bed of Sycamore Canyon Creek. JACK W. DYKINGA.

MCNARY BLACKS

The little town of McNary lies just inside the northern border of the Fort Apache Reservation. To the north are the old Mormon settlements of the Little Colorado. South are the Western Apaches. What, then, brought a sizeable number of blacks to this cool, high community in the Arizona outback?

The answer is ponderosa—hundreds of thousands of acres of it, one of the largest stands of ponderosa pine in the world. McNary is located on the eastern edge of Arizona's timber belt. In 1923–24, the predecessor of Southwest Forestries transferred an entire lumbering operation, including 500 black workers and their families, from the piney woods of Louisiana to the ponderosa forests of the White Mountains by train. Many of the first blacks left, but others from the same small Southern lumber towns arrived to take their place during the Depression and at the end of World War II.

The result, according to anthropologist Curtis Wienker, was Milltown, or "the Quarters," "a thriving town within the town." Blacks in McNary had their own churches, their own school, their own cemetery, and their own masonic lodge. Their restaurant served "down home" cooking, and most of them lived in simple wood-frame houses surrounding the mill. Segregated from their neighbors by the same laws and prejudices that existed in Louisiana, Mississippi, and east Texas, McNary blacks recreated a society that had developed more than a thousand miles to the east. Pocketed among the cowboys and Indians was a little piece of the Old South.

Times have changed since the early 1950s, when Milltown was at its peak. Schools are no longer segregated. Some of the old boundaries among ethnic groups have weakened or broken down. More to the point, periodic layoffs have forced many McNary blacks to leave the ponderosa stands for Phoenix or Los Angeles. And no new migrants enter the community from the piney woods anymore. Milltown itself is just a memory, bulldozed to make way for a plywood manufacturing plant after the remaining black families moved up to Hilltown, a part of McNary once restricted to whites.

Nonetheless, the history of McNary's black community is not as anomalous as it seems at first. Just as lumber drew mill hands there, cotton lured thousands of black farm workers to places like Eloy, Yuma, and the Salt River Valley. The great majority of the newcomers, however, came from farms or small towns in Texas and the rural South. Arizona's black population is largely urban today, yet traces of the Southern countryside linger on, in language and traditional health care, in church affiliations and family ties. You can still find remnants of southern black America like McNary scattered across Arizona. Even in cowboy and Indian country.

THOMAS E. SHERIDAN

HIGH CHAPARRAL

The central Arizona mountains formed such a rich larder for Apaches and Yavapais that they surely were one of the gifts from Sun. The Apaches hunted everything from deer to woodrats, grew a little corn, and with the arrival of the Spanish, raided southward for horse-meat and beef. But wild plants were their mainstay, and they wandered the mountains following the seasonal ripening of pinyon nuts, acorns, juniper berries, cactus fruits, wild grasses, mesquite beans, and, above all, agave (mescal).

Agave expert Howard Scott Gentry maps *Agave parryi* and its allies northward to the slopes of the Mogollon Rim, "the cold fringe of Agaveland," and notes "a remarkable coincidence between the distribution of this group of agaves and the tribes and clans of the wide-ranging Apaches." The great rosette of the agave could be roasted even in winter when other foods were scarce. This was a major chore that took four days of cooking in an underground pit, but once cooked, the mescal hearts could be transported, cached, or even traded to neighboring bands.

Navajos, too, or Mormon ranchers from Fredonia, would feel halfway at home in central Arizona: they could recognize characteristic plateau plants like juniper, pinyon, ponderosa pine, snakeweed, cliffrose, and Fremont barberry. Desert dwellers would spot a few familiar plants: creosotebush, catclaw acacia, Arizona white oak, jojoba, sotol, and agaves.

Cowboys from Bagdad, Prescott, or Sunflower, miners from Globe or Morenci, and above all the Western Apaches know all of Arizona's plant communities, for in the central uplands, north and south meet in a ragged mosaic, interlocking with chaparral.

Not too hot, not too dry, but neither too wet nor too cold. That describes central Arizona, and the climate favored by chaparral. The land here goes up and down endlessly. When it rises, chaparral gives way to oak woodland (encinal) in the south, pinyon-juniper woodland in the north, and, even higher, throughout the state, to ponderosa pines.

Where the land drops away to basins and plains, chaparral gives way to desert grassland and scrub. And throughout, fire and livestock-grazing interact with climate in ways that have revolutionized the mountains in the last century.

The word *chaparral* comes from Basque and Spanish words meaning "place of the dwarf evergreen oaks." No word could be more appropriate, for shrub live oak dominates the Arizona chaparral. More than fifty other shrubs grow in the community, but the most common companions to the live oak are mountain mahoganies, manzanitas, sumacs, ceanothus, silktassel, and snakeweed.

These shrubs often cover more than half the available ground.

When cover approaches sixty percent, virtually no other plants grow underneath the shrubs. Chaparral thrives with fifteen to twenty-five inches of precipitation, but the contorted topography of its home ground makes elevation, exposure to the sun, and soil all crucial. With their deep and complex root systems, the shrubs need well-drained soil and often grow in decaying granite and porous limestone.

Chaparral has a dynamic history. Relatively ancient in its southwestern habitat, it formed a refuge for northern plants driven south by the glacial climate in the Pleistocene, and a foothold for desert plants moving north as the climate warmed when the glaciers retreated. Chaparral maintained the middle ground throughout, not always in the same places it does today but always with a complicated mixture of associated plants.

The pinyon pines of central Arizona show this same evidence of changing climates. In these mountains grow isolated populations of the single-needled Great Basin pinyon, relics of the days more than ten thousand years ago when pinyon-juniper forest had shifted south with the cool glacial climate. Most of the single-leaf pinyons now grow far to the north, leaving these telltale trees behind, where they now hybridize with the common two-needled Colorado pinyon.

Fire has much to do with the stability of chaparral; indeed, chaparral species have been adapting to fire since the Miocene, more than five million years ago.

But the interplay of ecological succession with the shrubby landscape is delicate. In some places, trees seem to replace chaparral if fires diminish. In other places, chaparral seems to take over grassland. The interior mosaic is a puzzle with an elusive solution. Its dynamism continues.

By 1891, Captain Bourke could say in *On the Border With Crook*, "...the wild grasses of Arizona always seemed to me to have but slight root in the soil, and my observation is that the presence of herds of cattle soon tears them up and leaves the land bare."

In 1924 forester Aldo Leopold wrote of cattlemen who swore the central Arizona foothills carried ten, twenty, or thirty cattle in the old days; in Leopold's day they would carry "not one cow." Another cowman told him "about how in the 1880's on a certain mesa he could see his cattle several miles, whereas now on the same mesa he can not even find them in a day's hunt."

Leopold unraveled the following story, still accepted as accurate:

Previous to the settlement of the country, fires started by lightning and Indians kept the brush thin, kept the juniper and other woodland species decimated, and gave the grass the upper hand with respect to possession of the soil. In spite of the periodic fires, this grass prevented erosion. Then came the settlers with their great herds of livestock. These ranges had never been grazed and they grazed them to death, thus removing the grass and automatically checking the possibility of widespread fires. The removal of the

grass relieved the brush species of root competition and of fire damage and thereby caused them to spread and "take the country."

Take manzanita. This red-barked shrub, its stiff leaves held like green coins along its twisted branches, reproduces only from seed. Manzanita seeds accumulate in the soil over decades but rarely sprout except after fires. Without fire, manzanita stands likely give way to one of the more common shrubs (shrub live oak or silktassel) or trees (Emory or Arizona oak, juniper, or Arizona cypress). Since manzanita favors the higher elevations of chaparral country, trees rather than shrubs are the safest bet at takeover.

Most of the other chaparral shrubs can sprout from roots after fire, and the vigor of their root systems rivals their jungle-like thickets aboveground. In this way, individual plants whose branches and leaves date only to the last fire actually have lived many centuries. Within five to ten years after a fire, shrubs are back to pre-fire coverage, and the same species dominate. With root-sprouting, many of the same individuals resume their former places. Fire could sweep through chaparral every decade and the landscape still would remain chaparral. In the world of long-term ecological succession, this is a remarkable feat.

Decrease in fires combined with the introduction of heavy grazing have taken their toll. What once was grassland (semi-desert grassland in the Verde and Gila valleys, the Tonto Basin, Aquarius Mesa west of Prescott, and around Cordes Junction; plains grassland in Chino Valley and on the San Carlos Reservation plateaus) has suffered remarkable transformations. Grass has disappeared, or introduced annual grasses have replaced native perennial bunchgrasses. Shrubs, trees, and cacti have invaded. Burroweed and snakeweed cover millions of acres and indicate where grassland once existed. Mesquite, juniper, agave, and prickly pear, though native species, today are much more widespread in grassland, living up to their designation by range managers as "invaders."

Chaparral stretches across Arizona from its western outposts in the mountains edging the Mojave Desert (the Virgins, Cerbats, and Hualapais) eastward above the Gila into New Mexico and Mexico. Its transitional nature means that its animals also are transitional, desert-like in the lower reaches, plateau-like in the north, scrub-loving species in the chaparral proper, tree-dwellers where oaks and pines take over.

Fragrant ponderosa pine forest stands above Prescott on Mount Union and follows the base of the Mogollon Rim from Strawberry to the New Mexico line. Along interior streams grow cottonwoods, Arizona walnut, sycamore, alder, box elder, velvet ash. Grassland ranches in the Chino, Skull, or Verde valleys could be dead ringers for ranches in much of the Intermountain West.

Pockets of distinctive vegetation, however, give the interior its own flavor. Groves of Arizona cypress shade the reflecting pools of canyons in Sedona's Red Rock Country. Rough, unbroken thickets of bright green cloak the Mazatzals and Pinals like a fleece and seem lush on first encounter after the desert. Savanna-like oak woodland on the Natanes Plateau is reminiscent of California mother-lode country.

As Priestley said, the sum is greater than the parts. Arizona's Apachería is unique.

Again a voice spoke to Changing Woman. It instructed her to go to the lush places, to go where the water was dripping from the cliffs at seeps and springs, and to let it drip inside of her.

Changing Woman did this. She went to Oak Creek and to Salt River Canyon and way up onto the plateau in Glen Canyon. She did as the voice had commanded three times, and nothing happened. Then the voice told her to return once more. And on the fourth time the water dripped inside of her and she became pregnant.

Her son Tobatc'istcini, Child Born of Black Water, helped his twin brother kill off the evil creatures in the world. Together, they made the land safe for Apaches.

Opposite: Horsecamp Canyon, Aravaipa Wilderness. JACK W. DYKINGA.

C THE WHITE AND THE GREEN, THE BLUE AND THE BLACK

entral Arizona is a land of many rivers, some of which carry water only a few times a year. Not even the seeps "where the water is dripping" keep them flowing. But the rivers mark out the complicated topography, and their names and the names of the mountains they outline give the land its poetry.

In the northern part of the state, on the Colorado Plateau, the Colorado and Little Colorado pretty much take care of dividing the spoils of watersheds. It is the sequence of rock formations that gives the land its character and its vocabulary.

To the south, mountains stand like islands in the great desert sea of basins and valleys. The Gila theoretically drains much of this land, but its now-dry channel makes a puny organizing force. In this archipelago of mountains, the chant of alternating valleys and ranges charts the deserts.

The Gila heads in from New Mexico on a westering beeline for Yuma. In the interior, the Salt is its primary tributary. Born where the White and Black rivers come together deep in Apachería, receiving the Verde from the north when it reaches the edge of the desert, the "Rio Salado" flows through Phoenix to its master stream, the Gila.

What attention the interior receives mostly derives from these rivers, impounded by Coolidge, Roosevelt, and a half-dozen other dams. Their mountain water makes it possible for people to live and grow crops in the "Valley of the Sun" surrounding Phoenix, while the Apaches have seen their rivers shrink and their sacred lands inundated. Downstream, the Pimas saw their stretch of the Gila River dry up completely.

Manipulation of the central Arizona rivers seems never to cease. During World War II, the Phelps Dodge Corporation built Horseshoe Dam on the Verde to add to the water storage capabilities of the Salt River Project. As a reward, the corporation received a water credit, and they took it from the headwaters of the Black River to use in their mining operations at Morenci. To repay this drain, Phelps Dodge dammed East Clear Creek on the Mogollon Rim in the 1960s so they could pump water from newly formed Blue Ridge Reservoir in the Little Colorado drainage over the Rim and into the Verde drainage.

Farther west, the Agua Fria and the Hassayampa rivers drain Yavapai country. (An Arizona legend proclaims eternal inability to tell the truth if you drink from the Hassayampa; most times, you can avoid this danger because the river is dry.) In the far northwest part of the interior, the Santa Maria joins the Big Sandy to make the Bill Williams Fork of the Colorado, ancestral home to the Hualapai band called the Yavapai Fighters.

Along the east-west length of the Salt, streams flow due south in regular progression; major mountains stand between them. The Verde

Opposite: Sunset over the Gila River.
JACK W. DYKINGA.

Left: Salt River Canyon.
MICHAEL COLLIER.

Opposite: The Blue River, on the
Mogollon Rim. STEPHEN TRIMBLE.

River and Tonto Creek outline the Mazatzal Mountains, the major range in the interior. The Mazatzals stretch only fifty miles from near Pine southward to where the ancient resistant quartzite of Four Peaks looms over the desert, but their ruggedness makes them feel much larger.

After years of seeing the Mazatzal Mountains on maps and pronouncing the name of the range as you would in Spanish, you may do a double-take when you first hear the word spoken. Few Arizonans say it that way. The local favorite is "Matazal," but you will also hear "Matzal" and "Maztal."

Eastward, the Sierra Ancha rises between Tonto and Cherry creeks. The Mogollon Rim, Mazatzals, and Sierra Ancha outline the Tonto Basin. In the eastern extension of this lush grazing country the Pleasant Valley War broke out in 1887.

The Tewksburys were convinced that the Grahams' burgeoning cattle herds owed much to rustled stock, and the war took off from there. The intensity of hatred between the two families and their allies

seems startling today, but the passion of men carving out fortunes from new country knows no bounds. Five years after the infamous feud began, and with somewhere between twenty-five and fifty men dead, Ed Tewksbury shot Tom Graham, the only surviving Graham brother. The event gave Zane Grey the title for his book *To the Last Man* and a legendary spot to build his writer's retreat of a cabin. A lovely piece of Arizona acquired a permanent aura of violence.

At the eastern end of the Arizona interior lie the White Mountains and their southward-draining streams—the White, the Black, and the Blue (Apaches say if you drink four times from the Blue River you will be purified). The White Mountains rise to Mount Baldy, at 11,590 feet, the second highest range in the state. They obscure the Mogollon Rim with a pile of volcanic rock some 4,000 feet thick. White Mountain lavas also flowed south to obscure the bedrock of the eastern interior mountains, for the volcanics are recent—no older than 4 million years. Most of the central mountains are made from Precambrian rock some four hundred and fifty times older.

Through nearly 2 billion years, these Precambrian rocks have been

Opposite: Upland forest, Mogollon Rim. EDWARD J. PFEIFER.

uplifted repeatedly. Erosion has peeled away most of the rocks of middle age; only the ancient cores of the mountains remain, draped with massive outpourings of very young volcanic rocks. Even so, we know the story of major events in their history in remarkable detail, events as distant as the "Mazatzal Revolution" some 1700 million years ago, when continental drift propelled two crustal plates together, building mountains here that may have rivaled the modern Himalayas.

In the billion years before the end of Precambrian time, erosion planed these mountains flat. The sea encroached once more, leaving younger Precambrian sedimentary rocks visible today in Salt River Canyon and the Tonto Basin. In the next great era of earth history, the Paleozoic, seas and deserts left their strata of sediment. But central Arizona began a trend early on: it remained above sea level through most of geologic history. Geologists have called this Paleozoic highland "Mazatzal Land." In the Mesozoic, the central "Mogollon Highlands" shed sediment northward that became the Moenkopi and Chinle formations of today's Colorado Plateau.

With uplift came erosion, era after era, epoch after epoch. Over millions of years, the central highlands were uplifted more than either the deserts or plateau. Faults outlined mountain blocks, contorting the land more than the plateau but less than the basin and range desert country.

Today, the old Precambrian mountains survive, made from dark metamorphic rock that weathers to jagged angular ridges and from light-colored granite weathering to spheres and knobs (as at the Granite Dells, near Prescott). Here and there layers of Paleozoic sediments remain, below the Mogollon Rim around Cibecue and above the Verde Valley. In Salt River Canyon a Devonian formation yields fossils of primitive land plants—internationally significant finds from a time so thoroughly marine it is known as the Age of Fishes.

In the most recent era, the Cenozoic (the last 65 million years), erosion and faulting have created a chain of basins through the region, not as extensive as the huge desert basins but a welcome contrast with the mountains. Chino and Verde valleys abut the Mogollon Rim and form a sort of no-man's-land between the central mountains and the Colorado Plateau. The enormous San Carlos and Gila valleys lie at the southern edge of the interior mountains where they blend with the deserts. In the middle of the mountains, however, lie the Tonto Basin and many smaller basins, such as Peeples and Skull valleys west of Prescott.

Each of these basins has its own story distinctly different from the surrounding mountains. These sites are pockets of Anglo civilization. Prescott sits at the south end of Chino Valley, Payson in the Tonto Basin, Globe and Safford at opposite ends of the San Carlos/Gila Valley. And the Verde Valley has its miniature urban cluster: Clarkdale, Cottonwood, Camp Verde, and Sedona. Beyond these pockets and the mining towns (Bagdad, Jerome, Miami, Clifton/Morenci), the interior remains remarkably similar to nineteenth-century Apachería.

John Bourke appreciated familiar, picket-fenced, "American" Prescott after time spent in Spanish-speaking Tucson and after helping to blaze the Crook Trail along the unmapped Mogollon Rim from Fort Apache to Camp Verde:

> ...it was a village transplanted bodily from the centre of the Delaware, the Mohawk, or the Connecticut valley. Its inhabitants were Americans; American men had brought American wives out with them.... The houses were built in American style; the doors were American doors and fastened with American bolts and locks, opened by American knobs, and not closed by letting a heavy cottonwood log fall against them.

Prescott still has a distinctly middle-American feel. And Captain Bourke surely would approve of the flourishing real-estate market of the Verde Valley.

The Verde River is a microcosm of the interior. It has two small reservations for the Yavapai and Tonto Apache. It is bounded by moun-

tain walls, Mingus Mountains on the southwest and the Mogollon Rim on the north and east. Indeed, this is one of the most impressive stretches of the Rim, where Oak Creek slices through the escarpment in a canyon half a mile deep and flows out into the Red Rock Country. Here the Supai Group crops out in blazing red formations unknown to the north or south.

Even Carley Burch, Zane Grey's heroine in *Call of the Canyon*, fresh from New York City and "hostile and prejudiced" toward this "wild, violent, savage" West, could not fail to be awed by the country around Oak Creek Canyon. Carley's judgment: "How strange...it's not that way in the Adirondacks."

As erosion began to work on the rock layers here, the softer rocks of the Supai eroded faster than the hard Kaibab Limestone. The cliff of the Mogollon Rim (made from the Toroweap Formation and Coconino Sandstone) began to form because of this simple difference in erosion rate, possibly by 28 million years ago and certainly by 15 million.

Later, faulting began—associated with the development of the Basin and Range Province—and the Black Hills were left standing in a great block facing the Rim. The valley itself dropped lower in relation to both highlands. These same faults dammed the ancestral Verde River about 8 million years ago, and sediments began to accumulate in the valley in a series of small lakes and playas.

Today, rocks formed through the 6-million-year existence of "Lake Verde" make up some 3,000 feet of the Verde Formation—gravels, limestones, volcanics, gypsum, salt, and many fossils. This was the heyday of North American mammals, and Verde fossils include cats, bears, camels, elephant-like gomphotheres, primitive mice and woodrats, and then as now, a mixture of northern species such as voles and southern species such as cotton rats.

Similar events happened in many interior basins. Beginning about 2 million years ago, however, external drainage developed as basins filled, erosion took over, and the great network of interior rivers began to form. Anyone who has ridden the whitewater sections of the Verde or Salt can testify to the erosive power of the rivers today. Their rapids deserve respect; they have carved great canyons.

Winter brings half the year's precipitation, but its steady rains and snows have small erosional power. Summer thunderstorms, however, sweep through and drop several inches of rain that funnels into the washes, which boil and flood downstream, deepening canyons, cleaning away erosional debris. At night, lightning illuminates the rose-colored walls of Salt Creek Canyon and outlines sotol and agave stalks in dream-like flashes. Rain beats down in gray curtains on Apache homes and pickup roofs.

Whether dry or in flood, the branching fingers of waterways leading south from the Rim to the Gila define the landscape, water the desert, and dictate where roads and settlements can go. They keep the land rough enough still to be mysterious.

Opposite: Mountain lion. TOM BEAN.

DUTCH OVEN BISCUITS

When the Frost boys back their chuck wagon between the portables and the wood shop at Show Low Junior High School, they offer more than dutch oven biscuits. Jerry hollows a crater in a ten-pound mountain of Gold Medal. His rein hand fills the dent with fresh milk, his roping hand swirls and squeezes, till finally the dough pulls away from the side of the bowl.

"This is just the way my father, Aut, makes biscuits. He cooked for the hands on our cattle drives, up North, in the thirties. Sometimes that could be a hundred men." He nips the dough into perfect circles, flops both sides in a pool of Wesson Oil. Tucked in close in cast-iron dutch ovens, the little pillows rise three times their original size.

"He taught me and my brother, and I taught my boys. We don't run cattle so much any more, maybe twenty-thirty head, but these biscuits are our way of staying in touch, of holding on. They let us share a little history."

This time the Frosts are cooking for half of Show Low and plenty of out-of-towners, too. The crowds have gathered to celebrate two special events—the Junior High's Creative Writing Festival and Project Heritage Fair. In the gym, master quilter Elizabeth Nikolaus explains how her tiny stitches fly, forming the intricate wing of a dove. A Hopi kachina carver talks quietly about the spirit of the cottonwood, his blade smoothing the right shoulder of a mud-head. Notes from Charlie Thomas's old-time harmonica carry, gentle as pine scent, down the hall. Next door, the school's poet-in-residence helps a sixth-grade non-reader polish the persona piece that lets him become a champion brahma bull rider. In the art room, Sue Tilger, a mixed-media artist from Phoenix, guides housewives, lumberjacks, students, and millworkers. They marble paper, whirling the colors in patterns rich in texture and tradition.

People come in from Clay Springs, Linden, Pinedale, Heber, and from places too remote to have names. The students invite folks they've learned from all year—people who have taught them to make soap and saddles, to can plums and fan mandolins. Susan Permar, project coordinator, awards each guest a copy of the Project Heritage Yearbook—a thick anthology of interviews, stories, photographs, songs, essays, how-to articles, anecdotes, paintings, and poems. The book is a celebration: recognition of each one's part in the continuum. In putting it together, Permar says, students learn far more than grammar and punctuation. They revive dying skills and care for the elderly. They develop bonds that create a vibrant sense of what it means to be a productive member of an on-going community.

Marion McNamara, teacher and arts coordinator, wants to expand this active, community-based approach to education. "In a small town like Show Low, the school really is a natural center of the community. Now, after so many years combining Artists-in-Education with outreach, we're ready to expand—we've developed a receptive audience. We want our schools district-wide to be year-round educational and artistic resources for the entire community." This summer the schools will join forces with Northland Pioneer College and the city councils of Show Low and Pinetop-Lakeside. Together, they will sponsor concerts, writing workshops, and visual arts activities for kids and for adults. McNamara has big plans for the fall as well: "Next year, through the Arizona Commission on the Arts, we'll bring in a poet, a fiction writer, a kinetic sculptor, a drummer specializing in African music, and a fiber artist. We've chosen carefully, inviting people who will work well throughout the community. We want to take arts and education beyond the hours of school time and beyond the walls of the schools."

PEGGY SHUMAKER

When an Apache girl reaches maturity, she passes through the ceremony that makes her a woman. During these four days she assumes the power of Changing Woman, and this power will sustain her all of her life.

She wears an abalone shell dangling on her forehead. She kneels and dances in the same position in which Changing Woman was made pregnant by Sun. She runs to the four directions, four times toward the Sun, and her strong run assures her of strength and long life. In becoming Changing Woman, she goes right from being a girl to being a woman. She leaves her childhood behind. She leaves everything behind.

"May she run fast."

All the while, the medicine man sings the story of the creation of the earth, the story of Changing Woman, White Shell Woman, White Painted Woman. The power of Changing Woman comes to the whole community for these four days.

On the last day of the ceremony, the girl becomes White Painted Woman. She is painted white with earth; she will live until her hair, too, turns white. She dances under a wickiup made from the four kinds of trees that lightning never strikes. The whole community dances through behind her.

Changing Woman has brought her gift to the Apache people once again.

SUPERSTITION MOUNTAINS

J.B. Priestley said of Arizona: "There is no history here because history is too recent. This country is geology by day and astronomy by night." High in the Superstition Mountains, near Rogers Canyon, lies the grave of one man who succumbed to this starkness and ran naked through the night shooting at stars.

The Superstitions seem to focus the intensity of Arizona mountains in a single range. Their lower slopes are as cactus-studded and as difficult to traverse as any desert range, but their higher elevations hide chaparral and ponderosa pines. From their blunt profile to their geology, from their name to their legends, absolutely nothing about them is understated.

The Spaniards were reputed to have a gold mine deep in these canyons. American mountain men rounded the prow of Superstition Mountain in their explorations up the Salt and Verde rivers. James Ohio Pattie came first, in 1826. Three years later Ewing Young returned with a group of Taos trappers young Kit Carson included.

But these men were alone in their explorations until the Mexican War gave Apachería to the United States. Prospectors made up the next wave of explorers into the interior. For somewhere in the dry and bony hills lay glittering treasure, just waiting to be mined.

Most of Arizona's first strikes were gold and silver, and thus began the towns of Prescott, Superior, Clifton/Morenci, and Globe (the last two stolen from the Apache Reservation when Anglos hit pay dirt in land they previously had thought useless enough to be left for the Indians). Toward the end of the nineteenth century, copper replaced gold and silver as the true treasure of these mines, and copper towns like Miami and Jerome added their names to the list of "wide open" towns.

Nearly all of Arizona's copper strikes come from the same conjunction of rocks: granite of a particular texture called porphyry and in

contact with Paleozoic limestones. This granite rose as molten magma about 60 million years ago, during the time of crustal unrest associated with the building of the Rocky Mountains. In finger-like projections, these intrusions of magma cooled at intermediate rates—at just the right speed for the quartz, feldspar, and mica of the granite to crystallize first, leaving solutions with high concentrations of minerals, from which crystallized gold, silver, and copper.

Such "porphyry copper" deposits made Arizona "the Copper State." They occur in large bodies, usually low-grade, and thus have been mined in huge open pits, leaving remarkable scars (along with mountain-sized tailings piles). In order to make such gargantuan efforts worthwhile, the rock must contain at least a half a percent copper—ten pounds per ton of rock. Jerome's copper, though mined in an open pit, formed in a different way, its Precambrian ore sitting on a great stack of ancient metamorphosed volcanic rocks.

Arizona's most famous mine is a gold mine, but a lost one, the Lost Dutchman of the Superstitions. It may well exist, but the geology does not really seem right for it.

Three great collapsed volcanoes (calderas) have merged to form today's Superstition Mountains. Some geologists map as many as five overlapping calderas here. Largest is the Superstition Caldera, which poured out ash about 25 million years ago, collapsing on itself while still erupting.

Molten rock repeatedly surged toward the earth's surface here, forming unusually fine resurgent calderas. Each succeeding eruption blew up the previous configuration of mountains. Today, tuff (ash compacted into rock) from the Superstition Caldera stands high in the face of Superstition Mountain. Millions of years later came the Gold-field and Tortilla calderas. Together, the volcanoes spewed forth some 2,500 cubic miles of ash and lava that reached almost as far south as Florence, past Roosevelt Lake to the northeast, and left distinctive yellow tuff in the southern Mazatzals.

Jacob Walz and Jacob Wiser disappeared into this volcanic maze in 1871. Walz finally returned to Florence with a sackful of gold nuggets, but without Wiser, whom he had evidently killed. Walz was German, but his mine became "the Dutchman's" because on the frontier all Germans were "Dutchmen." Walz eluded (or killed) every pursuing prospector during the six years he worked the mine, bringing out gold for his sprees in Phoenix and Tucson, then disappearing into the Super-stitions again.

Finally, he retired. He settled down as a chicken farmer in Phoe-nix, acquired a girlfriend named Julia Thomas, and in 1891 survived a flood just long enough to dictate directions to the mine to Julia and another friend.

But they could not find the mine. And neither has anyone else. And so it is the Lost Dutchman Mine now, kept safe by the Superstitions. The Superstitions keep safe their treasure. The Apaches still know things no one else knows. The Arizona interior remains elusive.

Opposite: Open-pit copper mine at Morenci. RAY MANLEY.

THE PEOPLE

Part Two

THOMAS E. SHERIDAN

THE PEOPLE

Arizona history is not just a parade of cowboys and Indians and towns too tough to die. Rather, it is a chronicle of grids and niches, of networks and webs. Big business and big government built Arizona's infrastructure—its railroads, water projects, cattle industry, and copper mines. But the spaces in between were occupied by groups of people—not the rugged individuals of Western lore, but by families organized into neighborhoods, churches, unions, and mutual-aid societies. Even when they arrived alone, Arizona's immigrants soon came together as communities, recreating what they could of their pasts, incorporating new customs and beliefs from the other people they encountered. This dynamic mixture of assimilation and persistence has characterized all the ethnic groups—Native American, Mexican, Anglo, Black, and Oriental—who have lived in Arizona since prehistoric times.

The process has not always been a pleasant one. Like most frontiers, Arizona has been the scene of conflict as well as cooperation, its development determined by the establishment of an economic and political pecking order organized largely along ethnic lines. At the top were the owners and managers of the copper companies, the railroads, and the land-and-cattle companies. All of these individuals, without exception, were Anglo. The next rung was composed of middle-class merchants, farmers, and ranchers, mostly Anglo, but with a few Mexicans and Orientals as well. Finally, at the bottom, were the workers, but they too had their hierarchies. Irishmen, Slavs, Cornishmen ("Cousin Jacks"), and other Anglos dominated the relatively good-paying positions such as railroad engineer or underground miner. Mexicans, Chinese, and Native Americans, on the other hand, toiled as farm laborers, railroad section hands, and construction workers. But even at the bottom contention reigned, pitting Mexican workers against Orientals, and Anglos against Mexicans. In short, much of Arizona history has been a scramble for survival, for economic advantage, for a piece of the action and a place in the sun—ugly at times in its racism and exploitation, heroic at other times with its examples of friendship and familial self-sacrifice.

Overleaf: Apache Sunrise Ceremony. RICO LEFFANTA.

Above left: Runner at Hualapai Memorial Pow-Wow, Peach Springs. STEPHEN TRIMBLE.

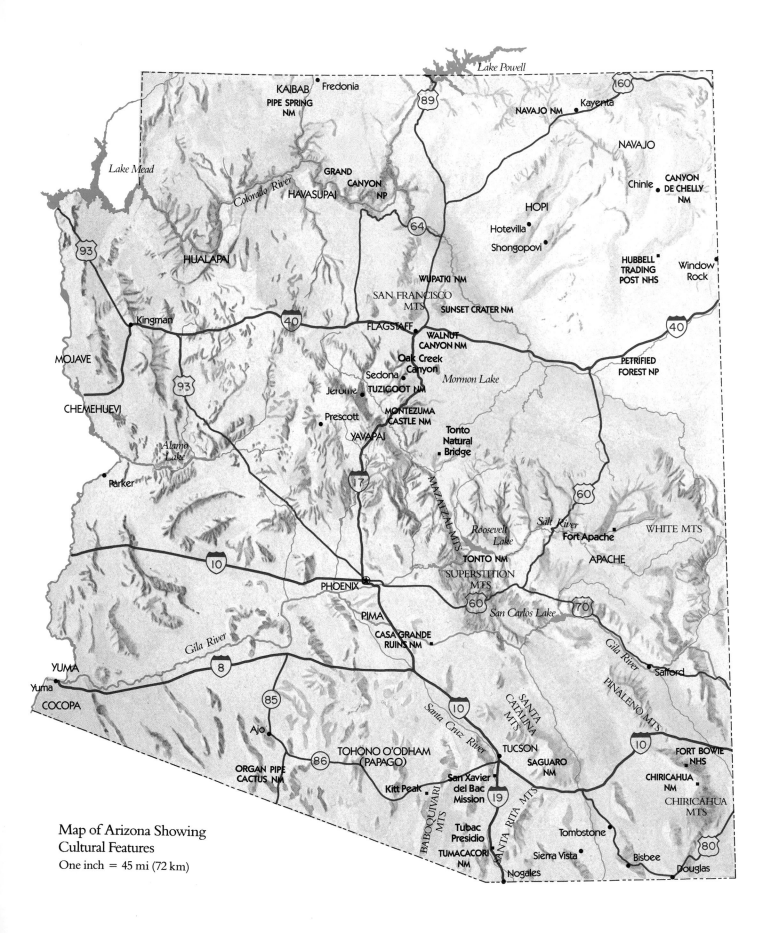

Map of Arizona Showing
Cultural Features

One inch = 45 mi (72 km)

The experience of the Chinese aptly demonstrates the basic, occasionally brutal trajectory that helped create Arizona as we know it today. Beginning in the 1870s, the Southern Pacific Railroad imported hundreds of Chinese immigrants to level the terrain and lay track across the desert for ten to twenty dollars a month. Despite such miserable wages, Mexican and Anglo workers resented the competition. In July 1882, for example, a mob of Anglos attacked a group of Chinese laborers outside Nogales and stole their money, broke their dishes, and burned their tents. None of the Chinese were killed, but management quickly got the mob's message. Chinese labor may have been cheap, but not cheap enough to compensate for sabotage or a violent work force. By the early twentieth century, the Chinese had been driven off the railroad and out of Arizona mines.

Arizona's emerging middle class joined workers in denouncing

the Orientals, who were labeled derisively as "celestials," "*chinacates*," or "sons of Confucius." Viewing the Orientals as threats to small businessmen as well as workers, both the English- and Spanish-language press repeatedly fulminated against "the most pernicious and degraded race on the globe: the Mongol race," as Tucson's *El Fronterizo* described them in 1892. In the minds of many Arizonans, the Chinese were clannish, opium-smoking pagans who stole "American" jobs and sent all their money across the sea.

Regardless of their hardships, however, the Chinese persevered. Denied employment in Arizona's major industries, many opened their own laundries, grocery stores, and restaurants, while others flourished as truck farmers along rivers such as the Gila and the Santa Cruz. And despite their reputation for aloofness, individual Chinese formed deep and lasting relationships with people of other races. A case in point was Lai Ngan, a resident of Nogales, who became the lifelong friend of an Indian woman named Doña García. Together the two women helped each other raise their children in the face of economic adversity and the frequent absences of their spouses.

Along the way, many of these Chinese immigrants, like immigrants everywhere, began to assimilate and succeed. The sons and daughters of "coolie" laborers became small businessmen and women. Their children, in turn, graduated from college to serve as professionals and politicians. Within three generations, the "sons of Confucius" were citizens of the Sunbelt like everyone else.

But like the larger American melting pot, Arizona's blend of people has always simmered over a very uneven flame. Not all cultural differences have been obliterated. Some have even been accentuated and preserved. Centuries after contact, there are still Papagos, Apaches, Navajos, and Yumas. Mexicans continue to celebrate Mexico's Independence Day—September 16, while blacks commemorate the Emancipation Proclamation on "Juneteenth." And even assimilation can be reversed, at least up to a point. Earlier this century, the children of Lai Ngan, dining at the home of a more conservative Chinese family, were embarrassed because they did not know how to use chopsticks and had to be given forks. "When we got back to Nogales," one of the children told historian Lawrence Fong, "we told our mother that we were ashamed to be Chinese and not be able to do things Chinese people do. She said, 'Hereafter you are going to learn to eat with chopsticks.' So she bought the bowls and chopsticks and the spoons and everything else and showed us how to do it."

Such an incident illustrates how people of all races preserve their heritage in countless small but important ways. Whether they emigrated from Europe or Asia—crossing the Bering Strait twelve thousand years ago or the international border today—Arizonans have always carried a part of their pasts with them. These pasts are what make the state distinctive. They bring a human richness to the desert and keep the homogeneity of the Sunbelt at bay.

Opposite: Lai Ngan, *right*, and her friend Doña Garcia.
PHOTO BY COURTESY OF MARIAN LIM.

ARIZONA'S INDIANS

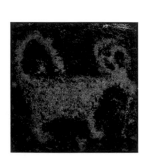

Once, in the magic and mystery of an Arizona desert dusk, I stood with a Hopi friend on the southern edge of Black Mesa above the springs and garden plots of the tawny, earthen village of Hotevilla. The Hopi man was anxious. There were rumors—it was the late 1960s—that a giant energy company was planning to stripmine coal from atop Black Mesa, which would destroy the aquifers that provided life-giving water to the Hopis.

"These are bad times," he said solemnly. "Over there and there and there and there," and he turned, motioning all about, "there are two kinds of human beings—the takers and the believers. Even among our own people there are the two kinds. To those of us who believe, this is the center of our universe. Sacred beings led us to it. The Great Spirit, Maasau'u, taught us the Hopi Way of peace and harmony with nature. He said, if we take care of this land, it will take care of us. If we lose our water, we will lose our way. We may no longer be Hopis. We will be something else."

I have recalled his words many times. Two years afterward, I accompanied an executive of the Peabody Coal Company from St. Louis to a meeting with Hopis in an Indian's home in New Oraibi. Mining was about to begin, and the company thought it might be a wise policy to calm the Hopis' fears with personal reassurances from a top official. It was a dramatic confrontation between representatives of two cultures. A young Hopi woman cried out to him, "You are destroying our land. We are tied to it, like it is part of our bodies. It gives our people the meaning of life. If we lose our water, we will lose our ties to our ancestors and to everything that is sacred to us." An old, white-haired grandfather leaned on his cane and nodded. The two sides were irreconcilable. When we left, the Peabody executive was embarrassed, but he had not understood. "We'll have to do a community relations job here," he said.

Again, when one of the Southwestern tribes was appealing for the return of some of its sacred lands, I sat in on hearings before a U.S. Senate Committee. Indian elders told of their annual pilgrimages to

Above left: Petroglyph at Picture Rocks, west of Tucson.
TOM WEISKOTTEN.

Opposite: Hopi man from the Eagle Clan in cornfield. STEPHEN TRIMBLE.

their many ancient shrines in the area in question. In rebuttal, a white man, opposed to the return of the acreage to the tribe, assured the senators that he had been over every foot of the contested land and had not found a single shrine.

Such examples are evidence of an enormously broad and deep gap of perceptions and needs that exists between many of Arizona's 230,000 Indians and the rest of the state's almost 3,000,000 population. And yet, since non-Indians first appeared within the area of the present-day state, there have been those who, in varying degrees, have groped toward a shared experience of the forces that have shaped and molded the cultures and values of Arizona's eighteen different tribes.

If nothing else, the impact of Arizona's awesome land itself has been such a force, often providing the beholder with a deeply religious experience and a sense of oneness with nature. In *The Land of Journeys' Ending,* Mary Austin—wrote her biographer, Augusta Fink—reflected "the awareness of presences and powers unsensed by the casual observer" in the Southwest. When I think of that, I imagine the first infinitesimal bands of humans, mere specks in the huge, overwhelming landscape, who entered the Southwest more than 10,000 years ago. They were people who watched the clouds and the daily change of colors on the desert and mountains and who knew intimately the animals, birds, insects, and reptiles as their only everyday companions. They recognized that their rounds of life were largely in the hands of unseen "presences and powers" that dwelled within their universe and became vivid in the strike of a lightning bolt or the soughing wind through the pines. In the vast terrain, with all its magical hues and friendly and fearsome earthforms, I imagine that there must have been a pervasive, ever-present awareness of a tie to the supernatural. It was in the air, the storms, the mountains, canyons, forests, and deserts. Linked to the spirit of the individual and the group, the spirits of everything in creation were present during the day and in dreams at night to dictate conduct, preclude loneliness, and help secure survival. They lived on the "floor of the sky."

From such a cultural underlayer evolved the rich, intricate systems of belief of the native inhabitants whom the Europeans and Americans found, and still know, in Arizona. With all their manifestations of rituals, ceremonies, dances, songs, myths, art forms, dreams, and codes of behavior, the systems and their interrelated structures of society answered the basic questions of life: who am I and what is my proper role; what is my relation to other humans, to nature, and to the supernatural; where did I come from and where am I going; what is the meaning of my life? Most profoundly, they held together the group and ensured its survival from generation to generation in the face of adversity.

Expanded upon through the millennia, embellished and made more dramatic with increasing detail, the myths, legends, and stories were key vehicles in ensuring the continuity of the different peoples. Customarily, grandparents or another elder related them to the young, usually in the winter. Telling them in summer, said the Papagos, brought bad luck, for the scorpions and snakes were out then and might bite the storyteller. Often, the stories were moralistic, emphasizing proper conduct, or were instructive, explaining the natural world. Their substance dealt with gods and other supernatural figures, living creatures with human traits, mountains and other familiar landforms, shrines, and migrations of ancestors. They taught harmony—the great, overriding need to keep the world in balance, to avoid disturbing the link that bound the spirit of the human with those in all forces in creation. Man, they related, could disturb that link by wrong living and evil deeds. Do so, and the universe would go out of balance.

The fountainhead of oral traditions was inevitably the rich, and often epic-like, origin and creation myths. Everyone knew the outlines, but the religious leaders were familiar with their every detail. Each group had its own version, though among some they were quite similar. Often, there were variations within a tribe. Sometimes they were a melding of legend and history. One of two sources of knowledge of the past (the other is the archaeological record), they are the truth for Indian societies as are the Scriptures for Christians.

Led by Spider Grandmother, the Hopis, for instance, rose through three unpleasant Underworlds, finally leaving evil beings behind and climbing by a reed through a hole in the sky (known as *sipapuni*) into the Fourth, or present world. There, after instructions from the deity Maasau'u, the different clans began long migrations until they found the appointed place to settle, their present homes, the very center of the universe. The Navajos and Yavapais also tell of Underworlds. Predecessors of the Navajos, birds, animals, and Holy People, rose through a series of disharmonious worlds of different colors and symbols, at last reaching the present world. They worked to make their new world beautiful, harmonious, and blessed for humans. Somehow, evil monsters appeared and threatened to destroy them all. The monsters were finally slain by the twin sons of the magical Changing Woman, who then—in many versions told by the different Navajo clans—created humans with the help of the Holy People. The Yavapais ascended on the first maize plant through worlds wracked with fire and flood.

For the Papagos, Earthmaker created the earth from a small ball of dirt. After an errant start, making and destroying beings who turned corrupt, Elder Brother fashioned people out of clay. When they, too, became evil, he did away with them and gave their land to the O'odham (the Papagos and Pimas) and taught them such things as their ceremony to bring rain. In the northwest section of the state, the Great Spirit created the Walapais from a bundle of cane on the Colorado River, and another deity led them to their homeland.

The long narratives that convey these stories of faith are basically sermons on how to walk the proper road and survive. Their rich images and symbols speak of ancient peoples, wondrous events, and migrations of the past, not a little of which can find support from the second source of our knowledge, the findings of the archaeologists. The Southwest has been particularly favorable to that branch of study. Through the centuries, the dry climate has preserved many remains of vanished cultures. The terrain itself has helped. In many places, erosion has revealed evidence of the earlier peoples. And, finally, many of the present-day tribes have retained old cultural traits and values, or links to them, that can help illuminate archaeological findings.

No one knows when man first entered Arizona, but he was well established by 12,000 – 11,000 B.C. By about 10,000 B.C. the climate favored the spread of grasslands, which, in turn, attracted grazing mammoths, camels, bison, and other large Ice Age game. With them came their hunters—small family bands of Paleo-Indians armed with spears, who seem to have followed after the animals from the more lush grazing grounds farther east on the plains. Finds of the Paleo-Indians that have excited attention, like those at the Lehner site in the San Pedro River Valley, suggest that the animals and hunters frequented areas where grazing conditions were favorable. By about 10,000 B.C., the Ice Age glaciers were well into their retreat pattern, the Southwest became drier, and the outsized animals and their hunters drifted back east to the better grasslands.

In Arizona, the Paleo-Indian hunters may have been succeeded by newcomers. Though they trapped, snared, and hunted small game and birds, they were essentially gatherers of wild plants and seeds. The earliest evidence of them in Arizona was found at Ventana Cave in the southeast corner of the state and dated to about 9500 B.C. But for thousands of years after that, the foragers held sway, processing their food with milling stones, grinders, choppers, and scrapers. Within that

long, somewhat stable period, the Archaic, archaeologists have given names to their three slightly different cultures. The people from the west are encompassed in a San Dieguito-Armagosa tradition, those from the north in an Oshara tradition, and those from the southeast in a Cochise tradition. Each of those divisions has been further divided into successive stages, marking levels of change and advancement.

In the first millennium before Christ, knowledge of argiculture diffused slowly into southern Arizona from Mexico. The first important product was a small, primitive type of maize, accompanied perhaps at the same time by squash, and later by beans. The discovery made little impact for another 1,500 years, until a more productive variety of maize appeared from the south. Then, gradually, the nomadic foragers added the cultivated crops to their diets and underwent a profound revolution. To tend their gardens, they settled down over many hundreds of years in semi-permanent, and then permanent, villages. Surpluses of food gave them more security and leisure time than they had ever known. With leisure, they could innovate, experiment, and make things that satisfied aesthetic impulses and provided pleasure. Population became concentrated, and villages grew. Social, political, and religious systems became more intricate to ensure harmony. Pottery, diffusing northward also from Mexico, was introduced to take its place beside basketry, and arts flourished, producing outpourings of religious, functional, and ornamental objects for the developing societies. By the first centuries of the Europeans' Christian era, with all these changes, most of Arizona's former nomadic foragers had coalesced into four major cultures.

One of them, the Mogollon, dating from perhaps as early as 500 B.C. until about A.D. 1450, evolved among the people of the last, or San Pedro, phase of the Cochise tradition in the forested mountain country astride the southern part of the present Arizona-New Mexico border and in northern Chihuahua and Sonora in Mexico. Until approximately A.D. 1000, the Mogollon people continued hunting and gathering wild foods, but also used stones to terrace hillsides for gardens, dam stream beds for water, and line slopes to halt erosion and channel runoff. Their villages were comprised of pit houses, occasionally lined with masonry to stabilize the walls. They included a single Great Kiva used for communal religious and social activities.

After A.D. 1000, the proliferating Mogollon villages were influenced by the spread of another, more advanced culture, the Anasazi (a Navajo word for "the ancient ones"), which had arisen farther north. In Anasazi style, the Mogollon people now built apartment-like, aboveground homes of stone set in mud mortar, joined to each other at first in lines or squares and expanded later into large, two-storied complexes. The making of pottery, known to the Mogollon since perhaps 300 B.C., took on Anasazi techniques. From about A.D. 1050 to 1200, however, one Mogollon group in New Mexico's Mimbres River Valley displayed a genius of its own. Portraying on their ware the naturalistic images of creatures and spirits to which they were bound,

Opposite: Baboquivari Peak, sacred home of the Tohono O'Odham creator god, I'itoi. JACK W. DYKINGA.

they produced what is unquestionably some of the world's finest known painted pottery. By that time, much of the Mogollon culture was becoming that of the Anasazi, and the development of the two people was coinciding. What became of the Mogollon we will see when we turn to the Anasazis.

Meanwhile, a highly creative, desert-oriented culture, the Hohokam (from a Pima word meaning "all used up" or "those who have gone"), had been flourishing in southern Arizona. It is not agreed upon yet who the Hohokams were, where they came from, or where they went. Some believe they were another group that evolved from the gatherers of the final stage of the Cochise culture. But more popular today is a premise that they migrated from northern Mexico about 300 B.C., bringing with them skills of the more advanced, irrigation-using Mexican civilizations. They overran or dispossessed the Cochise people. At any rate, during their first, or Pioneer, period that lasted until about A.D. 550, they spread across the arid country between present-day Tucson and Phoenix, establishing homes. They were made of brush and layers of mud and built above pits. They hunted desert creatures and gathered mesquite beans and the wild fruits of cacti. From the beginning they were expert desert farmers, irrigating fields of corn, squash, beans, and cotton with water conveyed through canals from wells or from the Gila and Salt rivers.

During their second stage of development, the Colonial Period, from about A.D. 550 to 900, the Hohokam expanded toward present-day Flagstaff, Prescott, up the Verde and tributaries of the Salt and Gila, and into the San Pedro and Santa Cruz valleys. Trade contracts with the south brought them many more influences from Mexico, including the use of ballcourts for ritualistic games and flat-topped mounds on which to erect religious structures and conduct rites. They increased their awesome networks of irrigation canals. They made clay figurines, possibly for fertility rites, handsome jewelry of all sorts, mosaic-backed mirrors of iron pyrites, sculptured stone bowls, and wonderfully wrought pottery effigy jars. During a third, so-called Sedentary Period (A.D. 900 – 1100), their culture continued to flower. From Mexico they received copper bells and from the Gulf of California and the Pacific highly prized shells. Their etching of shells, with fermented saguaro juice, was perhaps the earliest etching anywhere in the world.

During the final Hohokam period, the Classic (A.D. 1100 – 1450), their territory contracted back toward their original core area. At that time, there were numerous migrations in the Southwest, and it appears that they may have been joined temporarily by Mogollon-influenced Salado people from the Tonto Basin and then by Anasazi-influenced Sinaguas from the Verde Valley. Though the Hohokams continued living in their own ways, new traits, including the building of aboveground, single- and then multi-storied houses with thick clay or stone walls, like those seen at Casa Grande, suggest that the newcomers, with their Anasazi customs, lived side-by-side among the Hohokams. In time, they departed, leaving behind the mystery of what finally happened to the Hohokams.

Opposite: Keet Seel, Tsegi Canyon, Navajo Reservation. RICO LEFFANTA.

In the north, centered around the Four Corners country, the Anasazi, a third great culture, had arisen. Emerging about A.D. 1 from the hunting and gathering Oshara Tradition, the Anasazis left abundant remains by which they can be traced through steadily ascending stages of cultural development. Agriculturally based (though they also gathered and hunted), they were talented in basketry. By A.D. 700, the people were building aboveground stone and adobe homes, making many kinds of utilitarian pottery, spinning and weaving cotton into blankets and garments—all giving rise to the Pueblo periods.

Organizing into systems of clans and religious heirarchies, the Anasazi-Pueblo peoples attained a Classic Period after about A.D. 1100, building splendid towns of single- and multi-storied structures in many parts of the Southwest. Among their best-known sites in Arizona, where they are known as the Western Anasazi, are the cliff dwellings in Canyon de Chelly, Keet Seel, and Betatakin. But their expansion was

widespread, telling of a once thriving population that mastered the skill of accumulating agricultural surpluses in a land of little water.

And yet, at the end, something happened. Sometime before A.D. 1300, the Anasazi-dominated territory, which now included that of the Mogollons, contracted. At first, the northernmost areas were depopulated; people just moved away. Then more and more of them abandoned their homesites. No one knows exactly why it occurred, but undoubtedly the reasons were many: extended droughts, overpopulation, and breakdowns of internal religious, social, and agricultural systems. In the years before the coming of the Spaniards, however, there were many migrations that were marked by separations, joinings, and mixtures, not only among the former Anasazi populations, but among fringe peoples, who had continued to follow many of the old ways of their foraging ancestors. In the mosaic of movements, some of these latter groups joined the Anasazis and, with them, began to concentrate in three distinct Southwestern areas, where the Spaniards were to find them. One major region was the present-day Pueblo country of New Mexico's Rio Grande Valley. Another was the present-day home of the Zunis, also in New Mexico just forty miles south of Gallup. And the third was the Hopi mesas in northern Arizona. All three of those historic Indian peoples of today, living in areas settled by Anasazis well before the late thirteenth-century disruptions (the Hopis' Third Mesa village of Oraibi, the United States' oldest continuously inhabited town, dates from approximately A.D. 1150), are descendents of Anasazis. Some, like the Hopis, possess among their strains the legacies, also, of the Mogollones and perhaps of several fringe peoples who did not participate in the central Anasazi experience.

Under the name Hakataya, archaeologists group a number of other peoples in still a fourth culture. These people, living principally between the Colorado and Gila rivers, from the Mogollon country west into California, indulged in some agriculture, but were mostly hunters and gatherers. They contributed relatively little in the way of innovation, but borrowed heavily from neighbors in all directions. Stemming from the forager San Dieguito-Armagosa Tradition and its somewhat similar succeeding cultures, they adapted to a wide variety of terrain in which they lived, including the South Rim of the Grand Canyon, the upland plateaus and valleys of western Arizona, and the deserts of the lower Colorado River. In general, they lived in temporary camps, made simple pottery, and established networks of trade routes through their territories. Some of them adopted the ballcourt and other Hohokam traits. Others copied Anasazi architecture and lifeways. The culture of one of the best known Hakataya groups, the Sinagua, became a kind of melting pot of all the other cultures, particularly at Wupatki, near the San Francisco Peaks, where colonists from the Hohokam, Mogollon, and Anasazi regions joined them after the eruption of Sunset Crater in A.D. 1065. Other Sinagua ruins can be viewed at Montezuma Castle and Tuzigoot in the Verde River Valley and at Walnut Canyon east of Flagstaff.

By historic times, the Hakataya, divided by archaeologists into upland and riverine peoples, depending on their environments, had evolved into many of Arizona's tribes, including the upland Yavapai, Walapai, and Havasupai and the riverine Mojave, Quechan, Cocopa, and Maricopa. Largely semi-nomadic, the Yavapais ranged in bands over a huge area of their ancestral lands, between the Bill Williams and Gila rivers and from the Verde Valley to the lower Colorado. The Walapai, limited agriculturists who also hunted and gathered, lived north of them on the plateau that extended toward the Grand Canyon. The Havasupai were to their east, occupying the plateau country from Bill Williams Mountain and the San Francisco Peaks to the Grand Canyon. The other tribes were ranged in the hot, desert country along the lower Colorado, though the Mojaves and Quechans eventually forced the more peaceful Maricopas to leave the Colorado and migrate up the Gila to the Pimas' country.

Because all these tribes speak Yuman dialects, and are thus linguistically related, they are sometimes grouped collectively as Yumans, contrasting with Arizona's Uto-Aztecan speakers, the Hopis, Papagos, Pimas, Yaquis, and small groups of Southern Paiutes who dwell in the Arizona Strip north of the Grand Canyon. The ancestors of the Southern Paiutes are not descended from the members of Arizona's four major prehistoric cultures already enumerated. Instead, their ways of life, like those of their Southern Paiute relatives who inhabit much of the arid Great Basin country of southern Nevada and Utah, retained until late historic times many of the traits of the less advanced nomadic and semi-nomadic gathering and hunting traditions that preceded the Anasazis and their contemporaries.

Another group of nomadic peoples—the Athapascan-speaking Apaches and Navajos—are relative newcomers to Arizona. Breaking away, possibly about A.D. 1000, from the original heartland of Athapascan speakers, in northwestern Canada, the ancestors of the Apaches and Navajos began a dramatic southward migration, united possibly for three hundred years as a single people. Some of them may have pursued the bison along the eastern side of the Rocky Mountains, turning westward across New Mexico toward Arizona. They may have been in northern New Mexico and perhaps Arizona as early as A.D. 1400 or as late as 1525. The early Spaniards learned that they were already there, but that they had only recently arrived and were making life miserable for the Pueblos and other original inhabitants.

Across the Southwest and on the southern plains, where their different groups came finally to rest, the Spaniards gave them many names. Eventually they were all called Apaches—a Spanish variation of a Zuñi word for enemies. Even the people who became the Navajos were known originally as the Apaches of Navajo. In time, Arizona became home for seven Apachean groups: part of a central band of Chiricahuas in the southeastern portion of the present state; five of the most westerly Apache peoples—known to whites as the White Mountain, San Carlos, Cibecue, and Northern and Southern Tontos—from

Flagstaff and the Verde Valley to the Chiricahua country; and the Navajos in the northeast.

Hunters and gatherers, those we call today the Apaches were comprised of independent local groups made up of from ten to thirty extended families. A number of local groups comprised a band that roamed over a wide area. They lived in conical or dome-shaped wickiups, constructed—usually by the women—of mesquite, willow, or cottonwood poles, covered with brush, beargrass, or skins. Their religion included the use of shamans, both male and female, who interceded with the supernatural to effect cures, ward off sickness and evil, ensure success in hunts, raids, and amorous affairs, and foretell the future. They endowed their universe with many spirits and greatly feared witches and ghosts of the deceased, who in their loneliness, they believed, came back to claim the lives of others for the sake of companionship. It was wise, therefore, to avoid attracting the ghosts by abandoning places of death, forgetting the deceased, and shunning creatures like bears, coyotes, and owls whose forms the ghosts assumed.

From their first appearance in the Southwest, the Apaches gained a

reputation as fearsome raiders, and their name continues to be associated with that former image. "Glorified by novelists," wrote anthropologist Keith H. Basso, "sensationalized by historians, and distorted beyond credulity by commercial film makers, the popular image of 'the Apache'—a brutish, terrifying semihuman bent upon wanton death and destruction—is almost entirely a product of irresponsible caricature and exaggeration." The abundant foodstocks and rich possessions of the sedentary peoples—from the Anasazi and Mogollon descendents in the north to the Pimas in the south—were attractive to the Apaches, and they often raided these peoples' settlements and towns. But periods of peaceful trade were also common. Moreover, the Apaches made a fine distinction between raids for food and booty, recognizing the need to limit their aggression so the source would not disappear, and outright war, conducted usually to avenge the death of one of their own.

What has not come down in history so clearly is the cycle that gave the Apaches their dread reputation. After the arrival of the Spaniards, the Apaches' raids, often for horses, mules, cattle, and other food, provoked the whites into retaliatory raids, frequently accompanied by atrocities and the taking of Apaches as slaves. Inevitably, the Apaches struck back, this time with a ferocious vengeance. The pattern remained the same for centuries, under the Spaniards, Mexicans, and Anglo Americans, and the Apaches got their reputation. It is best not to forget that to the Apaches, the white man, who hunted them down and ultimately conquered them, was equally fearsome and unrestrained.

Emphasis on their raiding, also, obscures the dominant, peaceful side of their lives. The Western Apaches of Arizona, learning agriculture from the older inhabitants, grew staples, gathered wild foods, and hunted deer, rabbits, and other creatures. Lacking food surpluses, they had no permanent settlements, but moved from summer camps and gardens along high-country streams to wintering spots along the lower rivers. During cold months raids for food became necessary for survival.

In their camps, the Apaches raised their children with moralistic myths and teachings. The women made fine basketry, patterned with human and animal figures, tanned hides, fashioned buckskin clothing, and produced handsome saddlebags and other articles of leather. One of their major rituals was the four-day Sunrise Dance, a puberty ceremony in which girls were instructed symbolically in the ways and responsibilities of womanhood.

The Navajos, who call themselves Diné (People, or Human Beings), expanded westward into Arizona from the Dinetah, their original southwestern home in northern New Mexico. At first, they were much like the other Apacheans, but they also possessed traits of the less-advanced nomadic hunters and gatherers of the Great Basin, suggesting that they may have migrated south through that region. They used disguises to stalk game, drove it into ambushes, and employed pitfalls. Their clothing was simple, made generally of fibers twisted together. In cold weather, they wore blankets of rabbit skins.

Opposite: Navajo hogan.
TERRENCE MOORE.

Apache girl's puberty ceremony.
Opposite: Changing Woman with sponsor. Above: Pollen blessing.
RICO LEFFANTA.

Beginning in the seventeenth century, however, they became greatly influenced by the Pueblos, many of whom were sheltered and absorbed by them during and after the Pueblo Revolt against the Spaniards in 1680. From the Pueblos, the Navajos learned farming, weaving, the use of new clothing and ornamentation, and many new spiritual and ceremonial ideas, which they adapted to their own basic systems. As their culture changed to a joining of Athapascan-Apache and Anasazi-Pueblo traits, it also felt impacts from the Spaniards. From them they acquired fruit trees, oats, wheat, sheep, goats, horses, and a few cattle. A final strain was added to their heterogeneous population and culture when various groups of Southern Paiutes also joined them. Forming still another element of Arizona's present-day Indian population, some Southern Paiutes live today on the Kaibab Reservation in northwestern Arizona.

By the end of the eighteenth century, the Navajos, with a large and growing population, had become a distinct people with unified characteristics. The society was matrilineal, and the position of women was very strong and influential in all aspects of life. The basic social unit was the nuclear family, but extended families, composed of all married daughters and their families, often lived close to the mother of the nuclear family. Two or more extended families, tied by marriage or identity with a specific area, might live near each other, creating a circle of from fifty to two hundred people under the leadership of the male head of the most prominent family. In turn, a number of such groups, occupying the same general area, might compose a loosely knit community guided by a commonly acknowledged headman. The communities were widely scattered, and each was autonomous. Later, communities came to possess a peace *natani*, or leader, who served for life, as well as one or more war chiefs. Many large, matrilineal clans exercised strong social control over their members.

With their flocks of sheep and goats, the Navajos became increasingly pastoral. Their homes, scattered across and merging into the landscape, were hogans, at first conical, "forked-stick" dwellings, formed by a foundation of three poles whose forks were locked together at the apex. Additional logs were leaned against the foundation, and the whole was covered with mud or earth. In time, the hogan's style changed to a low, dome-shaped structure of logs and mud, covered with earth, and with a smoke hole in the center of the roof. But the "forked-stick" type continued in use, and its form, also, was used for sweat lodges. In modern times, hogans are often built of stone and have glass windows.

Following the lessons of their mythology—to keep their universe good, harmonious, and beautiful—the Navajos developed a rich and complex ceremonial system. It was designed to maintain everything that was considered blessed and favorable to man, as opposed to that which was evil and harmful. There were no priesthoods or religious societies: specially trained men known as singers conducted the ceremonies whenever they were needed. Illness was a sign of the disruption of harmony, and most ceremonies were held to cure the individual. They also served to secure blessings and harmony. With the song the most important element in the ceremony, the singer would combine his rites and songs with the making of symbolic paintings of colored sand, pollens, crushed flowers, minerals, and dry pigments. In effect, the result was frequently not unlike that of modern-day psychosomatic medicine.

Still another group of Indians are very recent newcomers to Arizona. They are the Yaquis, whose principal homeland was—and still is—along the Yaqui River in northwestern Mexico. In the seventeenth century, Jesuits taught them Christianity, but did not force them to abandon their own rituals. To this day, Yaqui spiritual and ceremonial life combines elements of seventeenth-century Spanish Christian beliefs and practices with those of their own ancient tradition.

Acculturated by the Spaniards, eighteenth-century Yaquis began coming north into the O'odham country with expeditions of soldiers, priests, settlers, and miners. In 1736, a Yaqui made a rich silver discovery near present-day Nogales in Sonora. The Spaniards called the location *Arizonac*, a Papago word for "little spring," and the name became that of today's state. In later years, Yaquis migrated into Arizona, working as laborers at the mines and on railroads and ranches. After 1890 and until well into the twentieth century, the migration became wholesale, as the Mexican government warred on the Yaquis and forced many of them from their homeland. Gradually, the families who came into Arizona clustered in a number of church-centered urban communities in and around Tucson, Yuma, and Phoenix. In 1964, Congress set aside land for them near the Papagos' San Xavier Reservation, and they established another community known as New Pascua. Long considered outsiders, they were finally recognized by the United States government in 1978 as an American tribe, eligible to receive federal services. Estimates of their population in Arizona in the mid-1980s range to more than five thousand.

The Yaquis' Easter ceremony, an intensely passionate mixture of Catholicism and traditional ritual, is conducted simultaneously each year at Old and New Pascua, Barrio Libre, and Guadalupe. It dramatizes in Yaqui terms, from the beginning of Lent through Easter Sunday, the final events in the life of Jesus.

The history of Indian-white relations in Arizona is essentially one of a conflict of cultures. The first Europeans searching for gold or souls to save, passed through parts of Arizona, leaving little but impressions of new goods, customs, and powers, and of horses and cattle. The

Opposite: Herding sheep in Navajoland. MICHAEL COLLIER.

INDIANS AND THE GOVERNMENT

About ten percent of the approximately 1.5 million Indians in the United States live in Arizona. Although the outsider's view of reservations traditionally credits them with an economy based on ranching, mining, construction, crafts, tourism, and the land, in reality it is government more than anything else that influences tribal cash flow. The schools Indians attend, the health care they receive, the roads they drive on, and the houses they live in are but a few of the projects whose funding begins in state and federal coffers. Money for such projects goes directly to the tribes, which act as contractors. Rare is the Indian whose life is sufficiently far from mainstream reservation economy that a government funding does not, for better or worse, touch his daily life. When Mae Chee Castillo, a seventy-two-year-old Navajo, journeyed to Washington from her reservation in 1985 to accept an award for heroism from President Reagan, she told him, through an interpreter, "In Indian country, there is little or no private sector. I ask for your support."

Indian-government relations go far deeper than money pumped into tribal economies, however. Indian control of land and water has had a marked effect upon municipalities off the reservations. Because arable tribal land requires no purchase, and sufficient water allocations keep the cost of irrigation down, reservation agriculture requires very little capitalization. Non-Indian farmers near reservations have found competition with the Indians difficult, and agricultural land—especially near reservations—has become gradually urbanized. Now federal laws allow tribes themselves to urbanize through long-term land leasing and water sales. Salt River Indian land adjacent to Scottsdale and Papago land near Tucson are two examples of this. "As more people move into Arizona," says Gordon Krutz, head of Indian Programs at the University of Arizona, "there is more pressure on the tribes to cooperate with developers."

Federal influence extends far beyond legislation and profits and losses. When the Army Corps of Engineers built Painted Rock Dam northwest of Gila Bend in the

WINDOW ROCK—Federal officials have told the Navajo Tribal Council that if it does not start building houses, it stands to lose up to $50 million in federal funds....

The director of Region 9 of the U.S. Department of Housing and Urban Development said that a new federal policy cracks down on tribes that have received federal funds for housing and have not been using them. He added that the federal government is thinking of taking back the funding for about 1,000 homes if the Navajo Tribe doesn't take action soon....

Associated Press

mid-1960s, Papagos living at San Lucy, a community in the projected dam's floodplain, were relocated to a reservation just north of Gila Bend. Their new homes, however, were planned without consulting the occupants. A woman whose new physical surroundings were meant to be a vast improvement over her old San Lucy home suddenly felt uncomfortable in her role as a grandmother. Why? She could no longer look out the back door at her grandchild. New houses in perfect rows separated by chain-link fencing ignored kin groupings.

Bureau of Indian Affairs homes conforming to Housing and Urban Development standards on the Apache lands in eastern Arizona have, within two decades, changed the living pattern from one dominated by wickiups to communities in which public housing is the norm. "If you want to see a wickiup in Apache country," Krutz says, "you have to go to the Ft. Apache Culture Center. The role of the federal government on reservations is very subtle, but it's very strong."

TOM MILLER

strangers' main thrust was toward the Zuñis and other Pueblo peoples of New Mexico.

From the Rio Grande Valley, the Spaniards' first area of colonization, soldiers and priests moved westward, trying at length to conquer and convert the Hopis. It did not work. In 1680, the Hopis joined the great Pueblo Revolt that drove all the Spaniards pell-mell out of New Mexico. When the Spaniards returned twelve years later, and priests appeared again among the Hopis, there was a disaster. A Franciscan missionary managed to convert almost half the population of the town of Awatovi. It created so much dissention that those who clung to their ancient beliefs feared for the future of all Hopi life. In a desperate attempt to preserve the Hopi Way the village leader of Awatovi appealed to other Hopi towns in 1700 to wipe out his own town and all its people, good and bad, himself included. The towns of Oraibi and Walpi responded and totally destroyed Awatovi, killing all its male inhabitants and clearing the earth of this threat to the Hopis' well-being. Tradition has it that women and children were spared and amalgamated into other Hopi towns.

For many generations after that, the Hopis were undisturbed by whites. Meanwhile, during the struggle for religious freedom, they had added a village of non-Hopis. Fleeing the Spanish oppressors in 1696, a group of Rio Grande Tewa Pueblos had asked for and received permission to live on the Hopis' First Mesa. The Hopis let them build their own town of Hano, which thereafter served the neighboring Hopi

Yaqui deer dancer. C. ALLAN MORGAN.

towns as a defensive buffer against marauding Navajos and Utes. Hano continues to be occupied by Tewa-speaking descendents of the refugee Pueblos.

The Spaniards' second thrust was into the ancient country of the Hohokams in southern Arizona, which they knew as the land of the Upper Pimans. It was a catch-all term for a vast expanse of shimmering deserts and mountains, extending from deep in Sonora northward to Arizona's Salt and Gila rivers and from the San Pedro Valley west to the Gulf of California. All of it was the territory of the Akimel O'odham (the people who lived along rivers) and the Tohono O'odham (the people of the desert).

Along the rivers near present-day Phoenix lived those who became known as the Pimas. Their homes were dome-shaped covered with brush and they were expert farmers, producing crops with water conveyed to their fields through networks of canals—an inheritance from the Hohokams. Between the San Pedro and Santa Cruz rivers were the Sobaipuris, Papagos who lived in year-round villages and also practiced canal-irrigation agriculture as did the Ak-Chin Papagos west of them. Far in the west, extending to the Gulf of California and occupying some of the hottest and most barren land on the continent, were the nomadic Sand people, also Papagos, collecting water from springs and *tinajas*, or rock tanks.

In 1687, Father Eusebio Kino and the Jesuits entered the land of the Sobaipuris and established a string of missions, including three in present-day Arizona along the Santa Cruz. Preaching kindness and goodwill, he gathered the Indians around the missions, introduced them to cattle, horses, and the growing of grains, and had much success in converting them to Catholicism.

Eventually, this proved to be a catastrophe for the Sobaipuris. Attracted by the herds of livestock and stores of food, Western and Chiricahua Apaches fell repeatedly on the missions, killing many of the Papago villagers who clustered around them. Hundreds of others died in recurrent epidemics of Spanish-introduced diseases. Regimented, and working more for the missions than for themselves, the Sobaipuris, as well as the Pimas, resented the taking of their own lands by Spanish farmers and ranchers. In 1695, and again in 1751, they revolted, on the latter occasion killing the missionaries and more than one hundred Spaniards, but Spanish soldiers came in, put down the uprising, and established a presidio at Tubac to protect the priests and settlers.

In 1769, the Franciscans succeeded the Jesuits, who had been expelled from New Spain, and among other things rebuilt the mission of San Xavier del Bac. One of its early pastors, Father Francisco Garcés, made three exploration trips westward through the desert, trying to convert and gather in Ak-Chin and Sand Papagos. He baptized some of them, but the people were remote and the country was harsh, and the Ak-Chins and Sand people remained beyond Spanish control. A tireless traveler, Garcés also visited the Hopis, who turned him away, as well as various Yuman-speaking tribes, including the Havasupais at the

Opposite: Sunrise, Old Walpi Pueblo, 1942. ANSEL ADAMS.

bottom of Grand Canyon and the Quechans at the confluence of the Gila and Colorado rivers.

Two Spanish settlements, a mission, and a garrison of soldiers were eventually planted among the Quechans to protect the Colorado River crossing to California, but in 1781, the Quechans revolted against the Spaniards' high-handedness and cruelty. Priests were killed, settlements destroyed, and Spanish control of the area was permanently ended.

Meanwhile, along the Santa Cruz, Apaches and epidemics continued to cut down the Sobaipuri population, and more Spanish settlers came in to take their lands. In 1786, the Spaniards attempted to buy peace from troublesome raiders with grants of farmland, rations, liquor, and gifts of obsolete guns with which to hunt. The raids lessened and matters were fairly calm until 1822, when Mexico, having won its independence, took over the administration of the area.

The situation deteriorated immediately, garrisons were weakened, and raids picked up again. Many of the missionaries were loyal to Spain and left. Mexico expelled the rest of the Franciscans in 1827, and the mission system fell apart. Large tracts of Papago land were given to Mexican settlers—even as the Mexican government's presence declined—and Apache raids increased. Finally, in 1848, Mexican troops left to fight the Americans in the Mexican War. Apaches staged a devastating raid that drove all non-Indians, as well as many Sobaipuris, out of the middle Santa Cruz Valley.

In other parts of Arizona, tribes had had conflicts with Anglo Americans as well. Exploring westward from Santa Fe and Taos, fur trappers had followed the Gila toward California, clashing with Apache and Yumans along the Colorado River. A party of Indian-fearing Anglo Americans usually started the trouble, killing or otherwise offending an Indian group. The next party of Anglo Americans then suffered the consequences.

At about the same time, Navajos were becoming locked in a vicious cycle of raids and counter-raids with the Hispanic and Pueblo towns and ranches along the Rio Grande. Raiding for livestock, food, and loot, the Navajos, like the Apaches, drew angry retaliations. For years, frustrated Spanish, and then Mexican, authorities in Santa Fe had been trying to punish the Navajos and stop their raiding. But their expeditions across the wild landscapes of the Navajo country had never been strong enough to accomplish the job.

With the acquisition of Arizona at the end of the Mexican War, the United States inherited the task of dealing with the many different tribes. The responsibility was increased in 1854, when the Gadsden Purchase pushed the international border southward, adding the northern portion of the Papago and Chiricahua Apache territories to the United States. Though the Indians had no say in the transfer of sovereignty, it was to have a great impact on their lives. Under Spain and Mexico, Indians had possessed the status of citizens. Moreover, when they lived in fixed communities, their title to their land had been recognized. There had been violations, of course, but on the whole the law had been observed. The United States, on the other hand, treated Indians as wards, and regarded their lands almost as public domain, open to settlers, miners, and ranchers. The idea, in the Age of Manifest Destiny, was to confine Indians to small reservations, out of the way of the expanding non-Indian population, and then turn them into whites.

During the Mexican War, American troops marching from Santa Fe to California had streamed through their lands, following the Gila River route. After the war, that and many other routes were taken by California-bound gold miners, official government exploring parties, and transcontinental stagecoach operators. By and large, their contacts with Arizona's Indians were peaceable. Setting a pattern of friendship and generosity that would last for many years, the Pimas on the Gila went out of their way to be helpful to the Anglo-American passers-by, supplying them with grain and other agricultural products at modest prices. The amply watered Pima villages became landmark resting stops for the weary desert travelers. Glad to be rid of their Spanish and Mexican foes, even the Apaches at first were friendly to the Anglo Americans.

But the favors were not always returned. Whites, crossing the Papagos' land, shot at the Sand people as if they were rabbits, and they left diseases among them that almost wiped them out. In the Santa Cruz Valley, Anglo-American miners and settlers arrived, building up the squalid pueblo of Tucson and fingering out aggressively to claim huge chunks of the Papagos' land, and the water that allowed it to be farmed. The Papagos protested, but they were a peaceful people and eventually they ended up on reservations, with barely enough water to stay alive. The Apaches were another matter. Inevitably, the new settlers offended the Chiricahua Apaches, and the area throbbed again with violence. U.S. troops were sent, forts were built, but raiding and warfare spread throughout southeastern Arizona. It only ended in the 1880s, when Geronimo and the last unconquered Chiricahua band surrendered. Geronimo was sent to prison in Florida and then to Fort Sill in Oklahoma, where he died. Meanwhile, the rest of the once-fierce Chiricahuas were confined on a reservation.

Navajo raiding ended more abruptly in 1864, when the Navajos met their match in Kit Carson, at the time a Civil War colonel of New Mexican Volunteers. Under orders from stern Gen. James H. Carleton, Carson and his volunteers invaded Canyon de Chelly, the sacred heart of Navajo country in snowy January of that year, destroying gardens, orchards, and foodstores, and threatening Navajos with immediate starvation. When some of them began to die, others surrendered. In all, some eight thousand gave themselves up at nearby forts. Carleton sent them all on a cruel, 400-mile "Long Walk" to the desolate Bosque Redondo reservation on the eastern New Mexico plains. Hundreds died of starvation, disease, and exposure en route, and many more perished during four years of exile. Finally, in 1868, they were allowed to walk back to Arizona, where a reservation was created for them.

Carleton's harsh treatment was visited also on some of the Western Apaches and the Yavapais, the latter of whom had had little previous contact with whites. In 1863, prospectors found gold near present-day Prescott, and miners and settlers flooded in, clashing with local groups of Northern Tonto Apaches and Yavapais, whom the Anglo Americans mistakenly called Apaches. Aggressions were committed by both sides, and as the fighting spread, Carleton sent troops from nearby Fort Whipple. Indian rancherias were destroyed and many Indians were killed. Some were lured into peace meetings with offers of tobacco and pinole, and then gunned down, and on one known occasion, poisoned by strychnine mixed with the pinole. Finally, tired of being hounded, the Yavapais agreed to live on a reservation. It took time to find an area that could provide them with sustenance, and as they were taken from one place to another, their lives were endangered by soldiers and Pimas, who were serving as scouts for the army. At one time, in 1872, an entire Yavapai band that had taken refuge in a cave in the Salt River Canyon

ALL AMERICAN

A red-neck drove his pickup into the parking lot at an Indian café south of Phoenix. Bumper-stickers and decals on all the other trucks indicated he was deep in Indian country. PROUD TO BE PIMA, read the one to his right. RED POWER advocated the one to his left. A.I.M.—AMERICAN INDIAN MOVEMENT announced the truck near the screen door. "You know," he said to no one in particular as he plopped down on a stool at the counter, "there was really only one good Indian—" all eyes turned toward the new arrival "—and that was Jim Thorpe. He could run, he could throw, he could jump—why, he was the most natural athlete that ever lived." He paused momentarily as his Indian audience listened attentively. "And *he* was half-white."

A few days later one of the same Indians found himself at a bar in Flagstaff. Bumper-stickers and decals on all the pickups indicated he was deep in red-neck country. COWBOY AND PROUD OF IT, read the one to his right. WILLIE NELSON FOR PRESIDENT advocated the one to his left. I LOVE RODEO announced the truck near the wood-frame door. "You know," he said to no one in particular as he plopped down on a stool near the bar, "there was really only one good white man—" all eyes turned toward the new arrival "—and that was Jim Thorpe. He could run, he could throw, he could jump—why, he was the most natural athlete that ever lived." He paused momentarily as his cowboy audience listened attentively. "And *he* was half-Indian."

TOM MILLER

was massacred by a group of soldiers. Yavapais still look back on the episode at "Skeleton Cave" as the most terrible event in their history. For twenty-five years, Yavapais were placed on the Western Apaches' San Carlos Reservation, where many of them intermarried with the Apaches. Finally, most of them were given their own reservations, including Fort McDowell, Prescott, and Camp Verde, Middle Verde, and Clarkdale in the Verde Valley. Others, finding jobs, established homes among whites outside the reservations. In all, today, the Yavapais are estimated to number about twelve hundred.

The Western Apaches were harder to bring to terms. The White Mountain and Cibecue Apaches were the first to make peace, and even agreed to serve as scouts for Gen. George Crook in campaigns against other Apaches. Gradually, the San Carlos and Northern and Southern Tontos were pacified, though not without occasional outbreaks of resistance that required new military actions against them. Eventually, all of them were induced by one means or another to stay on reservations. Today, they are spread among three reservations, the San Carlos, Fort Apache, and Payson, and they number more than fifteen thousand.

Assimilation was considered the only way Indians could survive and share the benefits of modern-day American civilization. Treated at worst as prisoners and at best as backward wards and children, they were subjected to pressures by government agents, missionaries, and the army to turn from their own religions, give up their languages, legends, and lore, dress and cut their hair like Anglos, abandon their traditional social and political structures, and send their children to government schools. Among the most notable Congressional attempts to smooth the road to assimilation were the Dawes Allotment Act of 1887 and the Indian Reorganization Act of 1934. The first, designed to break up Indian group-oriented societies by giving each Indian family its own plot of land on the reservation, was unsuccessful among most tribes in the arid environment of the Southwest. The second act, while encouraging a revival of Indian culture and restoring freedom of religion, contained provisions which kept the tribes dependent on the federal government.

Many Indians gradually learned to live like Anglo Americans and to accept Anglo values. Others among the Hopis and Navajos resisted. But the Hopis, for instance, who had once ejected the Spaniards, could not evict the Anglo-American government agents and missionaries who appeared among them in the late nineteenth century. The Hopi way of life was thrown increasingly on the defensive. Many Hopis were Christianized and encouraged to abandon the beliefs and ceremonies that reminded the people of the good way in which their ancestors had been taught to live. Children were forced to attend Bureau of Indian Affairs schools, and were punished for speaking their own language and made to feel ashamed of their parents' "superstitious" beliefs. Parents who resisted were sent to jail.

Inevitably, the pressures divided the Hopis between progressives, who accepted the new ways, and traditionals, who proclaimed that turning away from Maasau'u's instructions was threatening the balance of their universe and the future of their people. Old Oraibi itself was split in 1906, when a conservative faction left and founded the new town of Hotevilla. In the 1930s, the progressives accepted a tribal council form of government that undercut the position of the religious leader in each formerly autonomous town. The dissension it caused was exacerbated in the 1960s, when the tribal government, over the opposition of the traditionals, permitted the stripmining of coal on the Hopis' sacred Black Mesa.

Today, the Hopi tribe, numbering about nine thousand, is attempting to heal itself. Young Hopis are discovering a new validity in the people's ancient spiritual beliefs. Hopi artists and jewelers, with internationally recognized talents, are drawing on ancestral themes and motifs for inspiration. Even the more progressive are accepting once again traditional values, and finding meaning and comfort in the annual cycle of ceremonies centuries old. In the central plazas of the sun-baked towns, ritual dances are said to give deeply moving spiritual experiences also to non-Hopi visitors who are permitted to observe them. From spring until July, frequent kachina ceremonies are performed by masked dancers who impersonate the Hopi deities. In early August, the kachinas are believed to return to their homes on the San Francisco Peaks near Flagstaff, and from then until the following spring, the towns are the scene of unmasked and women's dances. The much-publicized Snake Dance, a dramatized prayer for rain sometimes barred to visitors, is held in August, in the town of Shungopovi in even-numbered years, and in Mishongnovi in odd-numbered years.

Arizona's tribes are beginning to emerge from years of poverty and hardship brought on by the abrupt ending of their ancestral ways of making a living, the inability of the reservations to support them at the same time it made them dependent, and the difficulty in adapting to the white man's economy. Many problems can be traced directly to white men's greed and the lack of governmental protection. For their many years of generosity in providing the army and other travelers with the fruits of their agriculture, the Pimas, for example, were

Below: Hopi pottery in the making.
STEPHEN TRIMBLE.

Opposite: Tohono O'Odham woman preparing yucca for basketmaking.
C. ALLAN MORGAN.

rewarded by the taking of their productive fields and the robbery—for no other word will do—of their water, which white settlers farther upstream were permitted to divert away from the Pimas to their own fields. As the base of the Pimas' economy dried up, the federal government advised them to move to the Indian Territory—in effect, "to get lost." The Pimas refused to leave the home of their ancestors. In recent years, after decades of living in poverty on small, dry farms, in the midst of booming non-Indian farms and sprawling urban developments, they finally instituted court action in the hope of gaining recognition of their right to some of the water that was taken from them.

Today, numbering more than fifteen thousand, they live on the Salt River reservation east of Phoenix and, with some eight hundred Maricopas, on the Gila River reservation south of Phoenix. In addition, a mixed group of about six hundred Pimas and Papagos inhabit the Ak-Chin reservation near Maricopa, which was established for them in 1912. Farming nearly six thousand acres, the Ak-Chin people in 1978 successfully settled a water-rights claim with the United States government, which agreed to supply them with water to offset what had been mined away from the water table under their land by surrounding non-Indian farmers.

Above: Supai, the Grand Canyon home of the Havasupai. STEPHEN TRIMBLE.

Opposite: Navajo woman feeding newborn lambs. MICHAEL COLLIER.

Like the Pimas, the Papagos, also, lost land and water to the whites. Today, their main reservation, extending across the desert of the old Ak-Chin country, covers 2.7 million acres and is the second largest U.S. reservation (after that of the Navajos). In addition, the Papagos, numbering in all about sixteen thousand people, inhabit three smaller reservations, at Florence, Gila Bend, and at the San Xavier Mission south of Phoenix. The widely scattered villages were autonomous until 1916, when they found themselves joint possessors of the main reservation, and became a single, unified tribe. In January 1986, the Papagos officially changed the name of their tribe to Tohono O'odham as they were known prior to the arrival of the Spanish.

The descendants of able farmers, the Tohono O'odhams have been handicapped by a lack of water, much of which was taken from them during the last century. The government has more recently dug a few wells for them, and some deliver water by deep-well pumps powered by solar energy systems. After legal battles and Congressional approval, the Department of the Interior in 1981 agreed to assign them water from the Central Arizona Project, but it is uncertain how much they will receive in any given year after 1992. In the meantime, their principal income is from cattle ranching, copper mine leases (in recent years, a hard-hit industry), federal and tribal jobs, and employment in agriculture and the mines. Basketmaking is a profitable industry of Tohono O'odham women.

On the Fort Apache (better known today as the White Mountain Apache) and San Carlos reservations, the Apaches are also struggling to improve their economic lot. More than two-thirds of the 1.6 million-acre White Mountain reservation is mountainous and covered with pine and aspen. The tribally owned Fort Apache Timber Company's logging and milling operations are a major source of income. But the tribe has also developed the White Mountain Recreation Enterprise, which employs tribal members to supervise, for use by fee-paying visitors, twenty-six mountain lakes and earthen water tanks, one thousand campsites, and more than three hundred miles of cold, clear trout streams (more than exist in all the rest of Arizona). Outsiders make heavy use of the cool area in summer, and in the winter come for skiing at the Sunrise Park Ski Lodge, which the tribe also owns and operates. Other sources of income for tribal members are cattle ranching and farming along the lower parts of the rivers.

The 1.8 million-acre San Carlos reservation was once three times its present size and included desirable farmland along the Gila River as well as rich copper deposits in Clifton and Morenci, and the land was eventually stripped away from the reservation. Today, the tribe owns a herd of high-quality Herefords, some timber stands, and a few thousand acres of farmland along river bottoms in the south. However, much of the reservation is suitable for recreation, and the tribe is beginning to develop that potential. Dozens of ponds and streams already attract permit-paying fishermen; others buy licenses from the tribe to hunt elk, deer, bears, mountain lions, javelinas, rabbits, squirrels, quail,

doves, ducks, and geese. Peridots—greenish, semi-precious stones—
are also found on the reservation, and a number of Apaches are
employed at tumbling, cutting, and polishing the gems.

On the western edge of Arizona, along the lower Colorado, most
of the Yuman-speaking tribes still live in their traditional homelands.
In the hot south, near the delta of the Colorado, about five hundred
Cocopas possess more than forty-five hundred acres. Above them,
some two thousand Quechans inhabit the Yuma reservation, most of
which lies in California. Farther upstream, Mojaves share the Colorado
River Indian Reservation with Chemehuevis, a small, formerly semi-
nomadic group that migrated from the Mojave Desert in the eighteenth
century, and some Navajos and Hopis, who moved in after World War
II. A large part of the reservation's irrigated lands along the river are
leased to non-Indian farmers. On the Fort Mojave reservation, above
Needles, are more Mojaves, whose population altogether is about
twenty-five hundred.

The Havasupais, the most isolated tribe in the United States, number about five hundred and live on a reservation of more than 250,000 acres in the western end of the Grand Canyon. Cataract Canyon there, a favorite of photographers, contains a series of high waterfalls that cascade into deep turquoise-blue, shaded pools. Until the late nineteenth century, the Havasupais followed an annual cycle of farming in the canyon until the fall, then migrating to the plateau above, where they hunted game. In April, they would return to the canyon to plant their gardens. In 1882, the government took their plateau hunting grounds away from them and confined them to living year-round in the canyon. By 1906, their population had dropped to 166. In 1975, after a bitter fight with environmentalists who wanted the area added to Grand Canyon National Park, Congress returned a portion of the plateau to the tribe. Since then, some of the Havasupais have revived their traditional migration pattern. Today, they support themselves mainly by outside wage work, and a small tourist industry caters to campers.

On the plateau west of the Havasupais, some one thousand Walapais make a living from stock-raising and timber. Though they once practiced a limited agriculture, early miners and cattlemen drove them

Inauguration of Navajo Tribal Chairman Peterson Zah, 1983. TIM FULLER.

from their best lands. When they complained, they were threatened with extermination by poisoning. Today, the tribe is considering developing recreational facilities of its own.

The Navajos, occupying the nation's largest reservation (about fifteen million acres extending into parts of Utah and New Mexico) have grown in numbers to more than one hundred and sixty thousand and are also the U.S.'s largest and wealthiest tribe. Possessing plentiful reserves of oil, gas, coal, uranium, they realize millions of dollars in leases and royalties each year. Today the tribe is engaged in renegotiating leases originally made for them by the federal government to get fairer prices. Although they have realized partial success, income from these natural resources still comes nowhere near meeting the needs of the growing Navajo population, and poverty is widespread. After the Navajos returned to the reservation in 1868, the economy rested for many years on farming and the raising of sheep and goats. By the 1930s, much of the reservation was seriously overgrazed, and despite the Navajos' angry objection, the government forced them to reduce drastically the number of their livestock. Little work is available on the reservation. In 1985, the unemployment rate was about sixty-five percent. As a result, many Navajos each year are forced to leave the reservation to seek jobs in the major cities. At the same time, Navajos have made great strides in educating their children on the reservation. The number of elementary and high schools has greatly increased and the Navajos have established their own Community College. Finally, young Navajos are enrolled in colleges and graduate schools throughout the United States.

The expanding Navajo population has brought problems with the Hopis. Since much of the Navajos' land is rugged and inhospitable, the government accommodated the tribe's needs from time to time by enlarging the reservation. Eventually, it completely encircled the Hopi reservation. Still, the Navajos extended their boundaries inward until they occupied three-fourths of the Hopis' territory. Despite the Hopis' outrage, a federal court in 1962 declared part of the Hopi reservation onto which many Navajos had moved a Joint Use Area. The issue remained a bitter one, and twelve years later, Congress divided the Joint Use Area between the two tribes. The decision satisfied neither tribe. The expensive and delicate job of forcing the Navajos to move onto the Navajo section and the Hopis onto the Hopi section was to have been completed in 1986, but the difficulties in settling the complex dispute have so far prevented a satisfactory resolution.

The rancor and dissention has been particularly disturbing to the traditionals of both tribes, who feel that they could have solved the issue peacefully among themselves, without government intervention. Their common viewpoint, contrasting with the hostility shown by the rest of the people of the two tribes, should not have been unexpected. To the traditionals, once again, harmony has been disrupted, and the teachings of the gods ignored. The world is out of balance. The future of the peoples' life is threatened.

Chapter Eight

HISPANIC HERITAGE

The concept of the "West" conjures up in most of us visions of movement and adventure—the "wild West" of prospectors, bandits, lawmen, saloons, and gunfights in the streets of such towns as Tombstone. Life seemed to be lived for the moment and nothing lasted, nothing was permanent. How different from that view are the memories of people like Ramón Soto, who lived his whole life in Arizona. His family had been there for generations, and his descendants are there still. Any member of the Romero family, or the Sosas, the Ramírezes, or the Carrillos would attest to the sense of stability and permanence of their families in this area. They belonged; they were part of the land, part of the history, part of the future.

Ramón Soto led a life that was full and varied, but one that certainly departed from the cowboy and gold-rush stereotypes. In every way we would consider his life quite ordinary, even while recognizing it as full of achievements. Ramón was an optimist. As a clerk in the Zeckendorf Store (later Steinfeld's) he saved his earnings and invested them in real estate—vacant lots that sold for a song but later gained in value and proved young Soto to be an astute investor. His holdings expanded to include ranches, and his activities as a contributing member of the community grew with them. He became a journalist and wrote for local newspapers. Sensing a need for unity among Tucson's Hispanics, he wrote a series of articles which led to the creation of the Alianza Hispano-Americana, an organization that became known internationally.

Ramón Soto's memories of the Tucson of the 1880s were filled with camaraderie, and his visions of the future were optimistic. He also looked back to the earliest presence of his ancestors, recognizing the intertwining that had taken place and the significance these relationships had to the future. This emphasis on continuity is one of the vital elements in Arizona's Mexican-American legacy.

Above left: Detail from "Blue Wall." LOUIS CARLOS BERNAL.

Opposite: The south wall of Tumacácori Mission. ED STILES.

THE LURE OF THE NORTH

Traditionally, historians have distinguished between the Mexican and Spanish roles in the Hispanic heritage of Arizona and the Southwest. But only in a limited sense can they be dealt with separately. The Spanish explorers who crossed Arizona in the sixteenth century came via Mexico, where the existing society influenced them and where many mixed with native populations. The complement of expeditionaries and their accompanying soldiers was made up of Spaniards, mestizos, Indians, *coyotes* (people of mixed Indian descent other than mestizos), and mulattos. Each of these groups contributed in different but important ways.

Most of the early expeditionary groups were headed north in search of wealth—Quivira, Eldorado, and the Seven Cities of Cibola were believed to possess more of the great riches the first Spaniards had encountered in Tenochtitlán. Expeditions were led by Marcos de Niza (1539), Vásquez de Coronado (1540), and Antonio de Espejo (1583), among others. Although the explorers passed through Arizona without leaving any permanent marks, they provided the first detailed written description of the natural characteristics and inhabitants of the area, forming what Luis Leal has called "the first image of Aztlán." (Chicanos, in looking back to their Aztec heritage, gave the name Aztlán to the southwestern part of the United States.) These excursionary groups were the predecessors of the colonizing entrepreneurs.

In the early seventeenth century a new kind of expeditionary

began to come north. Earlier expeditions, such as the one led by Vás-quez de Coronado, were criticized for seeking only gold and other riches and not staying to colonize the area. The new colonizers were mostly Spaniards and castas (different racial mixtures) who had become disenchanted with colonial life, and Indians and mulattos. They felt the oppressive weight of the system in central Mexico and saw adventure and resettlement in far-off places as their only means of escape. The North offered them the possibility of amassing land and wealth as well.

In spite of the desire of the new arrivals to shake off the worst of colonial Mexico, they soon realized they could not achieve their goals in the North without depending heavily upon two basic Spanish institutions: the church and the army. The church served as a con-science-soother for the adventurers and settlers who were displacing the inhabitants of the area, and usurping their land and belongings. In addition, the new settlers encountered Indians who were vastly differ-ent from those of central Mexico. The colonizers were not prepared to defend themselves against the Apaches and other bellicose tribes opposed to making peace with the invader. The merging of army, church, and adventurer allowed settlement to take place and produced a string of presidios, missions, and pueblos throughout the Southwest.

Because the Spanish Crown lost interest in overt military expan-sion, most expeditions to the North in the seventeenth century were led by missionaries rather than soldiers. Because the Dominicans had settled and evangelized the south-central region, and since the Fran-ciscans had done the same in the north-central region, the Jesuit mis-sionaries found themselves reaching into the remote northwestern areas of Mexican territory. From 1587 on, they founded missions along the Sinaloa, Mocorito, and Ocoroni rivers and from there continued north-ward to Arizona. The settlements at Guevavi, Tumacácori, and San Xavier del Bac were part of this extensive chain of missions.

In keeping with the less militaristic orientation, new missions were built without presidios, although some were added on in the eighteenth century in response to uprisings of the Yuma and Pima Indians. Such was the case of the Tubac and Tucson presidios built in 1752 and 1775, respectively.

In the process of evangelization, an attempt was made to abolish native rituals and religious beliefs. When this did not work, Christian beliefs and rituals were superimposed upon native ones, producing such blends as the Easter ceremonies still performed in Yaqui villages in Phoenix and Tucson. The imposition of Spanish culture on the native populations met with mixed success as well, as shown by the careful preservation of Indian languages and customs among mission Indians. Many of today's mission tribes are bi- or trilingual, their cultural manifestations are both Indian and Spanish, and their family and group relations are based as much on Indian tradition as on Spanish custom.

The Arizona mission system provides a clear example of the colo-nizing attitude the Spaniards brought to the New World. Octavio Paz described this attitude as "inclusive." In his words:

Opposite: Branding cattle at the Ramón Soto Ranch, Sierrita Moun-tains, 1949.
ARIZONA HISTORICAL SOCIETY.

...the notions of conquest and domination were allied to conversion and absorption.... An inclusive society founded on the double principle of domination and conversion had to be hierarchical, centralist and respectful of all the peculiarities of each group: a strict division of classes and groups, each of them with laws and special statutes, and all believers in the same faith and obedient to the same Lord.

When the Mexican War of Independence broke out in 1810, the troops in the Southwest were sent to fight against the revolutionaries, and the missions were left without military protection. The mission system began to decline, and a new era for the region began. The mission period had had an overwhelming impact on the area. Carey McWilliams wrote in *North from Mexico*:

...the Spaniards, in a triangular relationship with Mexicans and Indians, succeeded in laying the foundations for the present-day economic structure of the region. Anglo-Americans in the Southwest have been the beneficiaries of three hundred years of experimentation, adaptation and innovation. If one thinks of the Southwest in terms of mines, sheep and cattle, and irrigated farming, then it is readily apparent that the underpinnings of the economy are of Spanish origin.

Opposite: San Xavier Mission, the white dove of the desert, southwest of Tucson. JACK W. DYKINGA.

MEXICAN INDEPENDENCE

In 1824 most of what is today Arizona was governed from Santa Fe, capital of the new territory called New Mexico; the region south of the Gila River was part of Sonora. At that time, Tubac and Tucson were the two major Mexican population centers in Arizona. Many of the soldiers who had been ordered from the area to fight in the Mexican War of Independence returned to work in agriculture along the Santa Cruz River. The change in government had little effect on the system which continued to keep mestizos and Indians in the position of peons. The geopolitical circumstances of the Southwest, then the frontier of a new country, prohibited the new wave of egalitarian values from influencing significantly the social and political realities.

Many social and economic advances took place in the border area during the next ten to fifteen years. The printing press was introduced to New Mexico by Antonio Barreiros in 1834 and to California by José de la Rosa a year later. Barreiros started the first newspaper of the territory, *El Crepúsculo de la Libertad*, in Santa Fe.

Commerce also became an important part of the area's economy. The Santa Fe–Los Angeles trade route, opened in 1829, was a major commercial highway and allowed for a great deal of social and political contact among communities along the way. Even more important was the route which ran between Guaymas and Tucson. Guaymas was a major port and received merchandise of all sorts from around the world, goods which were then shipped overland to southwestern communities.

The majority of Arizona's residents at this time were farmers and cattle ranchers. In spite of the fact that Apache Indian attacks continued to be frequent, many families from farther south took advantage of the land-grant programs offered by the Mexican government and settled in such areas.

AFTER THE GADSDEN PURCHASE

After the Mexican American War, more than half of Mexican territory was turned over to the United States under the Treaty of Guadalupe-Hidalgo in 1848. The ceded land included all of what is today California, Nevada, and Utah; most of New Mexico and Arizona; and portions of Colorado, Kansas, Oklahoma, and Wyoming; the treaty also acknowledged the United States' annexation of Texas in 1845. Southern Arizona south of the Gila River and the Mesilla Valley in New Mexico were the only parts of Mexican territory north of the present international border that were not transferred. Lucrative min-

ing ventures and the desire for a transcontinental railroad route soon made the acquisition of the small section that remained a top priority for the American government. In 1853 James Gadsden was authorized to make several offers for more land to General Antonio López de Santa Anna, commander in the war with Texas and the Mexican American War and three-time president of Mexico. Santa Anna accepted the offer that included the least amount of land, and nearly 30,000 square miles of what is today southern Arizona and southern New Mexico were sold under the Tratado de la Mesilla, or in U.S. history books, the Gadsden Purchase.

Confusion and contention surrounded property ownership after the Purchase. Anglo-American settlers arriving in the area were neither aware of nor in harmony with the Spanish and Mexican legal traditions that had established proprietorship up to that time. Hispanic residents and landowners tried to protect their property rights, but often their ignorance of court procedures in the U.S. made them easy prey for unscrupulous lawyers. Overtaxation of the land also caused some of the residents in the area to lose ownership.

In 1863 New Mexico was divided into the separate territories of Arizona and New Mexico. Arizona's territorial capital was first located at Fort Whipple, then moved to Prescott, to Tucson, back to Prescott, and finally, in 1889, established at Phoenix. The movement of the

Opposite: Domestic scene at the Sanders Ranch in the Sierrita Mountains.
ARIZONA HISTORICAL SOCIETY.

capital away from Tucson was based on a number of factors, including the rapid expansion of population in the central and northern parts of the Territory, the need for a location accessible to outlying areas of Arizona, and the desire on the part of some recent arrivals to place the seat of government where the Anglo population predominated.

The most important development in the second half of the nineteenth century in Arizona was the great increase in mining activity. Ever since the day in 1583 when Antonio de Espejo first discovered copper in the Verde River, the Spanish-Mexican residents of the area had developed mining activity throughout the region. In 1800 José Carrasco founded the Santa Rita Copper and Silver Mine in western New Mexico. In 1804 this mine employed six hundred workers and sent copper to Mexico City to be melted into currency. About thirty miles outside of Tucson, the Heintzelman Mine was developed. In 1859, 800 Mexican Americans worked in this mine and produced $100,000 worth of silver. These mines used a peonage system in which the workers' salaries were paid in tokens that had to be used in the company stores. In protest, the miners organized into a protective collective-bargaining type of organization.

When Harry Lesinsky first started to work the mine in Clifton, Arizona, in 1872, he went to Ciudad Juárez, Chihuahua, to find good smelter operators. These miners built the first smelters for the melting down of copper ore in Arizona. They were made of adobe and fired with mesquite charcoal. The smelter capacity was two tons a day, and the fire was kept hot by using bellows. Miners loaded the raw ore on to burros for transport to the smelter. Once melted down, the copper was loaded on mules and oxen and taken as far as Kansas City. In 1875, when the Bisbee copper mines opened, they used the same techniques refined at the Santa Rita and at mines in Sonora.

The Spanish-Mexican legal system, as well as tools and techniques, was important in the development of the mining industry in Arizona around the turn of the century. For example, the still-prevalent system of leasing mining privileges on a piece of land instead of selling the land outright is a legacy of the Hispanic tradition.

CITY LIFE IN ARIZONA TERRITORY

Life in Arizona in the second half of the nineteenth century varied according to the principal economic endeavors in different parts of the territory. Ranching was stable and permanent, while mining communities usually flourished and then faded. Established urban centers were based on government bureaucracy and small businesses, and the military was often present until the threat of Indian attack was greatly reduced, around the 1880s.

Carlos H. Tully described the Tucson of 1870 in an account pub-

lished almost fifty years later in the Tucson newspaper *El Tucsonense*. In 1870 Tucson's population was approximately 3,200, the majority of the residents being Mexican Americans, who owned almost all of what was then Tucson. The cemetery, the military barracks, and San Agustín Plaza were on the outer edges of the community. San Agustín, built in 1868, was the only church in town. The only newspaper being published at the time was the *Arizonan*. Business with Sonora was lucrative for both Mexicans and Americans, and the Territory imported flour, fruit, hats, blankets, mats, mescal, cigars, and cigarettes from across the border. Soldiers at nearby Fort Lowell were the best customers for local businesses.

Most Tucson houses were made of adobe and had high ceilings and large open spaces, a design well suited to the desert climate. Few homes had wood floors. The interior walls were coated with mud and then whitewashed. Roofs were flat and made of mud and saguaro ribs.

Levin Park, one of many entertainment centers, had a large hall used for theatrical productions and dances, a beer parlor, and an elegant

Above: San Agustín Cathedral, Tucson, built in 1868.
ARIZONA HISTORICAL SOCIETY.

Opposite: The Samaniego family parlor, Tucson.
ARIZONA HISTORICAL SOCIETY.

cantina where families and friends gathered. Tucson had a strong sense of community, and the residents considered themselves part of a large extended family. Carrillo Gardens was another gathering place, with ponds and many flowers. Silver Lake provided swimming and boating for the public.

Ramón Soto—merchant, entrepreneur, landowner, and journalist—described the everyday life of Tucsonans as well as the observance of holidays. On Sundays, he wrote, people gathered to worship and socialize. San Agustín Day, August 28, was the most important holiday of the year. During the two-week-long fiesta a ramada of tree branches was constructed to provide a refuge from the hot sun and the frequent late afternoon showers. Square dances were popular, as were the Pascola, Zapateado, and Danza Andaluza. Booths were set up for food and drink and games of chance. The fiesta concluded on September 16 with the celebration of the Gloria de los Heroes de la Patria Mexicana.

Toward the end of the nineteenth century, the presence of Ameri-

TALES TOLD IN OUR BARRIO

What credentials are necessary to be a historian—a professorship? A college degree? Students at Carrillo School know that the only requirement is curiosity. These elementary school children set out to tell the story of their neighborhood, on the western edge of downtown Tucson next to the Community Center, through the words of its longtime residents coupled with their own observations. First they went to the Arizona Heritage Center to see what others had written. Then they mapped out an approach of their own: walk the streets, talk to dozens of people, and explore the history, traditions, folktales, and landmarks which decorate their small corner of town.

The project, aided and guided by Carrillo's staff and outside friends, resulted in a remarkable 64-page book, *Tales Told In Our Barrio*. Students at Carrillo—designated a bilingual "magnet school" in a 1980 desegregation plan—asked each person, "What has 'barrio' meant to you?"

"Barrio means a lot of things to me, but the most important things are *familia, religión, y cultura,*" explained Bertha Santa Cruz, who has lived in the neighborhood since 1933. "Barrio also means working together and doing without."

" 'Barrio' means my neighborhood," said Adalena Cervantes Hall, who lived there until she was twenty-two years old, "and it means my old home."

"It was mostly desert, and there were only a few houses," recalled Anita Palafox, who moved to the barrio when she married at age eighteen in 1935. "A ditch used to go past my house, and my two boys use to play baseball in the desert. There were a lot of Chinese stores."

Isabel D. Urías, whose mother arrived in Tucson from Mexico in a covered wagon, remembered the schoolground at the corner of Simpson and South Main: "Where Carrillo School is now there was a zoo. One day, a bear at the zoo killed a baby. They had to kill the bear and close the zoo. Sometimes on the playground of Carrillo School there appeared apparitions of the lake that used to be here that dried up."

One neighbor pointed out where her house used to stand; a Holiday Inn has replaced it. No one hesitated to comment on the shrinking community. "I don't like changes very much because when the Urban Renewal System came some people had to leave," lamented Beatrice Pérez, whose backyard includes an old artisian well from which her husband's family used to draw water. Alicia Córdova, who has lived in the barrio all her life, looked at life there another way: *"Las amistades no han cambiado. Yo creo porque no han tumbado nada para acá donde yo vivo."* My friends haven't changed. I think that's because nothing's been knocked down over here where I live.

"One day some construction workers for the city were going to remove a mesquite tree that is on the corner of the Carrillo School playground" on 17th Street, related Mrs. Urías. "My husband and some of his friends sat in the tree and would not let the workers tear it down. The tree is still standing there." Another landmark was a skating rink where the school now stands. "My father used to skate there every weekend. One time he told us they were all skating," the young historians learned from Socorro B. Haro, whose adobe home is across the street from their school, "and this lady was dancing with this man and he was very handsome. Then the lady said, 'How beautiful you dance!' She bent down to look at his feet and they were devil's feet. She fainted and everybody ran away. Later the place was sold and they made a swimming pool."

Carrillo students also learned first-hand about their little community changing from a peaceful barrio to one where random violence can strike. Not long after they interviewed a man well-liked throughout the neighborhood, he was shot and killed by a stranger during one of his regular early evening strolls to a local bingo game. But another generation of community pride is starting to take its place. "As I walk along the cracked old sidewalk, I notice lots of trash and fallen leaves along the street," wrote Rosemary Galvez, a sixth-grader at Carrillo. "It might be dirty, but it smells like flowers and pine trees."

TOM MILLER

Below: The Southern Pacific Band in concert at the Carrillo Gardens, Tucson.

can military troops in Arizona greatly reduced the risk of traveling. This new sense of security allowed for an upsurge of cultural activities along the different routes across Arizona. Traveling theater and musical troupes made regular stops in Phoenix and Tucson and the less permanent mining camps that dotted the territory. Troupes from Spain, Cuba, and Mexico came north from Sonora and traveled as far as San Francisco. There was something for every taste, from comic and serious drama to opera and *zarzuelas* (musical comedies).

Literary get-togethers, called *tertulias*, were also common. Regularly scheduled recitals, discussion sessions, and poetry readings took place in the Tucson and Phoenix areas. These gatherings were the focus of intellectual life, and discussion topics included literature and politics. Many newspapers were born as a result of the tertulia movement, providing a means of spreading the views of these intellectual groups.

The Spanish-language newspapers of Arizona and the Southwest generally included a section in which appeared works by well-known literary figures and local authors. A look at their pages suggests that the region was not as isolated and intellectually barren as novels and films portrayed.

A RESPONSES TO DISCRIMINATION

As the end of the nineteenth century drew near, Anglo-
American immigrants to Arizona started to develop nativist senti-
ments, perceiving the Mexican Americans as obliged to adopt the
views and ways of life of the nation to which they now belonged.
Polarization between the two groups in Arizona became more pronounced and conflicts more frequent. The economic depression of 1894
further aggravated this developing situation, especially in mining

towns where Anglo Americans were competing with the more experienced Mexican-American miners for a limited number of jobs. Mines in Prescott and Bisbee refused to hire Mexican Americans, and the members of the all-Anglo Western Federation of Workers went on strike at the Old Dominion Mine to protest the employment of Mexican-American miners. In communities where Mexican Americans were still employed, a double standard existed. Mexican workers tended to get the lowest paying jobs, they received less pay for equal work ($25 to $30 a month for 60-hour work weeks compared to $70 a month for Anglo workers), housing was segregated, and wages were paid in tokens which could be used only in company stores. In Arizona copper mines, Mexican Americans were denied skilled positions, and as extraction of copper in a given mine became more difficult and complicated, Mexican workers were frequently obligated to participate in dynamiting if they wanted to continue to work. Anglo-American workers could refuse to do this kind of work.

Mexican Americans encountered similar discrimination and prejudice in their daily life. The union movement and the creation of *sociedades mutualistas* (mutual-aid societies) grew in response to this new set of circumstances. In Tucson the Sociedad de Obreros Unidos (Society of United Workers) was formed in 1883. Within the next twelve years it was followed by the Sociedad Protectora de Artesanos Unidos (Protective Society for United Craftsmen), the Sociedad de Beneficencia Mutua de la Raza Latina in Phoenix, the Sociedad Hidalgo, and, the most important and long-lasting of all, the Alianza Hispanoamericana.

Another response to discrimination was the attempt to unify the Mexican-American vote. Bernabé C. Brichta wrote the following letter to the editor of the newspaper *El Fronterizo* on August 12, 1890, speaking for many Mexican Americans:

Fellow Mexican Citizens:

Territorial and county elections are upon us and as citizens everyone who has the right to vote should exercise it, and it is imperative that he be highly interested in the elections, though in a different way from times past.

In California, New Mexico and other states of this great Republic, there are Mexicans that occupy honorary and important positions such as members of Congress, members of the Legislature, Supreme Court judges, city managers, etc. Why then does this not happen in this territory? Don't the members of our race have the same rights in Arizona as in other states?

.... The population of Tucson is three-quarters Mexican and it is time that the other one-fourth realizes that we exist and that we have the same rights as citizens as they do and that our rights must be respected.

Opposite: "Ernesto Villa," before a family shrine. LOUIS CARLOS BERNAL.

Brichta concluded his letter with the following statement:

> Let us unite, then, because there is strength in unity and putting
> aside personality and differences, when election day arrives, let us
> all cast our votes in favor of the Mexican candidates and this union
> and harmony will produce marvelous results for all people of our
> race in Arizona.

At the beginning of the twentieth century, a new wave of Mexican
immigrants came to the Southwest and joined the already sizable
number of Mexican Americans who were now aware of themselves as a
group apart. Almost all of these immigrants settled in the borderlands.

In Arizona the number of immigrants rose from 14,171 in 1900 to 114,173 in 1930.

Events on both sides of the border during the first quarter of the twentieth century account for this wave of immigration. In Mexico, dissatisfaction mounted among the working class during the last years of the Porfirio Díaz dictatorship. Trapped in an agricultural system based on peonage, many Mexicans moved farther and farther north in an attempt to remedy their situation. A little later, the rifts that existed between the various factions of the Mexican Revolution also produced large numbers of exiles.

Meanwhile, in the United States, the Southwest was emerging as a powerful economic empire as a consequence of the arrival of the railroad and the increasing demand in the East for the products from the area. The Mexican-American population continued to play an important role in the enterprises they had helped to develop—transportation, mining, agriculture, and cattle ranching. New immigrants joined with them as these sectors of economic importance grew.

In transportation a significant number of the workers on the railroad were Mexican or Mexican-American. In 1908 alone, more than 16,000 Mexicans were recruited to work on the railroad lines; an estimated sixty to ninety percent of workers on eighteen southwestern railroad lines were Mexican American. The 1930 census shows that 70,799 Mexicans worked in transportation and communication.

In mining the increasing need in the East for Arizona mineral products caused owners to send recruiters called *enganchadores* (literally "hookers") into Mexico to find the additional laborers needed. Immigration laws which barred Orientals and set strict quotas for some European immigrants made the Mexican labor force attractive. These laws, coupled with the increasingly intolerable social situation in Mexico, made the *enganchadores'* job an easy one. Between the years 1900 and 1930, about 60 percent of the common laborers in southwestern mines were Mexicans.

During World War I the demand for long-staple cotton rose sharply. The Arizona Cotton Growers Association recruited more than 30,000 Mexican workers during the war years to help plant and harvest the crop. Mexicans and Mexican Americans also made up sixty-five to eighty-five percent of the work force in agriculture.

Mexican Americans played an important role as intermediaries between the new arrivals and the Anglo-American working system. They eased the transition for the immigrants and aided in deploying the crowds of new workers successfully.

In response to the hardships suffered by the newcomers and the sense of a common bond, Mexican Americans formed organizations that fostered pride and provided assistance. The *sociedades mutuas* were groups of people who each year contributed sums of money to a fund to help defray the costs of medical, legal, and funeral services. Society members could request funds when needed; at other times the money was contributed toward community-wide campaigns and to legal bat-

Opposite: "Dos Mujeres" (Two Women). LOUIS CARLOS BERNAL.

tles when they affected the Mexican-American population as a whole.

Ligas protectoras were another type of association common in Mexican-American communities at the turn of the century. Their purpose was threefold: political, educational, and fraternal. Members worked in the political arena to eradicate institutionalized discrimination and in the public arena as an anti-defamation league. The most important *liga* in Arizona was the Liga Protectora Latina (LPL). This group was based in Phoenix, but its 5,000 members in 1920 were spread throughout Arizona and other southwestern states, and a Liga Protectora Lodge was even opened in Philadelphia. The Liga published a monthly bulletin called *Justicia*. One of its early major efforts was to fight the passage of the Claypool-Kinney Bill in the state legislature, which proposed to prohibit any business employing more than five people from hiring more than 20 percent non-English-speaking personnel. The bill would have also prohibited any non-English-speaking person from performing hazardous work, thus in effect limiting the Mexican Americans' access to mining jobs.

The Liga also addressed examples of discrimination and defamation. For instance, it publicized a Tempe theater's practice of segregating Mexican patrons, took a Tempe cotton grower to court over poor working conditions, and filed a complaint against the *Phoenix Gazette* and the *Arizona Republic* for publishing anti-Mexican comments. In the area of education, the LPL established a committee in 1918 to present a bill to the Arizona legislature establishing bilingual education in the elementary grades.

Another important organization was the labor union. It underwent great change when in 1904 a great number of Mexican progressives, including the Flores Magón brothers, crossed the border into U.S. territory as exiles. Other liberals joined the ranks of the working class in the fields, on the railroads, and in the mines. They joined the more progressive labor unions and had a profound impact on them. A new philosophy of being equal members of a group, as opposed to representatives and represented, changed the make-up and size of some of the local unions. The large network of Spanish-language newspapers made the transmission of progressive ideas possible and their effect extensive.

The Mexican-American union movement, especially in the mines, was able through negotiations and well-organized nonviolent strikes to assure Mexican workers' rights and to obtain improved conditions, higher wages, a formal grievance procedure, and a shorter work day for all miners. Many workers, however, fell victim of hard times. Large numbers of Mexican Americans lost their jobs in the pre-Depression era when cotton growers no longer needed the thousands of Mexican workers they had only recently imported. An estimated 3,000 to 10,000 Mexicans were homeless and destitute in the Phoenix area alone in 1921, and conditions continued to worsen in the following years.

This was a period also of Anglo dominance, and towns and cities reflected the new developers and decision-makers. Zoning regulations

Opposite: "Jácomes." From left to right are Alex F., Alex G., Augustine E., Henry G., Jr., and Margarita E. A family portrait.
LOUIS CARLOS BERNAL.

changed, and housing construction took on a distinctly Anglo-American flavor. Even the oldest and most traditional of Mexican towns and cities were slowly transformed into something more like eastern communities. The Mexican-American population protested the rapid and poor construction of new buildings and the lack of public gardens, open-air markets, and kiosks in the development plans.

In the 1920s there was a tendency in the United States to define a nation by the racial homogeneity of its citizens, and immigration quotas began to be set according to race and nationality. Assimilation was stressed in the schools. Organizations like the Ku Klux Klan and the All American Protective League, among others, created fear and

mistrust of peoples of different races and religions. In 1922, M. A. Hudges published an anti-Catholic newspaper in Phoenix called *The Crank*. In 1927, crosses were burned on A-Mountain in Tucson to intimidate Blacks and Catholics.

The Mexican response to the situation was to criticize this racist point of view and to emphasize the positive aspects of integration. In the newspapers of the 1920s many editorials appeared counteracting the general philosophy of the times by citing the integrationist ideas of Enrique Rodo, José Vasconcelos, and Maurice Davis. The Mexican Americans stressed their historical presence and natural right to be in the region as well as their contributions to the area's development and to the economic growth of the United States in general.

Despite all the attempts to alter the Anglo-American perception of the Mexican Americans, not much changed. According to Abraham Hoffman's *Unwanted Mexican Americans in the Great Depression*, during the depression years of 1929 to 1937 almost a half million Mexicans and Mexican-Americans were deported from the United States, with little consideration for citizenship rights or familial ties. Long-standing Mexican-American communities were broken up and their members dispersed to diverse places. Cultural and political activities that had integrated the Mexican-American population even during hard times almost ceased. Dispersion created an identity crisis among the Mexican

Above: Jerome celebrates Mexican Independence Day, September 16, 1928. ARIZONA HISTORICAL SOCIETY.

Opposite: Women workers at Tucson's Southern Pacific railyard at the height of the Second World War. ARIZONA HISTORICAL SOCIETY.

Americans, aggravated even further by their view of the Anglo-American perception of them. The 1930 census separated "whites" and "Mexicans" for the first time.

In World War II, 875,000 Mexican Americans joined the armed services. They received the highest proportion of congressional medals of honor of any minority group in the United States. Yet, upon returning to their home towns, many felt the same type and degree of discrimination that had existed when they left. Their sense of disillusionment led to the creation of the Pachuco movement.

The Pachuco movement was the first protest that Mexican-American youth made against both the American system and the traditional values of their own communities. They defied the establishment by wearing their hair and dressing in a distinctive and flashy manner. They defied their own communities and value systems by developing a language of their own and by making independent decisions. In Phoenix and Tucson, where the movement was strong, many Pachucos were

¡VIVA LA CHIMICHANGA!

Who invented the chimichanga? One might as well ask about trees falling in the forest or the sound of one hand clapping. "There is no doubt in my mind how it came about," insisted Carlotta Flores of El Charro in Tucson. "One day my aunt Monica accidentally dropped a burrito into a vat of boiling lard. The next day it was on the menu." El Charro's "disaster redeemed" story is countered by others who claim Ronquillo's Bakery, also in Tucson, first served up chimichangas. "I can remember seeing chimichangas at the Yaqui Old Pascua Village in the mid-1950s," answered Jim Griffith of the University of Arizona's Southwest Folklore Center. "Definitely it was at Mi Nidito," replied Cora Borboa, who runs Cora's Cafe in Tucson. A professor of Latin American Studies in Texas put the chimichanga in perspective: "It's hard to believe that some Mexicans and Papagos in Arizona haven't been frying their burritos for generations. It simply took until the 1950s before they were served in restaurants."

Regardless of where it came from, the chimichanga is a staple of Mexican restaurants throughout Arizona. It is that most curious of foods—a Mexican dish neither born in Mexico nor served there. Briefly: the chimichanga is a large flour tortilla, so thin you can read the Gadsden Purchase through it, wrapped cylindrically and sealed tightly around a filling (refried beans, stripped beef, chicken, or chile, for example), then deep-fried. Many chimis are garnished with lettuce, cheese—often melted—salsa, and sour cream. The chimichanga is the regional equivalent of creole gumbo or Florida stone crabs. It gives you 580 calories to burn off. (There is no such thing as a "light chimichanga.") You know your chimichanga is authentic if, an hour after eating it, you feel a log gently rolling around in your stomach. In many parts of Arizona, it is a first-class misdemeanor to be caught carrying a concealed chimichanga. The chimichanga is the gastronomical equivalent of war.

The chimichanga—the word loosely translates to "thingamabob"—has spawned its own culture and fanciers. In 1982, when Congressman Morris K. Udall had to choose which of two redrawn congressional districts to represent, he opted for the one with the best chimichangas. Since the late 1970s chimichangas have crept onto menus far from home—in New York, Washington, San Francisco, Minneapolis, and elsewhere. Easterners have been known to ask friends flying in from Arizona to stop on the way to the airport and pick up authentic chimis to bring with them. A transplant living in Australia wrote an Arizona acquaintance: "Please," he begged, "send me a chimichanga!"

The best made chimis offer three textures in one bite: the soft cheesey outside, the crisp tortilla shell, and the well-cooked interior. Rarely is the chimichanga ever ordered in the plural, although once after polishing off his very first chimichanga, a visiting Californian leaned back and smiled slowly. "That was great!" he said, patting his stomach. "I think I'll have another."

The name has often been bastardized, and almost always enjoyably so. At one place near Calexico, California, you can order a chivillanga. A New York gastronome reported a chingachanga on one menu. But please, do not confuse the chimichanga with chimurenga, which means war of liberation in Shona, the principal Bantu language in Zimbabwe; nor with Chickamauga, the Civil War battle in Georgia; nor with chimba-chaca, in Ecuador, a crudely built cable suspension bridge; nor with Chitchen Itza, the ancient Mayan sacrificial center in Yucatán, Mexico; nor with "Cushingura," Hiroshi Inagaki's Samurai epic. But no matter what you call it, you can always take the uneaten portion of your chimichanga home and have it cold for breakfast the next morning.

TOM MILLER

TIM FULLER

picked up by the police, and the most common sentences they received were prison terms, haircuts, and military service. The Pachuco movement was one of the antecedents of the Chicano movement.

Once again, the Pachucos' protest and the youths' contributions did not change the situation of the Mexican Americans substantially. In 1950 the Mexican-American community in Arizona numbered 128,318. Of the 41,430 who reported income, 8,130 earned less than $500 a year, and 1,760 earned $500 to $900 a year; 36.2 percent of the Mexican-American population was under the subsistence level. At the other end of the spectrum, fewer than 500 earned $6,000 or more. The average annual income for an Anglo was $2,051 and for a Hispanic was $1,406.

THE CHICANO MOVEMENT

A surge of cultural pride and identity began in the late 1950s and early 1960s. The civil-rights activities of blacks and the election of a Catholic president were seen as indications of a societal move toward acceptance of previously excluded groups and a wider, if not complete, tolerance of cultural pluralism. John F. Kennedy was an inspiration to the Mexican-American communities of the United States, and many "Viva Kennedy" groups were formed. But the passage of time with few tangible achievements and the assassination of President Kennedy combined to dampen the spirits of the Mexican Americans, who became increasingly dissatisfied with the results obtained from working "within the system." The birth of the Chicano movement may be traced to this time.

As a search for social, economic, and political freedom, the Chicano movement works for equality in civil rights, and educational and occupational opportunities within the majority society. To obtain these objectives, the movement fostered resurgence of cultural awareness and the reaffirmation of the language, cultural heritage, and contributions of the Mexican Americans as a group to the social and economic development of the United States.

The Chicano movement brought about a renaissance in the Mexican Americans' perception of themselves. It touched all aspects of life, including family, education, legal matters, political activity, the organizational tradition, and the participation of youth in bringing about change.

In Arizona, education was a main area of Chicano activity. In 1966 the National Education Association met in Tucson, and the case for bilingual education was made. A report entitled "The Invisible Minority" came out of the meeting, stating that Spanish, properly used, could be a bridge instead of an obstacle in learning English, and that Mexican-American students could become truly bilingual and bicultural. The report focused national attention on an issue that had been of interest to the Hispanic people of the region since the first Anglos had arrived. In 1940 Rafael Granados had made a strong case for language as the single most important element of cultural retention and as the element which binds an individual to a group. A child who is not instructed in the language of his parents and ancestors is, in effect, disconnected from himself. This view was restated by the sociolinguists and others in the early 1970s. They considered the first step of retention to be linguistic, that is, that the linguistic element precedes the socioeconomic and psychological processes in the phenomenon of retention. These ideas have continued to form the philosophical basis of the movement to support and expand bilingual education.

Above: Low rider. TERRENCE MOORE.

Opposite: "Blas and Pauline Flores," at home. LOUIS CARLOS BERNAL.

The concern for cultural and linguistic retention brought a special awareness to the Mexican-American community of the importance of effecting change in a variety of areas through grassroots organization and participation at local, state, and national levels. Many of these efforts were successful in obtaining legislative gains, in broadening the curriculum of schools, in instituting Mexican-American studies programs and research centers at the state universities, in providing better health care and obtaining parks and community centers in the barrios, and, in general, in achieving a better-balanced society.

Art and literature in Arizona also became more imbued with the rich cultural tradition of the Mexican-American community and the perception of the arts as an instrument of social change. Mural art, Chicano theater groups, collective writing endeavors, and serious poets and novelists have been recognized in Arizona since the 1960s, with a consequent clarification and enhancement of Arizona's cultural legacy.

Arizona's Mexican-American population in the mid-1980s faced many challenges. They still perceived a need to battle certain inequities, but they carried on the struggle in a mood of hope based on the sound social and political structure they had built and used successfully for almost three decades.

ANGLO SETTLEMENT

He called himself the "Father of Arizona"—Charles Debrille Poston, mining entrepreneur, territorial delegate, frontier visionary. As a man of twenty-nine, he first entered southern Arizona the year the Gadsden Purchase was being ratified. A year later, he formed the Sonora Mining and Exploring Company, one of capitalism's first ventures into the Arizona frontier. During the late 1850s, he considered himself the uncrowned king and benevolent patron of the town of Tubac, where he ran his company's mining operations, supervised a large force of Mexican laborers, and even married couples who wanted to avoid the fees charged by priests in Sonora. According to Poston, Tubac was an earthly paradise where there was "no law but love, and no occupation but labor. No government, no taxes, no public debt, no politics. It was a community in a perfect state of nature." Presiding over this "Athens of Arizona," Poston must have felt that his future, and his fortunes, were secure.

Like many other dreamers Poston's reach always exceeded his grasp. Apache raids destroyed his mines and ran off his work force. By 1864, according to Poston's friend, journalist J. Ross Browne, Tubac was a ghost town, "a city of ruins—ruin and desolation wherever the eye rests." Poston himself survived, but he never prospered, never regained the preeminence he craved. For the next three and a half decades, he made a meager living as a lobbyist, newspaperman, and government employee, winning and quickly losing a series of federal appointments: registrar of the Land Office at Florence, superintendent of Indian affairs among the Pimas, consular agent at Nogales, and agricultural agent in Phoenix. He died in poverty in 1902 after spending the last years of his life alone in a crumbling adobe house in downtown Phoenix. Only the contributions of his friends spared him a pauper's grave.

The strange saga of Charles Poston did not end with his death. On April 25, 1925, in a solemn ceremony attended by Governor George W. P. Hunt and other Arizona dignitaries, Poston's remains were removed from a Phoenix cemetery and formally reinterred beneath a small

Above left: Charles D. Poston, ca. 1900.

Opposite: Poston's Pyramid. Before it, second from left, stands Arizona State Historian James H. McClintock. ARIZONA HISTORICAL SOCIETY.

white pyramid resting atop a place called Primrose Hill, northwest of Florence. It was there, nearly a half century earlier, Poston had hatched his most fantastic scheme. During an extended trip to the Orient, he had become a convert to Zoroastrianism, a true believer in the struggle between light and darkness. When he returned to Arizona, he dreamed of establishing a cult of sun-worshippers, of Parsees, in his beloved desert. Primrose Hill was the site he chose for his great temple of the sun. As usual, his dream never materialized, even though he carved a road up the hill and appealed, with no success, for financial assistance from the Shah of Persia. "Poston's Folly," his detractors called it. They were both right and wrong. Poston never became a rich man or a religious leader. He never recovered his early power in Arizona politics. Yet, in his pyramid on Primrose Hill, renamed Poston's Butte in his honor, he managed to capture, in death if not in life, the essence of Arizona history: sunlight, transience, and dreams, always the dreams.

Poston and those who followed him came for every reason under the sun, and the sun gave them their reasons for being here—the ranchers, farmers, loggers, and lungers, coughing up their dreams in the dry desert air. Arizona, Apachería, Zion, the Frontier: a blank slate

on which they could etch their visions of the future. Some dreamed of an empire of grass, others of deserts blooming under a web of canals. Dreamers and builders, Mormons and gentiles, loners and colonial agents of the corporate world, they came to Arizona in cycles, all of them convinced they would find that for which they were looking. What they found instead was a land where all cycles come to an end, or are absorbed in other cycles, where one generation's vision of the future becomes the next generation's discarded past.

RANCHERS

Ranching was the first major industry established by the Spaniards in Arizona. Even after Hispanic Arizona declined and the Apaches destroyed such great haciendas as San Bernardino and Babocomari, large herds of cattle remained, feral, more dangerous than the buffalo of the Great Plains. In 1846, at the height of the Mexican War, Col. Phillip St. George Cooke led his Mormon Battalion across southern Arizona. The only resistance his forces encountered came not from the Apaches or the Mexican troops stationed at Tucson, but from

Above and opposite: Scenes on the open range.

wild bulls who attacked Cooke's wagon train, goring his mules and even wounding some of his men.

Anglo cattlemen soon brought more tractable animals into the region. At first, Arizona was merely a dry, desolate stretch of the trail between Texas and California, through which cowboys drove herds down the Gila River to feed the Forty-Niners and their economy fueled by gold. Relatively few cattle were raised on Arizona ranges because of the sparse population and the constant danger of Apache attack. Paradoxically, though, the Apaches triggered the early development of the cattle industry in Arizona. As the Civil War ground to its bloody conclusion in the east, the U. S. military turned its attention to the "Indian problem," and certainly no Indians presented as many problems to the Anglo settlement of Arizona as the Western and Chiricahua Apaches. Military posts proliferated across the newly constituted Arizona Territory, which was separated from New Mexico in 1863. Soldiers needed beef, and Texans needed a market for their cattle, so the boom began.

In 1870 there were only 5,132 cattle in the entire Territory. Most contracts for beef at army posts and Indian reservations were filled with cattle driven in from Texas, Oregon, Idaho, and California. But as the drovers plodded across Arizona, they noticed the lush grasslands of the

San Simon Valley, the vast ranges of the Colorado Plateau, the protected, well-watered valleys of the Santa Cruz, the San Pedro, and the Salt. In 1872 Col. Henry Hooker founded his famous Sierra Bonita Ranch in the eastern foothills of the Galiuro Mountains. By 1884, the territorial governor's office reported that "every running stream and permanent spring were settled upon, ranch houses built, and adjacent ranges stocked." The following year, the governor estimated that at least 652,500 head of cattle grazed Arizona ranges. Stimulated by the arrival of the railroads, the expansion of the cattle industry was staggering. Easterners and Midwesterners exported their cattle to Arizona. As investors across the United States and abroad jumped on the bandwagon, "a great ballyhoo campaign waged by railroad prospectuses, livestock journals, and territorial legislatures trumpeted to an eager public that the West held easy riches and that grass was gold," according to Hastings and Turner in their classic study *The Changing Mile*.

The realities of semi-aridity quickly deflated those dreams. Grass may have been gold, but like gold it began to give out, trampled beneath thousands of hooves and cropped by far too many bovine teeth. Stockmen's associations tried to stem the tide of cattle, but they acted too late. As livestock numbers skyrocketed, prices dropped. And then the drought of 1892–93 devastated the Arizona range. Ranchers frantically shipped their starving cattle out of the territory at greatly reduced prices, but despite these last-ditch efforts, fifty to seventy-five percent of their herds died. According to Arizona pioneer Edward Land, "Dead cattle lay everywhere. You could actually throw a rock from one carcass to another."

One consequence of this cycle of boom and bust was the widespread deterioration of Arizona grasslands. Thousands of acres lost much of their vegetative cover, exposing the soil to accelerated erosion when the rains finally resumed. Increased runoff and the destruction of riverine vegetation by trampling, roadbuilding, and woodcutting also contributed to the incision of Arizona floodplains, seriously reducing the amount of land that could be cultivated along rivers and streams. Overstocking turned out to be a major ecological as well as economic disaster for the Territory, one which had profound repercussions for years to come.

Another consequence of death on the range was the decline of the small stockman. No one knows how many ranches existed in Arizona during the 1870s and 1880s. Anyone with a horse and a "long rope" could set himself up in business on the open range, and many ranching frontiers in Arizona were homesteaded or simply occupied by small, pioneer operations. By the 1890s, however, the trend was clear: survival on the ravaged grazing lands depended upon careful management and costly capital investment. Stock had to be improved, ranges enclosed by barbed wire, and supplementary sources of water developed. The era of the small rancher was over, destroyed by the railroads, the land speculators, and the great land and cattle companies which soon dominated the Arizona ranching industry.

National myths die hard. As author Charles Bowden observes, "Much of what is written as western history is a tale told and retold—a sort of creation myth treasured by the American people." A cornerstone of that fable is that Arizona was one of the last refuges of the rugged individual, a place where frontier virtues still prevailed—self-reliance, equality, free enterprise. But historical evidence contradicts this cherished image. Small ranchers, farmers, and businessmen existed in Arizona, but the major development of the territory, and later the state, was carried out either by large, private corporations or by the federal government. Despite America's Jeffersonian ideals, bigger proved to be, if not better, then at least more efficient in the evolution of Arizona's economy.

This pattern emerges more clearly in the development of the territory's two other major extractive industries, mining and agriculture. Nonetheless, ranching had its own economies of scale. As early as the late 1880s, ranchers began consolidating their holdings and pooling their capital. Railroads were granted nearly 8.5 million acres, much of which wound up in the hands of companies like the Aztec Land and Cattle Company (immortalized by Zane Grey as the Hash-Knife Outfit). This corporation controlled a range ninety miles long and forty miles wide between Flagstaff and Holbrook, running as many as 60,000 head of cattle in a single year.

Three cowboy generations: Bill, Skeeter, and Mack Hughes at the Diamond 2 Ranch, Kirkland.
JAY DUSARD.

These great land and cattle companies continued to depend upon the toughness and skill of men on horseback to care for their cattle, but they were businesses, not family operations. Above all, they were large enough to withstand both the vicissitudes of the Arizona climate and the fluctuations of the national livestock market. One of the best examples of these "big outfits" was the Greene Cattle Company's ORO Ranch on the Baca Float in northern Arizona. Sprawled across 257,000 acres of rugged terrain south of Seligman, the ranch in the 1930s and 1940s was run according to principles that wedded corporate America to the ranching frontier. All business decisions originated in the company's offices in Cananea, Mexico. Operational decisions, on the other hand, were made on horseback at the ranch itself. The ranch manager, Bob Sharp, received his orders from the company's general manager. He, in turn, gave orders to the wagonboss, who oversaw the cowboys. This chain of command, grounded in years of ranching experience, never varied. Men at each level knew exactly what their responsibilities were and what was expected of them. The managers and accountants looked after business, while the cowmen took care of the cows.

This system worked very well, at least for a time. Profits were made, but the romance of the Old West lingered on. Because of the hierarchical nature of the company and the isolated nature of their

Opposite: The Greene Cattle Company office in Hereford, about 1906. ARIZONA HISTORICAL SOCIETY.

work, the cowboys were largely insulated from the changes transforming twentieth-century Arizona. According to ranch manager Sharp, who wrote a memoir about his experiences, these "aristocrats of the range" lived in their own little world, a world "whose citizens had only occasional contact with the outside world, and they lived by their own rules."

Even the big outfits did not last forever. Despite unprecedented profits during and immediately after World War II, the cattle business changed once again. As Arizona's population soared, so did the demand for recreation. Thousands of acres of patented land were sold to real-estate developers, who turned places like Horse Mesa north of Payson into Mesa del Caballo, fenced to keep cattle out rather than in. Prime cattle country from Prescott to the White Mountains sprouted A-frames and mobile homes. Sharp captures this bittersweet transition when he quotes one old retired rancher:

> Hell, Bob, this old boy don't understand what's going on no more. Why nowadays these foreigners don't have nothing in front of their eyeballs but a dollar sign, and are mostly interested in making land deals. Sometimes I wonder what the cattle business has come to when I hear them bragging about their knowhow on how to beat taxes. Why, I've even heard the money-heavy jaspers say they bought their ranches only for tax purposes, 'cause they can write off their losses on their cattle outfit. They don't have to pay such big taxes on their other business. To my way of thinking, that ain't the cow business; that's tax business.

MINERS

As important as the cow business was, however, mining proved to be even more significant to the development of the state. It stimulated the early settlement of Anglo Arizona more than any other industry. No other activity wrapped itself so tightly in legend, lore, and chance. No other activity promised fabulous wealth overnight. Ranching was a known equation, one in which great profits could be made, and great risks taken, but one where there was at least a rough correlation between effort and gain. Mining, on the other hand, abounded with stories of prospectors who stumbled upon the mother lode. The work might be back-breaking, the life isolated and dangerous, but there was always the chance that sometime, somewhere, a man might find more gold and silver than he could spend in a lifetime.

Mining also was the tie that bound the Arizona frontier to the corporate capitals of the United States. Although most historians argue that the primary motivation behind the Gadsden Purchase was the desire for a southern, transcontinental railroad route, the first U. S.

citizens to enter Arizona with substantial capital behind them were not railroad engineers, but mining entrepreneurs. The railroads, in fact, did not cut across Arizona until the early 1880s. By 1856, on the other hand, mining companies had already established themselves on the southern Arizona frontier.

Charles Poston was one of these early pioneers. So were men like Samuel Heintzelman, Sylvester Mowry, and Herman Ehrenberg. During the late 1850s and early 1860s, these individuals founded large, semi-feudal mining camps at Cerro Colorado, Tubac, and Patagonia. Most of their laborers were Mexicans from Sonora, frontier jacks-of-all-trades who crossed an invisible, newly created border to extract and process the gold and silver ore that lured Eastern investment to the edges of the Apachería. Indian raids were a constant threat, transportation routes nothing but pack trails across the desert, military protection almost nonexistent. Conditions in the mining camps were further aggravated by the rising ethnic tensions between Anglo overseers and

their Mexican workers, tensions which on several occasions brought southern Arizona to the verge of racial guerrilla warfare.

Nevertheless, for a brief period these camps flourished, employing hundreds of laborers at their peak. They were also the prototypes for the company towns that evolved after Arizona's frontier days were over. In places like Tubac and Patagonia, the corporation—Poston's Sonora Mining and Exploration Company, Mowry's Silver-Lead Mine—dominated the life of the community. Workers purchased their supplies from company stores at greatly inflated prices, occasionally becoming debt peons in the process. Like the Bisbees, Cliftons, and Jeromes which followed, these early mining settlements were marked by clear divisions of class as well as cultural differences.

The Arizona frontier also gave birth to another type of mining community, one that contrasted dramatically with the company town. These were the boom-and-bust towns, bursting with miners one year, ghost towns the next. A prime example was Gila City, a sordid collection of tents, shacks, and clapboard bars located about twenty miles up the Gila River from Arizona City (modern Yuma). In 1857, Jacob Snively discovered gold in the alluvial deposits along the river. By 1858, more than one thousand prospectors, prostitutes, gamblers, and merchants were frantically panning for gold or preying on others who did. In the colorful words of writer J. Ross Browne:

> The earth was turned inside out. Rumors of extraordinary discoveries flew on the wings of the wind in every direction. Enterprising men hurried to the spot with barrels of whiskey and billiard tables; Jews came with ready-made clothing and fancy wares; traders crowded in with wagon-loads of pork and beans; and gamblers came with cards and monte-tables. There was everything in Gila City within a few months but a church and a jail, which were accounted barbarisms by the mass of the population.

Like many other camps, Gila City blazed like a meteor across the Arizona frontier, burning itself up when the gold gave out. By 1864, Browne noted that "the promising Metropolis of Arizona consisted of three chimneys and a coyote." Countless other mining communities followed the same basic trajectory. In 1877, for example, Ed Schieffelen discovered silver in the hills east of Fort Huachuca. Two years later, Tombstone, the town that sprang up around Schieffelen's diggings, was the largest community in the Arizona territory. In 1882, 5.8 million ounces of silver were ripped from Tombstone's mines. By 1888, the mine shafts were flooded and Tombstone's glory days faded into the pages of pulp fiction.

That same year, copper replaced silver as Arizona's most important ore, a change that revolutionized the territorial economy and transformed the political structure of the region. Small-scale copper mining had been carried out in the Ajo area by Anglo miners as early as 1854, but the development of this industry was hampered by primitive technology and poor transportation networks. By the 1880s, however, rail-

Opposite: Jerome, 1938.
EDWARD WESTON.

roads linked southern Arizona with the rest of the United States, and high-grade copper ore bodies in places like Globe, Clifton, Bisbee, and Jerome began to be mined in volume. These communities became the backbone of corporate mining in the territory.

Copper mining, unlike prospecting for precious metals, required capital investments far beyond the reach of single individuals. The Copper Queen Mining Company spent $2,500,000 to begin its operations in Bisbee; initial capitalization was equally as expensive for other copper mines. From the very beginning, Arizona's copper industry was a corporate affair run by companies with headquarters from San Francisco to New York. For decades these companies dominated Arizona's economy and politics. According to historian James Byrkit, whose *Forging the Copper Collar* analyzes corporate mining in Arizona,

"the mining men intimidated editors, threatened ministers, bought sheriffs, seduced lawmakers and bullied union leaders. They rigged elections and manipulated the legislature." In the process, these corporate leaders revealed Arizona's pretensions of frontier independence for what they were—myths and fables of an Old West that never was, romantic fantasies convincing urban dwellers across America and the world that there still existed a place where pioneer freedoms thrived.

The leader among these corporate giants was Phelps, Dodge and Company, an East Coast import firm that invested heavily in Morenci and Bisbee copper mines beginning in the 1880s. Under the management of James Douglas, Phelps Dodge developed some of the most modern and extensive mining operations in Arizona. It also spearheaded the attack on organized labor in Arizona, transforming the state from a stronghold of Progressivism into a quiet colonial backwater of corporate America.

Few people think of Arizona as a major battleground in the struggle between management and labor. During the first two decades of the twentieth century, however, the state experienced a series of strikes that reverberated throughout the nation and beyond. Since the Spaniards founded Tubac and Tucson in the eighteenth century, Arizona had been a multi-ethnic frontier. But copper towns such as Bisbee, Clifton, Globe, and Jerome were melting pots, hilly warrens of Serbs, Czechs, Mexicans, Irish, Italians, and experienced Cornish miners, or "Cousin Jacks." Within these communities, the great immigrant tides of late nineteenth and early twentieth century America collided with the Arizona frontier, a frontier controlled not by yeoman farmers and small, independent ranchers, but by railroad magnates and mining entrepreneurs.

The mining towns were also the only places where organized labor ever established a foothold in Arizona. During the late 1800s, there was little union activity in the Territory, although strikes in the Globe-Miami mining district erupted as early as 1884. By 1905, however, nine locals of the Western Federation of Miners were scattered across the territory, and organized labor enjoyed the support of Populist farmers and Progressive small businessmen alike. Together these groups formed a powerful if transient coalition, one which successfully counterbalanced the corporate interests until Arizona's "copper collar" was forged during World War I.

The leader of Arizona's progressives was George W. P. Hunt, the state's first governor and a self-educated man whose political views were as expansive as his corpulent frame. Hunt came to Globe as an itinerant miner and rose to become a banker, businessman, and the state's premier politician during the first two decades of its existence. Despite his success, Hunt remembered what it was like to labor in Arizona's dangerous mines, and he never lost his sympathy for the working man. He ramrodded a progressive constitution through Arizona's Constitutional Convention in 1910 and consistently supported the unions throughout the labor wars which followed. Railing against

Opposite: The Copper Queen smelter, Bisbee, at the turn of the century. ARIZONA HISTORICAL SOCIETY.

"dollar despotism" and "profiteering patrioteers," Hunt fought the copper companies in the press, the legislature, and the courts. It is a testimony to their power that the companies were able to seize such thorough control of Arizona despite Hunt's opposition.

Hunt's nemesis, the man who coordinated the campaign against organized labor in Arizona, was Walter Douglas. President of the Phelps Dodge Corporation, chairman of the board of directors of the Southern Pacific Railroad, Douglas moved behind the scenes. His name rarely made the newspapers, many of which he controlled. His style was coolly corporate, contrasting sharply with the florid rhetoric and populist displays of Hunt. But Douglas pulled the strings in a way Hunt never could, carefully manipulating public opinion against the unions, mobilizing the often antagonistic copper companies to unite against their common enemy, recapturing county and state governments and even the governorship itself in order to break the unions during the First World War. In the process, Douglas orchestrated one of the most audacious examples of corporate lawlessness in Arizona history—the Bisbee Deportation of 1917.

Byrkit points out that Arizona may have been a relatively progressive state before World War I, but wartime hysteria moved Arizonans steadily to the right. Fear of German sabotage along the Mexican border convinced many residents that union activities, especially strikes, were unpatriotic if not traitorous. Douglas and his colleagues were shrewd enough to capitalize on those fears. Using the radical Industrial Workers of the World as whipping boys, Douglas and other copper company executives managed to brand all union men as Wobblies. And even though there was no evidence of union violence, many Arizonans, including some of the miners themselves, came to believe that radicals and saboteurs financed by the Kaiser himself were plotting

Left: Governor George W. P. Hunt (in white) with labor committee negotiators, Clifton, 1916.

ARIZONA DEPARTMENT OF LIBRARY, ARCHIVES AND PUBLIC RECORDS.

Opposite: Phelps Dodge Corporation President Walter Douglas (second from right).

BISBEE MINING & HISTORICAL MUSEUM.

to destroy Arizona's copper industry. By the summer of 1917, they were ready to take the law into their own hands.

On July 10, two hundred vigilantes in Jerome, supported by the police department and the United Verde Copper Company, rounded up and deported sixty-seven Wobblies by railroad car. The deportees were released in Kingman the following day. Jerome, however, was merely a dress rehearsal for the events in Bisbee that followed. At dawn on July 12, two thousand members of the Bisbee Workman's Loyalty League and the Citizen's Protective League, many of them armed with rifles issued from the Phelps Dodge dispensary broke into homes, pulled people out of bed, and marched two thousand "undesirables" into the Warren ball park. A hundred of these men were card-carrying Wobblies. Another three hundred belonged to the I.W.W. as well as to other unions. The rest were striking miners or Bisbee shopkeepers and professional people sympathetic to the strikers. Those who promised to go back to work were quickly released. The rest—some 1,186 of them—were packed into twenty-three boxcars and deported to Columbus, New Mexico.

Few of the deportees ever returned to Bisbee. There were howls of outrage from a few sectors. Labor leader Samuel Gompers thundered against "capitalistic anarchists" to President Woodrow Wilson. Wilson responded by appointing a Mediating Commission to investigate labor problems in Arizona's mining communities. The commission condemned the actions of the deportation's organizers. In 1918 the federal government even indicted twenty-one Bisbee residents, including Walter Douglas and Cochise County Sheriff Henry Wheeler, on charges of conspiracy and kidnapping. Judge William Morrow of San Francisco ruled that the charges should be heard by the state rather than the federal court, and the U. S. Supreme Court upheld his decision. In 1920 Arizona tried 200 Bisbee citizens for kidnapping. After three months of testimony, the defendants were acquitted, and jury foreman J. O. Calhoun stated proudly, "The verdict of the jury is a vindication of the deportation."

By then, the copper collar had been forged. Unions such as the American Federation of Labor were broken along with the Wobblies. Pliant county and state governments wrote tax codes favorable to the copper companies. Pro-corporate ministers and newspaper editors convinced their flocks and readerships that what was good for the Arizona copper industry was good for Arizona. As Byrkit points out, "Between 1915 and 1918 the companies, led by Walter Douglas, completely reversed the direction of Arizona politics and destroyed the liberal influence in the state. By 1921 they had secured a closed society." He goes on to say:

> The Bisbee events reveal that a powerful colonial relationship existed between the East and the West, the old and the new. Crude habits and sensational events veiled the sponsorship and manipulation of the American Frontier by East Coast political and economic figures. But the Arizona experience shows that instead of independent, individualistic pioneers who founded a new and liberated western society, there existed, standing behind each frontiersman—trapper, railroadman, soldier, or miner—a speculating financier or an ambitious entrepreneur or an exploitive politician .... Grubstaking each significant newcomer to Arizona was a quiet patron who kept western settlers of importance tied to eastern interests.

Below: IWW workers and sympathizers being herded into boxcars during the Bisbee Deportation of 1917. ARIZONA HISTORICAL SOCIETY.

Opposite: Bisbee today. RICHARD BYRD.

TOMBSTONE JEWS

Josephine Sarah Marcus, a dance-hall girl from San Francisco, was Jewish. As Wyatt Earp's long-time lover, she has become perhaps the best known Jew to have lived in Tombstone. A business directory from the 1880s reveals Jewish-surnamed residents in professions such as miner, merchant, banker, grocer, gunsmith, and restaurant owner. Others were peddlers who drifted into town after the California gold rush. Most were first-generation immigrants. Gunslinger Jim Levy ran a bar in town; he died in a shootout. The more reputable Jews formed the Tombstone Hebrew Association. A Jewish mine superintendent, Abraham Hyman Emanuel, served as the town's mayor during its declining years from 1896 to 1900.

None of this was known to Israel Rubin when he and his family visited Tombstone from back east in 1982. A local historian they met casually mentioned that an abandoned Jewish cemetery adjoined the infamous Boothill Graveyard where some of the town's more notorious personalities are said to be buried. Together with the historian

C. Lawrence Huerta. TIM FULLER.

and their host, C. Lawrence Huerta, the Rubins made their way through catclaw and thick underbrush until they arrived at the crumbled remains of an adobe wall. That's it, the historian told them, pointing to a small field of desert scrub facing the Dragoon Mountains. No gravestones remained.

Rubin immediately recited Kaddish, the Jewish prayer for the dead, and mused about the possibility of restoring the site for the public. Moved by the scene, Huerta, a Yaqui Indian who has served as a judge and a community college chancellor, volunteered to help carry out Rubin's vision. The Jewish Friendship Club of Green Valley, the retirement community one hundred miles west of Tombstone, soon got in the act, and the operators of Boothill Graveyard lent a hand as well. Eighteen months later, Rubin and Huerta walked once more to the burial ground, this time in the company of 250 others gathered to celebrate the restoration of Tombstone's Jewish cemetery.

The crowd listened as Kaddish was again recited—through a bullhorn by a retired Army chaplain from Sierra Vista. The centerpiece of the 50'-by-50' cemetery, surrounded by a new wrought-iron fence, was a two-tier pedestal made of rock from nearby silver mines. Ceremonial items were sealed into a burnished safe adorned with Jewish and Indian symbols atop the pedestal. The contents included a yarmulke, a menorah, a Kaddish cup, prayer and hymn books, and an Israeli bowl filled with dirt from Jerusalem. "Why a full-blooded Indian would want to associate with a bunch of Jews," joked the head of the newly formed Tombstone Historical Jewish Graveyard, Inc., "is the unanswered question of the hour." For his part, Huerta donated a Yaqui bowl containing prayer sticks, deerskin, Apache tears, and corn pollen. Wearing both an Indian headband and a yarmulke over his braided hair, Huerta said, "In honoring my Jewish brothers I feel I am also honoring the lost and forgotten bones of my own people who lay where they fell when the West was being settled." He referred to the dedication ceremony as his own bar mitzvah.

Louis Broitman, the lay rabbi for Jews posted at Fort Huachuca, also attended. His county-wide Passover seder the previous year drew 125 Jews. "They came from out of the woodwork—from Bowie, Bisbee, Douglas, you name it." Broitman estimated that in all, 200 Jews live in Cochise County. Meanwhile, in Tombstone, "the town too tough to die," the Boothill gift shop sells "limited edition" pewter replicas of the newly dedicated monument for $25.

TOM MILLER

Below: Picking chiles at St. David.
ARIZONA HISTORICAL SOCIETY.

THE FARMERS

The development of agriculture in Arizona revealed this colonial dependence even further. When the Gadsden Purchase Treaty was ratified in 1854, Mexican Arizona was an isolated agrarian society clinging to the banks of the Santa Cruz River. People in communities like Tubac and Tucson made a modest living raising small herds of livestock and cultivating crops of wheat, corn, beans, and vegetables, their way of life no different from that of their fellow Sonorans to the south. A century later, Arizona farmers were enmeshed in a mighty web of dams, canals, and lawsuits. Their agricultural infrastructure was financed by federal reclamation projects. Their most basic decisions of resource allocation—how to divide up the irrigation water they needed—were being made, not by them, but by treaties, compacts, and rulings involving institutions ranging from the U.S. Supreme Court to the government of Mexico.

During the eighteenth and nineteenth centuries, Arizona's economy was based upon floodplain–irrigated agriculture. It was a system

grounded upon the acceptance and the intimate understanding of scarcity. Without rivers like the Santa Cruz, agrarian society in Arizona could never have taken root, for that society was a riverine one wedded to the waterways snaking through Arizona's rugged, semi-arid basin and range. Rivers supported the vegetation that provided wood for fuel and pasture for livestock. More importantly, their surface flow allowed farmers to irrigate fields laboriously cleared along the floodplains themselves.

Nevertheless, river water was often in short supply. In 1885, for example, Tucson farmers squared off against each other in court, those downstream complaining that they rarely received enough flow to irrigate their crops. Emerging from their testimony is a picture of traditional riverine water use, of farmers who tailored their cropping patterns and canal systems to the changing nuances of their river. Wheat, not corn, was the most important crop because it could be grown during the cooler months when flow in the Santa Cruz was relatively abundant. By late spring or early summer, however, that flow decreased. At a time when young corn plants desperately needed moisture, there was rarely enough water trickling into the earthen *acequias* (canals) "to give a horse a drink of water," according to one plaintiff in a court case. The constraints of their semi-arid environment limited Tucson farmers to one major crop a year. Interestingly enough, that crop was a winter one, introduced by the Spaniards from the Old World.

For nearly a century, Hispanic farmers accepted such limitations and learned to live within them. They were content with the low yields, cooperating with each other to maintain a system which guaranteed everyone a subsistence living but made no one rich. As more and more people came to the Tucson Basin, though, demand for agricultural produce rose. Entrepreneurs such as Sam Hughes, Solomon Warner, and Leopoldo Carrillo purchased the land and attempted to intensify production by wringing more water out of the Santa Cruz. Stretches of the floodplain were channelized. Ditches were dug to intercept groundwater. Reservoirs and flour mills were constructed. Not surprisingly, environmental devastation was the result. Within a few decades, the Santa Cruz was transformed from a sluggish river into an arroyo, which carried water away from Tucson with raging efficiency. Fields were either washed away by torrential floodwaters or left high and dry as the flow sank beneath the sands of the Santa Cruz. Under the impact of mismanagement and urbanization, the intricate system of floodplain agriculture broke down. And when it died, riverine society along the Santa Cruz died as well.

Subsistence agriculture also was a dying dream throughout the rest of Arizona, a victim of land speculation and the ever-growing economies of scale that devoured small ranchers and farmers in every county in the Territory. During the late nineteenth century, however, one group clung to the dream with religious tenacity, braving harsh environments and hostile neighbors to gather in their desert Zion.

Miramonte farm girls, 1914.
ARIZONA HISTORICAL SOCIETY.

That group was the Church of Jesus Christ of Latter-day Saints, better known as the Mormons. They alone wedded the Jeffersonian ideal of the small farmer to the economic and political strengths of corporate organization. Because of that union, Mormon subsistence farmers survived longer than many of their gentile counterparts, especially along the Little Colorado River in northern Arizona.

Fleeing religious persecution, Mormon pioneers endured hardships to establish their kingdom of God on earth in the Great Basin. Yet even the vast and relatively empty spaces of Utah soon filled up with the restless and industrious Mormons. Ever hungry for frontier lands where they could live apart from the urban Babylons of the gentiles, the colonists left Utah, crossed the Colorado River at Lees Ferry, and established a series of agrarian missions along the Little Colorado River. Many of these early settlements later developed into the most important towns of northeastern Arizona, including Show Low, Snowflake, Springerville, and St. Johns.

Historian Charles Peterson described nineteenth-century Mormon agriculture as "subsistence" rather than "speculative." With few exceptions, the Saints desired the righteous company of each other rather than the opportunity to expand their holdings and make a profit. Therefore, they pooled their resources and purchased land in common through trusted members of the church like William J. Flake, who acquired the acreage upon which the villages of Snowflake, Taylor, St. Johns, Nutrioso, Eagar, and Show Low were built. Small parcels were distributed among individual families, who rarely farmed more than

twenty or thirty acres. In their "gathering to Zion" along the Little
Colorado, the Saints could prepare for the Second Coming of Jesus
Christ far from the pernicious influence of the gentile world. Accord-
ing to Apostle Erastus Snow:

> Our people are an agricultural people and wish to...improve and
> cultivate the land. I believe that the Lord has selected this new land
> for His Saints to gather to, as in thickly populated places wicked-
> ness is more prevalent. Here you are not constantly thrown into
> contact with crime and sin....A race that grows up under such
> circumstances ... are more powerful and vigorous than other
> people. Here they will learn the art of self preservation and defense
> ....

The vastness of the Colorado Plateau could not protect the Saints
from corporate encroachment. First they were forced to battle the
Atlantic and Pacific Railroad, which received hundreds of sections of
land from the U. S. Congress—land that ran right through the heart of
Mormon country along the Little Colorado. Then they had to skirmish
with the large ranchers who followed the railroad into the region. As
Peterson notes, a particular problem was the Aztec Land and Cattle
Company, the notorious Hashknife Outfit, which employed gunmen
and desperados to drive small ranchers and farmers from their land.
Gentiles as well as Mormons were beaten, horsewhipped, and forced at
gunpoint from their claims until the law in northern Arizona finally
cracked down.

Because of the resources of their church, most Saints successfully weathered these storms. By the 1890s, Mormon settlers along the Little Colorado had justified their claims or purchased clear titles to their land from the railroad or neighboring ranchers. Yet the real challenge to Zion lay in the natural world, the world of aridity and intractable rivers. Like their fellow Saints in Utah, many Mormons believed that God would temper the climate in order to bless the efforts of His chosen pioneers. "Destiny's children," they called themselves, expecting an increase in rainfall and an abundance of production once they had sanctified the land with their toil. In the end, however, their destiny was no different from that of all the other Arizona farmers. Not even the Mormon church could tame the Little Colorado or the territory's other rivers. Like so many other dreams, the vision of a separate and independent Zion evaporated in the dry Arizona air.

And so a new dream slowly came into being, one that forever linked Arizona's agriculture to the federal government in faraway Washington, D.C. Farmers did not surrender their frontier independence without a fight. For years, many of them tried to make it on their own, throwing diversion dams across the rivers, forming local water users' associations, pouring private capital into ever-more expensive systems of water control. But slowly, grudgingly, farmers from the Little Colorado to the Gila began to realize that the freedom they cherished often meant the freedom to go broke.

The best example of this inexorable process was the Salt River Valley of central Arizona, one of the heartlands of the ancient Hohokam agricultural civilization. Farmers along the Salt-Gila watershed avoided much of the arroyo-cutting that destroyed floodplain agriculture in southern Arizona. Nevertheless, they faced their own set of problems, reeling beneath a climatic pendulum that swung between drought and flood. From 1898 to 1904, for example, a prolonged dry spell withered crops across the valley. Armed men jealously guarded their canals against their neighbors. Then, in 1905, record floods roared down the Salt, wiping out diversion dams and irrigation ditches. Desperately they searched for new solutions to the age-old problem of too little water or too much.

What they needed, the more foresighted of them decided, was a system of dams and canals large enough to tame the Salt's flow. At first, the water users envisioned a private corporation or one paid for by the sale of Maricopa County bonds. But the staggering cost of such a project soon drove them into the arms of the federal government, and it just so happened that the government was eager to embrace them. In 1902 Congress passed the National Reclamation Act, the purpose of which was to provide funds for irrigation projects. That fall, a group of progressive farmers and businessmen organized the Salt River Valley Water Users Association in order to unite the many diverse water-user groups under one umbrella agency. Cooperating with officials of the newly formed Reclamation Service, Association leaders undertook the difficult task of persuading their more conservative neighbors of the need for federal aid.

At first, many farmers balked at the very idea. They prized their control over local irrigation systems and feared that a large water users' association would deprive them of their autonomy. Furthermore, they hesitated to commit themselves to repay the federal investment, which bore an estimated cost of fifteen dollars an acre over a ten-year period. Nonetheless, the Association, led by such men as Joseph Kibbey and Benjamin Fowler, patiently chipped away at the opposition. By 1903, landowners controlling 150,000 out of a possible 250,000 acres had been persuaded to join the Association. That was good enough for the Reclamation Service, and the Salt River Project was born.

From its inception, the Project was monstrously ambitious. Association leaders and Reclamation Service personnel conceived of a mighty network of irrigation canals spreading across the valley from Glendale to Chandler, all of them integrated into a single system of water control. To that end, the Reclamation Service began buying up private canals and placing them under the administration of the Project. The government also constructed the Granite Reef diversion dam in 1906. But the crowning glory of the Project was the massive storage dam rising in a narrow canyon of the Salt River eighty miles east of Phoenix. Workmen, many of them Apaches, built the dam across one of the most rugged stretches of central Arizona terrain. Completed in 1911, the dam was named for Theodore Roosevelt, who had signed the National Reclamation Project into law.

In the years that followed, the Salt River Project transformed the Salt River Valley into an oasis of modern agribusiness, a vast, sunny plain of cotton fields, truck farms, date orchards, and citrus groves. Flood and drought, the twin specters of Arizona agriculture, became inconveniences rather than devastations. More than 200,000 acres of fertile desert soil were brought into cultivation, and five additional dams on the Salt and Verde rivers were built, greatly increasing the Project's storage capacity. Soon hydroelectric power for the growing city of Phoenix was also being generated.

Farmers outside the Salt River Valley were not so lucky. Throughout other areas of the state—on the flat, arid plains between Phoenix and Tucson, across the yucca-studded sweep of the Sulphur Springs Valley, or along the floodplains of the Gila, the San Pedro, and the ravaged Santa Cruz—other irrigation districts were formed. Unlike the Salt River Valley, however, these districts largely depended upon water sucked out of the bowels of the earth itself. In the words of water administrator Rich Johnson, "The powerful pumps hummed day and night—a symphony of sound gradually acquiring the rhythm of a dirge as the rate of groundwater mining grew ever more apparent in water-table-decline measurements."

The answer to Arizona's groundwater dilemma was the greatest scheme of all, the dream that has dominated Arizona politics from the early twentieth century to the present: the fabled Central Arizona Project. In 1918, the Arizona Engineering Commission recommended that water from the Colorado River be transported up its tributary, the

Theodore Roosevelt at the dedication
of Roosevelt Dam, 1911.
ARIZONA HISTORICAL SOCIETY.

Gila River, to irrigate three million acres of land in Yuma and western
Maricopa counties. A few years later George H. Maxwell raised funds
among Phoenix businessmen to survey the route of a proposed aqueduct from the juncture of the Colorado and the Bill Williams rivers to
central Arizona. Arthur Davis, Chief Engineer of the Reclamation
Service, checked Maxwell's route out himself. He pronounced it a
"Mad Man's Dream."

Nevertheless, the dream refused to die. That same year, negotiators from seven states along the Colorado River and its tributaries
met in Santa Fe, New Mexico, to hammer out the Colorado River
Compact. The Upper Basin states—Colorado, New Mexico, Utah,
and Wyoming—feared that the construction of a proposed dam in
Boulder Canyon, Arizona, would divert the bounty of their watersheds into the thirsty maw of southern California. The compact, which
assumed an average annual flow of fifteen million acre-feet along the

Colorado, allayed those fears by dividing the water equally between Upper and Lower Basin states.

Legislatures in the other six states immediately approved the compact. Arizona lawmakers, on the other hand, repeatedly refused to ratify the agreement, launching the state upon a single-minded quest for Colorado River water that grew increasingly quixotic as the years rolled by. Despite pressure from the other states and the federal government, Arizonans contended that they were entitled to as much of the river's water as they needed. The Colorado, after all, flowed within or along Arizona's borders for nearly half its length. "Save the Colorado for Arizona" became a powerful rallying cry, one which spelled certain defeat for any Arizona politician foolish enough to argue otherwise.

What followed was a crusade of bewildering complexity to

Opposite: The spillway at Roosevelt Dam. SALT RIVER PROJECT.

accomplish two major goals: the guaranteeing of Arizona's fair share of the Colorado, and the construction of an aqueduct to transport that water to the deserts of central Arizona. As pumps chugged and water tables dropped, farmers pinned their hopes for the future on the esoteric calculations of hydrologists and the Byzantine maneuverings of lawyers and politicians. In 1949 Carl Hayden and Ernest McFarland, Arizona's two senators, darkly warned that without Colorado River water "Arizona is doomed to wither away to the point of disaster." Uniting Democrat and Republican, conservative and liberal alike, the Central Arizona Project became a secular religion throughout the state.

Ultimately, the battle was fought and won in Congress and the Supreme Court. In 1963 the Court ruled that Arizona was entitled to the 2,800,000 acre-feet of Colorado River water mandated by the Boulder Canyon Act of 1928. This was in addition to the estimated 1,000,000 acre-feet contributed to the Colorado by Arizona tributaries. In 1968, Congress finally approved the Central Arizona Project itself. Victory must have tasted very sweet indeed to the businessmen and politicians who gathered to celebrate the Project's passage in Phoenix's venerable Westward Ho Hotel.

But even as they raised their toasts, new problems arose to delay the Project even further. And all the while, great changes were occurring in Arizona, changes which would make the Central Arizona Project little more than a chimera to the farmers who had waited for its water for so many years.

FROM THE SOUTHWEST TO THE SUNBELT

Some of the powerbrokers may have recognized the ultimate irony of the Project as they stared out the windows of the Westward Ho at the Salt River Valley below them. Beneath the hotel's great spire, the city of Phoenix was relentlessly expanding, devouring the citrus groves and cotton fields, demanding more water, more energy, more dams. If the Central Arizona Project had been constructed in the 1940s, agricultural interests would have dominated its flow. By the 1980s, however, farmers were being squeezed out of the Salt River Valley by city dwellers, and driven out of the rest of central Arizona by falling water tables and rising energy costs. The farmers had dreamed of a vast agricultural oasis in the Arizona desert. They never envisioned an urban center of nearly two million people paving over their irrigated fields.

Phoenix was settled by farmers. By 1919, in fact, a visiting reporter hailed it as "the agricultural center of Arizona," a place of "production, profit and contented human life." The following year, the city boasted a population of 29,053, overtaking its older rival, Tucson, as the largest urban center in Arizona. Just as its founders had dreamed, Phoenix was an agrarian prodigy rising out of the ashes of prehistoric Hohokam fields and canals.

The total urban population of the Salt River Valley, however, was much larger than Phoenix alone. Tempe, Mesa, Glendale, Chandler, and Scottsdale contributed an additional 8,636 inhabitants to the metropolitan fold. In contrast to Tucson with its large Mexican population, Phoenix and its satellites were predominantly Anglo communities, a demographic fact of which city leaders were inordinately proud. One representative of the chamber of commerce even proclaimed in the pages of the 1920 city directory that "Phoenix is a modern town of forty thousand people and the best kind of people too. A very small percentage of Mexicans, negros or foreigners." The great urban bird spreading her wings across the Salt River Valley turned a staunchly Anglo-Saxon face toward the rest of the world.

Many Anglo leaders were determined to preserve this racial and religious status quo. During the early 1920s the Ku Klux Klan wielded considerable power in the Salt River Valley and beyond. According to Sue Abbey in the *Journal of Arizona History*, the Klan numbered a secretary of state, a state treasurer, a Phoenix mayor, a superior court judge, a county sheriff, and a county attorney among its members at that time. At its height, the racist organization harassed Catholics,

Below: Phoenix Court House in 1900, as Arizona enters an urban century. ARIZONA HISTORICAL SOCIETY.

Opposite: Quarantine camp for tuberculosis victims, Phoenix, about 1903. ARIZONA HISTORICAL SOCIETY.

Blacks, Mormons, and Jews in Phoenix and across the state. It also spearheaded the recall of a Pinal County judge. And even though the Klan itself declined, its legacy lingered on in segregated schools, restricted public facilities, miserable farm labor camps, and occasional outbursts of racial violence directed against Mexicans, Asians, Blacks, and Indians. Maricopa County became the conservative stronghold of an ever-more conservative state.

As Phoenix grew, the power of the farmers decreased. Among the first newcomers were the health-seekers, searching for a cure for their maladies in the dry desert air. Ever since the nineteenth century, they had made their desperate pilgrimages to places like the Salt River Valley or to Tucson, hoping to cure the illnesses that consumed them. Some of these "lungers," as the tuberculosis patients were called, ranked among Arizona's most distinguished citizens: A. P. K. Safford, territorial governor and founder of Arizona's public school system; Hiram Hodge, one of the territory's most enthusiastic promoters; John C. Van Dyke, author of the classic natural history, *The Desert*; Harold Bell Wright, novelist and one of Tucson's leading literary figures. Many others, on the other hand, were desperately poor, crowding into the "tent cities" that sprouted up on the outskirts of Tucson and Phoenix. In the words of Dick Hall, these tent cities were "dreary places":

> The desert with so little vegetation seemed forlorn in contrast with the green fields and tall trees of Kansas and Iowa. The invalids were too sick to work. The nights were heartbreaking, and as one walked along the dark streets, he heard coughing from every tent. It was truly a place of lost souls and lingering death.

Nonetheless, the health-seekers brought millions of dollars into the

Arizona economy, stimulating the development of modern health-care centers and more extensive lodging facilities. More importantly, their desert odysseys drew attention to the state, and they were soon joined by thousands of more robust visitors.

During the 1920s, groups of businessmen such as the Phoenix-Arizona Club and the Tucson Sunshine Climate Club generated a flurry of promotional campaigns. Phoenix was touted as "the Garden Spot of the Southwest," a name which still retained agrarian as well as recreational connotations. The following decade, however, a local advertising agency dubbed the Salt River Valley the "Valley of the Sun," and the name stuck. By the winter season of 1939–40, roughly 35,000 visitors flocked to this young mecca of hotels, dude ranches, trailer courts, and resorts. Charles Poston must have chuckled a little beneath his pyramid. The sun-worshippers had finally arrived, ready to wrest Arizona away from their predecessors—the ranchers, the miners, and the farmers.

But even Poston at his most grandiose could never have predicted post-war Phoenix and Tucson. During World War II, both areas with their year-round sunshine served as training grounds for thousands of pilots who flew off to do battle with Germany and Japan. Because of their protected inland locations, the two cities were also chosen as sites for a number of important defense plants—the Aluminum Corporation of America, AiResearch, and Goodyear Aircraft in Phoenix, Consolidated Aircraft in Tucson. These installations poured millions of dollars into war-time Arizona. More importantly, they laid the foundations for a phenomenal post-war boom.

In 1940, Phoenix and its surrounding communities had a combined population of about 83,000 people. Forty years later, more than 1.5 million urban dwellers sprawled across the Valley of the Sun. Tucson's growth was almost as spectacular. Motorola and General Electric, attracted by the state's favorable business climate and tax laws, joined industry in creating still more jobs. By 1955, manufacturing had replaced agriculture as Phoenix's number-one source of income.

For years, Arizona's economy revolved around mining, ranching, and agriculture. These industries brought the first Anglos to Arizona and dominated the political and economic life of the state until World War II. For most of its history as a part of the United States, Arizona was a colonial outpost of industrial America, its natural resources converted into commodities and shipped away.

By 1978, only two percent of Arizona's work force labored at agrarian tasks. Even fewer people toiled in Arizona mines. Copper, cattle, and cotton clearly had been overwhelmed by a highly urban, service-oriented economy. New immigrants transformed the state from an extractive colony into a recreational one.

What people want from Arizona has changed. Newcomers bring their own dreams, ones which view Arizona increasingly in the abstract, as little more than a place for the sun to shine upon. The old visions were more visceral.

Opposite: Pima County Courthouse, Tucson today. JOSH YOUNG.

Chapter Ten   TOM MILLER

MODERN ARIZONA

Paul Winter was playing his soprano saxophone on a raft floating down the Colorado
River deep in the Grand Canyon. A cello and
flute provided the obbligato. Ravens soaring
overhead and eddies swirling below offered
additional counterpoint. Portable taping equipment recorded this most wilderness of concerts. An underwater microphone picked up
the mysterious sounds of the river in flow. Later, Winter and others
recorded music in New York City at the Cathedral of St. John the
Divine—what Winter calls "The Grand Canyon East." These recording sessions, along with others in both locations, were blended to
produce the first of a series of records musically interpreting the evolution of the Canyon and of the Indian life which complemented it.

Winter, whose previous records have featured whales and wolves,
must have been reading the journal of John Wesley Powell. In 1869
Powell led the first party to explore the Colorado River through the
Canyon. "Mountains of music swell in the river," he wrote. "The
Grand Canyon is a land of song." The sound of a motorized boat did
not reach the Canyon for another eighty years, during which time no
more than one hundred adventurous souls had rafted the Canyon's
rugged Colorado. Today, 15,000 people take the trip every year.

One reason for the dramatic rise in river running is the presence of
Glen Canyon Dam, whose construction, along with that of three other
dams downriver, has radically altered every form of life in the state,
from single-cell plants to air-conditioned night clubs. The Colorado
River has become the preeminent force in contemporary Arizona. In
both nature and politics it has no rival.

Glen Canyon Dam is part of the Colorado River Storage Project,
an ambitious plan authorized by Congress in 1956, after years of interstate wrangling and court battles, to harness the river's water for
hydroelectricity and other uses. (The Project includes lesser dams and
reservoirs in Wyoming, Colorado, Utah, and New Mexico.) To build
the dam, engineers had to divert the river around the construction site
through man-made tunnels in the Canyon's walls. The dam was complete in 1963, the lake began to fill, and the Colorado River gave up its

Above left: A young sun-lover.
KIM VIVIER.

Opposite: The Paul Winter Consort
in the Grand Canyon.
STEPHEN TRIMBLE.

wild and natural rampages into the Grand Canyon. Its flow became smooth and steady. The lake formed by the dam was named for John Wesley Powell, who had, in his visits a century earlier, named the pristine Glen Canyon which his lake now engulfs. To form the lake, magnificent Navajo sandstone canyons, Indian ruins, oak glens, and remote wildlife were sacrificed. In 1980 Lake Powell was completely filled, backing 180 miles into Utah. Walking its perimeter now, around every grotto and fold, you would cover 1,960 miles—the entire length of the United States' southwestern border from the Gulf of Mexico to the Pacific Ocean.

Veteran river runners recall the stretch of the Colorado now filled by the lake as tranquil, hospitable to rafts, its shores a pleasure to camp on, its walls overwhelming. The tallest red sandstone canyon walls remain visible, and the natural stone Rainbow Bridge forms a stunning setting. The young lake now attracts two million visitors annually who come to swim and water-ski, boat and camp, or just go fishing.

Opposition by preservationists was not strong enough to prevent the dam's construction. The most recent generation of dam opponents is "Earth First!," a group which divides environmental approaches into two categories: shallow ecology and deep ecology. Shallow ecology

Opposite: The heart of the Grand Canyon. COLLIER/CONDIT.

Right: A channelized Salt River flows into Scottsdale. TERRENCE MOORE.

involves compromises, trade-offs, and planned development; its practitioners include a wide range, from Arizona Congressman Morris Udall to former Interior Secretary James Watt, from the Sierra Club to the Del E. Webb Corporation (the company which operates Lake Powell's tourist facilities). Deep ecology rejects this attitude, arguing that every trade-off and compromise, no matter how well-intentioned, forever reduces the earth just a little bit more. In an actively growing state, that philosophy finds receptive ears.

Electricity generated by the dam's power plant travels along high-voltage lines to energy companies in Arizona and all the states which feed the Colorado River, plus Nebraska. Visions of hydroelectricity have been with us for generations. "Large cities will light up," wrote William Hamilton Nelson, an Arizona booster in the 1920s. "Women will come out of the kitchen with hours for leisure," Nelson said in his book *Alluring Arizona*, "for they will cook with electricity, and use it

Below: Parker Dam, on the Colorado River. SUZI MOORE.

Opposite: Lake Powell, 1966, after partial filling of Glen Canyon. TAD NICHOLS.

in a dozen ways about the home .... The Middle Ages believed in Black Magic, but the conservation of water power will furnish electricity, which is the 'white-magic' of a more enlightened age."

First of the white-magic dams along the Colorado River was Hoover Dam, on the Arizona-Nevada border just below Las Vegas. Behind the dam weekend water enthusiasts play on Lake Mead, while electricity from the plant keeps the lights of Los Angeles burning. The Colorado heads south here to fill Lake Mohave, whose southern end is held back by Davis Dam at Pyramid Canyon, just north of Bullhead City. Below lies yet another major dam and generating plant at Parker.

Just above Parker Dam in Lake Havasu, however, aqueducts are in place to siphon off some of the Colorado and carry it to the state's interior, supplying water and power for Arizona's smaller towns and ever-expanding major cities, a few Indian reservations, mining operations, ranchers, and farmers. This is the Central Arizona Project, an

undertaking so unwieldy on the drawing board, in Congress and the state legislature, that its feasibility has been in doubt since it was first proposed in 1918. Controversies of substance have arisen: will the advent of the CAP encourage further growth which the desert cannot, in the long run, support? Should Indian land be usurped for the CAP? When it is finally working at capacity, officials may recall the observations of John S. McGroarty in 1910: "Water is no longer a problem," he wrote of Arizona. "Water is everywhere throughout the whole length of the Territory .... Every city has its own ample supply of pure and sparkling water for every domestic need and demand." The Central Arizona Project, operating at full strength, may match that pre-statehood claim. Our sunbelt thirst will, for a while, be quenched.

From Parker, the Colorado River, having been dammed, diverted, harnessed, and channeled, flows past the "Parker Strip," then to Yuma, and finally into Mexico. Once a muscular and temperamental river with a mind of its own, the Colorado River ends its 716-mile trip through the state limp and lobotomized.

Water stored behind the dams is carefully measured so that its use for electricity, irrigation, and for cities is maximized. Its cycle is easy to foretell now that its current is regulated by man and machine. When winter snows melt in the Rockies, runoff increases, the river gains temporary strength, and the amount of water stored in Lakes Powell, Mead, Mohave, and Havasu must be adjusted by releasing an increased amount of water from the dams. The system has worked well, allowing for its top priority—water conservation—as well as its other uses, flood control among them. Decades of engineering and construction along the river coupled with seemingly endless lobbying in Washington benefit Arizonans, residents of the six other watershed states, and Mexico's far northwest.

A curious sequence of events in mid-1983 tested the entire system. The Rocky Mountains had received much heavier snowfalls than usual the previous winter, and because the temperature remained low far into the spring, the massive snowpacks stayed on the mountains as well. A sudden and unexpectedly warm late spring thaw melted the build-up, sending a lot more than the anticipated runoff into the upper Colorado River and into Lake Powell. As the lake quickly filled to capacity, water came crashing through the spillways of Glen Canyon Dam into the Grand Canyon and on to Lake Mead. Next, Hoover Dam allowed its excess to spill downriver into Lake Mohave, which quickly overflowed Davis Dam. Then the water descended on Lake Havasu and its retaining wall, Parker Dam.

The Parker Strip, with its mobile-home parks, boat docks, motels, and riverside restaurants was hit particularly hard by the once-again raging Colorado River. Damage to businesses built in and near the river's floodplain came to an estimated $10.6 million as the river roared beyond its banks and explored land it hadn't dampened in generations. The river overran all compacts, accords, and treaties. It temporarily drowned water-user obligations, commissions, and statutes.

Opposite: The Rillito of Tucson during the flood of 1983.
TERRENCE MOORE.

The National Weather Service was blamed for not forecasting the unusually high late-season runoff until too late. The Bureau of Reclamation was blamed for its handling of water releases from the dams. The Bureau of Land Management was blamed for permitting property owners to build in the floodplain. In the end, however, the Colorado River got back at us. It showed no respect for our resource management systems, political jurisdictions, engineers, steel retaining walls, or concrete barriers. The widened Colorado turned carefully irrigated farmland into jungle marsh. From the air, the expanded river looked magnificent; only tree-tops emerged where solid ground once appeared. The Colorado was doing a little reclamation of its own.

Just below the confluence of the Colorado and the Gila, Interstate 8 veers northerly over the river to cross from Yuma westward into California, a spot first recorded in 1539. Since then it has been a natural meeting ground for Indians, explorers, surveyors, soldiers, adventurers, and in the mid-nineteenth century, gold-seekers en route to California. The name of this section of the Colorado changed from time to time, depending upon the moods of the river and its many explorers. Its first recorded name, according to *Arizona Place Names*, reflected the faith of the early Spaniards: El Río de Buena Guía. "The River of Good Guidance" failed to live up to its calling when, in 1540, Captain Hernando Alarcón waited there in vain to deliver supplies to Coronado's expedition. The following year another Spaniard, Melchior Díaz, arriving at the same place, noted that the Indians on the riverbanks warmed themselves by holding burning brands next to their bodies, hence El Río del Tizón, "Firebrand River." Don Juan de Oñate, leading an expedition in 1604–05, came upon the river and optimistically called it El Río Grande de Buena Esperanza, "Great River of Good Hope." Starting in the 1700s explorers learned of various Indian names for the river: the Pima called it Buqui Aquimuri, "Red River"; the Cocomaricopa name was Gritetho, "Great River"; for the Yuma it was Javil, "Red"; the Havasupai name, Hackatai, has no satisfactory translation; Pa-ha-weap was the Paiute name, "Water Deep in the Earth." English-speaking travelers contributed variations of their own—Red River, Grand River, and borrowing from the Spanish, Colorado ("red," or "ruddy") River of the West. Gradually, consensus, following political power, settled on the English-anointed Colorado River.

From the early travelers to the present, Yuma's ties with the states to its south and west have been stronger than its relations within its own state. Today, travelers pass through Yuma, cross the river into California and on to San Diego with such familiarity that they scarcely recognize the historic significance of their route. To rectify this, a group has undertaken the creation of a Yuma Crossing Cultural Park. The project involves acquiring acreage near downtown and along the Colorado. When complete—even the most active supporters estimate the early 1990s—the passage westward will, through museum exhibits and restored nineteenth-century buildings, commemorate early Indian life on the riverbank, Spanish exploration, national expansionism, the gold rush, military outposts, ferry and steamboat travel, and the establishment of the city of Yuma. The Territorial Prison and the old Custom House will become part of the park, and, as envisioned, so will restaurants, beaches, a boat dock, playing fields, and a bike path.

First-time visitors to Yuma and its surrounding communities on both sides of the Colorado River may be surprised at the number of trailer settlements housing "snowbirds" from the chilly north. The average winter temperature is 72 degrees, which along with the underground water table and diverted Colorado River water, makes the southwestern corner of the state ideal for agriculture. Richard Kaighn, an accountant for California investors who transferred him to Yuma to manage their 1,600-acre farm, understands this well.

"Blowsand," Kaighn declared, running his fingers through the light grains thickly covering the ground. "We farm here on pure blowsand. There are no nutrients in the ground. Everything the plants get they get from us." Yet from the blowsand, Kaighn is testing the growth of asparagus, a crop which requires careful tending, but if nurtured properly, yields immense profits. His experiment shows signs of success.

"Asparagus takes three years to reach full maturity," Kaighn began. "The land I'm planting it on used to support alfalfa, squash, melons, cabbage, parsley, turnips, and beets." He maneuvered his pickup through the adjoining field. "I still grow watermelon," he said, getting out to slice a peacock melon from the vine. "And I'm experimenting

Opposite: Snowbirds.
TERRENCE MOORE.

with grapes, too," he added as he drove a bit farther to his arbor. "They're called 'Flame Seedless.' May is their harvest season. Try some," he offered, handing over a newly cut bunch. "Sweet as sugar, huh?"

A small plot of asparagus grew next to Kaighn's double-wide trailer office. He plucked a few seeds from a plant. "Look at them." He passed them from one hand to the other. "They're gorgeous. Just gorgeous. The best ones have no cracks in them. They're all black. The more lustrous they are, the better. Another test of the seed is its uniformity. You can't bite them either—they're too hard."

As farming becomes increasingly sophisticated, more variables enter the picture. To arrive at the right conditions for growing his new crop, Kaighn consulted with experts from the University of Arizona Experimental Farm and the U. S. Department of Agriculture County Extension Service. How much water is necessary? Should he use flood or drip irrigation? What fertilizers should be applied, when, and how? Is asparagus susceptible to insects? Will weeds overwhelm the plants?

How should they be warehoused and cooled after harvest? Where should they be shipped to, and more importantly, when? Once the shipping dates are determined, Kaughn must figure backwards to determine on which dates the earlier process should be carried out.

When Kaighn finished calculating all the factors in his equation to grow the best and most profitable asparagus during his twelve-week harvest season, he decided upon drip irrigation, two hours a night, pumped by a 250-horsepower engine from the water table a hundred feet underground. The water goes through a filtration system which adds twenty-five pounds of nitrogen for each acre planted; in all, Kaighn's asparagus drinks only seven acre-feet of water a year. (One acre-foot of water is enough to cover an acre—43,560 square feet—with water one foot deep.) At the height of the season, asparagus doubles its size overnight. As soon as the plants reach eleven inches, nine inches out of the ground and two beneath the surface, they are cut.

Asparagus is extremely delicate. Machines can't harvest it—people must. Like virtually every other farmer in the region, Kaighn relies upon Mexican labor. "My pickers are all green card workers," he said; that is, they are permitted to work north of the border. Although a "green card" allows them to live in the U. S. as well, Kaighn's workers commute from San Luis Río Colorado, Sonora, five miles from the farm. "The Mexican labor season around here begins in September with lemons. Then comes lettuce. I'd rather hire a family of ten than ten separate individuals, because that family has a purpose in life. I have an advantage in that this is the first farm they come to after crossing over. Asparagus is a very labor-intensive crop."

To cut asparagus, the workers use a specially designed knife with a hard rubber pistol-grip handle and a sharp rectangular blade at the end of a six-inch steel bar. During a daily six-hour shift beginning at dawn, workers fill fifteen to twenty boxes of asparagus apiece, each weighing about thirty pounds. Kaighn pays between $5 and $6 a box.

After briefly storing the newly picked plants in hydro-coolers, he ships them seventy-five miles west to the distribution center in Calexico, California. From there they go throughout the United States and to Europe and Asia. Kaighn expects close to $30 from produce brokers for each of 11,000 boxes he ships his first year.

•

Signs on Highway 95 north of town announce the U. S. Army's YUMA PROVING GROUNDS. One turnoff is reserved for AMMO TRUCKS. Another cautions RESTRICTED AREA. Just past a Border Patrol roadblock, at which drivers and passengers are asked their nationality, another warning tells motorists to KEEP TO PAVED ROADS and stay clear of the YUMA PROVING GROUNDS. After four or five such announcements for the Proving Grounds, the question begs: Just what is it they're trying to prove?

"Right now we're trying out the new M1E1—that's an up-gunned version of the Abrams M1 Main Battle Tank," answered Jim Coles III, public affairs officer at the Proving Grounds. "We'll give it a thorough

Opposite: Picking lettuce in the Yuma Valley. TERRENCE MOORE.

TURN ON TO ASTRONOMY

After a three-year survey of mountain ranges in the United States, astronomers chose Arizona's Kitt Peak in 1958 as the best site for the national center for ground-based astronomy. Kitt Peak, west of Tucson, is a sacred mountain belonging to the Tohono O'odham, or Papago, Indians, from whom the astronomers had to obtain permission to use the mountain for their telescopes. When negotiations with the Tribal Council stalled, Edwin F. Carpenter, then director of the University of Arizona's Steward Observatory, invited the Council and their families to Tucson to view the moon with the Steward telescope. Impressed by what they saw, the Council members decided to lease Kitt Peak to the astronomers, but only for use as a research facility.

Since the national observatory's establishment, nineteen telescopes have been built for use on Kitt Peak or moved there from other locations. They range in size from 16 inches to the giant Mayall 4-Meter Telescope, the majestic white dome of which can be seen for miles from the desert floor. The large size of the Mayall telescope allows study of distant objects such as quasars, as well as the search for planetary systems surrounding other stars, study of new stars forming in molecular clouds, and investigation into the age of the universe.

The McMath Solar Telescope, the largest of its kind, is also located at Kitt Peak. It is used exclusively for observing the sun. Since the sun is a "garden-variety" star, knowledge gained by study of its emissions, sunspots, and flares can be applied to similar stars in other parts of our galaxy and beyond.

"An astronomer doesn't look at objects directly through an eyepiece with these large telescopes. That's obsolete," says Tony Encinas, a tour guide at Kitt Peak. "These telescopes are used to gather and intensify light." Data is recorded on magnetic tape and analyzed after completion of the observing run. Data collected in two nights of observing on the Mayall 4-m, for example, may be studied for months before the astronomer's work is complete.

Dry, clear skies, lack of air turbulence, and mountaintop locations have drawn astronomers to Arizona since before the turn of the century. In 1894 Percival Lowell built a telescope in Flagstaff to observe Mars and its recently discovered "canals." A few years later, comparison of the predicted and observed positions of Uranus and Neptune led Lowell to hypothesize that there must be a ninth planet in our solar system. The hypothesis was proved correct when, in 1930, fourteen years after Lowell's death, Pluto was discovered by an astronomer at Lowell Observatory. More recently, a Lowell Observatory astronomer participated in the discovery of a ring system around Uranus.

Mount Hopkins, in the Santa Rita mountains, is the location of the Fred Lawrence Whipple Observatory, home of the revolutionary Multiple-Mirror Telescope, a joint project of Steward Observatory and the Smithsonian Institution. While bigger and better telescopes are needed to collect data about the farthest reaches of the universe, conventional single-mirror telescopes reach a practical size limit at about 6 meters. Mirrors larger than this are so heavy that they sag under their own weight. The MMT is the first telescope of a new design that uses six smaller mirrors working together to give the light-collecting area of a 4.5-m single-mirror telescope.

Space exploration is based in part in Arizona. Astronomers here have participated in Ranger, Surveyor, Lunar Orbiter, Mariner, Pioneer, and Voyager space missions. At the University of Arizona Lunar and Planetary Laboratory, scientists help plan the missions, develop instruments for the spacecraft, and analyze the data received from space.

As the state's population grows, increased light from the cities causes the sky to glow, creating "light pollution" which interferes with astronomers' delicate instruments. Flagstaff, Tucson, Phoenix, and twenty other cities have lighting ordinances aimed at controlling this type of pollution. In Tucson all street lamps are shielded to direct light to the ground, and the trend may be to replace mercury-vapor streetlights with low-pressure sodium light that astronomers can filter out. To remain a world center for astronomical and planetary research, Arizonans must heed the advice of a popular bumper sticker: "Turn Off Your Lights—Turn On to Astronomy."

MELANIE MAGISOS

Above: The Aircraft Maintenance and Regeneration Center, Davis-Monthan Air Force Base. USAF.

going over." The Proving Grounds is one of twenty-six test facilities the Defense Department maintains to work the kinks out of its latest warfare equipment. Trucks, bombs, parachutes, helicopters, guns, ammunition, tanks, computers, cameras, artillery, aircraft—in short, anything used to fight a war—undergoes evaluation here.

General George Patton's Third Army trained near here shortly after the Corps of Engineers opened the facilities in 1943. Today, the terrain includes a "Mideast Course," a vast stretch of gypsum sand eighteen inches deep on the desert, where equipment designed for the Middle East and Africa goes through exercises. Hardware used in the 1980 attempt to free the American hostages in Iran was tested here.

Coles flashed slides on his office wall of two current experiments. One appeared to be of a helicopter wearing a beanie; the other looked like a regular tank. "Let's say you are flying along in this helicopter and you see a column of enemy tanks on the other side of the ridge. You go below the ridge and pop up the mast-mounted site system. You can see them, but they can't see you. That way you can call in artillery and pinpoint the location. You can even call in a B-52 if you want to. We also have a sixty-ton tank out here which can go ninety miles an hour.

It has a first shot capability of ninety-five percent. In other words, if we see Ivan before Ivan sees us, we're almost certain to get a kill."

Jake Taylor was equally proud of his work at the Marine Corps Air Station, also at Yuma. "We teach pilots air-combat maneuvers here," said Taylor, manager of the Tactical Aircrew Combat Training System (TACTS). "We send them up for simulated dog-fights. We can watch every move they make on our computer screens."

The TACTS computer can track practice jet runs for miles on display monitors the size of barroom television screens. As two jets square off against each other over the desert, trainers sit in front of the screens, watching blips indicating the jets' altitude, distance from each other, speed, and direction. The pilots are coached by the trainers through a two-way intercom system. After each mock air fight, the pilots come in to watch a computerized rerun of their flights. "This is carried out in real time," Taylor said. "We do this to improve their kill ratios." Practice in launching missiles, firing mortars, and dropping bombs rounds out the pilots' routine.

The desert floor which now absorbs these daily bombing runs and air strikes was first cleared of its cactus and scrub in 1928 for an Army Air Field. During the next three decades it was used as a Civilian Conservation Corps Camp, a municipal airport, a World War II pilot training center, and an Air Force Base. In 1959 the Marines landed at Yuma and have been there ever since.

Although relatively small by military standards, the seven-square-mile air base uses most of the skies above the southwestern quadrant of Arizona and some of California for its runs. Because of its climate, which offers near-perfect flying conditions, and its clout in Congress, Arizona has fourteen separate military installations. The smallest is the five-acre Air Force Auxiliary Training Field at the Coolidge airport, and the largest is the Gila Bend Gunnery Range, covering 4,100 square miles. A total of 5,870 square miles of Arizona land is devoted to U. S. military operations, with many times that amount of its airspace used for flight tests.

•

WATCH FOR ANIMALS say the signs on Highway 95 as the lonely eighty-mile drive to the town of Quartzsite slices through the raw Sonoran Desert. In truth, there is little else to watch for, save the next WATCH FOR ANIMALS sign. Is the statement intended as a cautionary warning or a friendly suggestion? To the west, the Imperial National Wildlife Refuge hugs the Colorado River from both the California and Arizona side for thirty miles. The Kofa National Wildlife Refuge, surrounded on three sides by the Yuma Proving Grounds but largely unaffected by it, lies to the east. The Refuge takes its name from the long-defunct King of Arizona Mine, and on its thousand-plus square miles run desert bighorn sheep, deer, mustangs, feral burros, foxes, bobcats, ringtail cats, cottontail rabbits, and the trickster coyote. Dove, quail, and waterfowl roost nearby. You may keep watching for animals, but all you'll likely see are signs.

Opposite: Kofa National Wildlife Refuge. JACK W. DYKINGA.

In the summertime, something else about the drive north between the river and the Refuge seems vaguely unsettling, a disquieting notion which becomes clear after a half-dozen cars and pickups pass heading south. Drivers on Highway 95 do not return the standard country wave. On Arizona's rural highways and county roads from Springerville to Kingman, from Douglas to Fredonia, the sight of a driver going the other direction is cause for a nod and a wrist-flick salute. Eye contact, however fleeting, gives a sense of companionship on the highway; you are not alone. Why is this custom—almost a reflex, really—ignored on Highway 95? No one, it appears, seems to enjoy the drive in the summer.

At Quartzsite, handwritten advertisements for dogs, trailers, and drip-irrigation tubing clutter the community bulletin board, along with a note from Blackjack Ben offering "classes on how to beat the Las Vegas odds." Inside the Roadrunner Market hangs a large aerial color photograph of one of the world's biggest parking lots—tens of thousands of cars, campers, trucks, and mobile homes gathered at Quartzsite for the annual Rock and Mineral Show. The checkout clerk motioned to the picture: "Bet there aren't things like that in Tucson."

•

Driving east toward Phoenix on Interstate 10, you are constantly struck—no, assaulted—by Arizona's headlong urbanization. The state's 1980 population, 2.7 million, will double by the end of the century, the U. S. Census Bureau estimates. Some of these newcomers will settle in Goodyear, Litchfield Park, Avondale, and Tolleson, touted as the "Western Gateway." Despite the aerospace industry in their midst, development in these towns has always centered on its agricultural resources. Small farms have been swallowed by larger ones, family truckfarmers have yielded to agribusiness. One ranch in Goodyear has joined corporate hands with an Israeli company to increase its productivity. Small towns which Arizonans drive past on the highway to Los Angeles are now called "bedroom communities." One development boasts ROOM TO BREATHE—COUNTRY LIVING MINUTES FROM PHOENIX—ONE ACRE MINI-RANCHES—HORSE PRIVILEGES AND BRIDLE PATH.

"The Western Gateway Team," a group of civic leaders, real-estate brokers, bankers, builders, landowners, architects, economists, and others with a professional and financial stake in the area's future, meets monthly to hammer out a plan strong enough to meet the population onslaught. At one meeting, a research consultant displayed slides with graphs and charts to explain how expansion should best be handled. Where scarcely more than a generation earlier local growth involved words like "lettuce," "acreage," "homes," "frontage roads," "investment," "irrigation," "schools," "Mexican labor," and "warehouses," Gateway leaders now bandy about "scenarios," "impacted interface," "variable utilization," "substantial component," "associated capital outlay," "marginal model," "dimension coefficients," and "conceptualization." A planner for Tolleson said its "small town atmosphere should be retained as a very marketable commodity." Utility wires, bikeways, and chainlink fences figured into his draft, along with a view of the mountains. Perhaps as a reminder of the years following Word War II when Tolleson claimed to be the "vegetable center of the world," the Team agreed "to keep some land in agriculture."

Arizona's first modern planned city was Chandler, founded by veterinarian Alexander J. Chandler. By selling off his 18,000-acre ranch in parcels ranging in size from 10 to 160 acres when statehood was conferred in 1912, Chandler became one of Arizona's first real-estate developers. His original town center drew upon the popular "City Beautiful" concept which called for orderly streets and a plaza. The San Marcos Hotel was its centerpiece, drawing wealthy visitors from all over the country for golf and other genteel activities. Farming and ranching thrived in this Salt River Valley community twenty-five miles southeast of Phoenix, living on water from the newly completed Roosevelt Dam. "Here," wrote George Wharton James in 1917, "the desert and civilization clasp hands." By the time Dr. Chandler died in 1950, the city had let itself grow aimlessly, and many of its elegant landscape features had been allowed to wither away.

Starting in the 1970s, when high-technology manufacturers began looking for sites outside of California's "Silicon Valley," Chandler began competing with other sunbelt cities for the new industries. Soon cotton, corn, and alfalfa gave way to Motorola, General Instruments, and Honeywell. Some started referring to Chandler as the "Silicon Desert." Intel's semi-conductor plant on West Williams Field Road employs 12,000 at full capacity; in the adjoining fields farmworkers continue to harvest cantaloupe, beets, lettuce, onions, greens, and cabbage for Maggio, Inc., a large Salt River Valley agribusiness. To watch Mexican *campesinos* hand-pick crops in suburban fields adjoining a high-tech plant is to witness three generations of Arizona history at once.

With thousands of engineers, technicians, and other highly skilled workers moving to town, Chandler civic leaders talked about redefining their city. They spoke of the "quality of life," more open spaces, expansion, a jogging trail, a performing arts center, and a major league baseball spring training camp. Others urged maintaining the city's ethnic make-up, and retaining the flavor of Chandler's past. Realtors eased away from subdivisions where houses resemble each other and moved toward neighborhoods with distinctive homes. A red-top survey stake, one woman suggested, should be the city's new emblem. At Sideburn's Cafe and Serrano's Bar, old-timers gave the changes ambivalent approval. The center of the city's new plans highlights a refurbished San Marcos Hotel, Alexander Chandler's original drawing card.

About seventy-five families live in small tidy homes set apart from the rest of Chandler at the far west end of the city in a Yaqui Indian neighborhood called Pueblo Alto, "High Town." Most Phoenix-area Yaquis live a few miles farther north in Guadalupe, a town of fewer than five thousand. Yaquis make up a third of Guadalupe's population; almost all of the rest are Mexican and Mexican American.

Yaquis started crossing into Arizona from Sonora in the late nineteenth century after long resistance to Mexico's policy of occupation, subjugation, and enslavement, and settled in what is now southwest Tempe. From there they were shoved onto forty acres of worthless land known as La Cuarenta, "The Forty." President Woodrow Wilson confirmed the land as theirs in 1915. Everyone called the settlment Yaqui Town until the end of World War II, by which time more and more non-Yaquis had moved there and it took on its current name.

Guadalupe, more than any other town in the United States, bears striking resemblance to small-town Sonora. On a hot, windy, summer day, dust-swirls on the main plaza partially obscure the white facades of the Yaqui Temple and the Roman Catholic Church. You can easily believe you are in a small town somewhere west of Santa Ana on Mexico Highway 2.

Four flags fly over Guadalupe's town hall: The Stars and Stripes, Mexico's Eagle and Serpent, Arizona's Copper Star, and the blue,

white, and red striped Yaqui banner—gold stars shining in each corner, with a black cross, a crescent moon, and a full sun filling its center. The town conducts its business multilingually—signs announce the police are PARA SERVIR, "to serve"; street names are almost all in Spanish (Calle Iglesia, "Church Street") or Yaqui (Calle Vauo Nawi, "Follows the Water Street"); one elementary school teaches three languages; and Town Council agendas are printed in both Spanish and English. Still, it is a patriotic town. It sent its young men off to Germany, Japan, Korea, and Vietnam. Most returned. A monument for those who didn't faces a major intersection. A Yaqui Deer Dancer is painted prominently on it.

Because a handful of businesses provide only a limited tax base for the town, Guadalupe depends upon outside funds. Community Development Bloc Grants are a constant topic at Town Hall. Aggressive community organizing groups provide the catalyst for much of the town's progress. Lights to illuminate the town's baseball field for the Liga Guadalupana came from an Arizona Outdoor Recreation Grant. Money for a youth and a senior citizens center, a clinic, and many other facilities is available to Guadalupe because of its high unemployment,

Above: On the shores of Big Surf, an artificial lake in Tempe.
TERRENCE MOORE.

Opposite: Lake Havasu.
ARIZONA OFFICE OF TOURISM.

low income, limited town services, and substandard housing. "Most houses here are in such bad shape," lamented the assistant town manager, "that you can't even rehabilitate them."

At a Town Council meeting which included debates on road construction bids, a waste management contract, and the town budget, Teresa Torrez stood up. Señora Torrez appeared to be in her fifties. She complained in alternating English and Spanish that the schoolboys who play baseball in the street in front of her house are rude when they enter her yard to retrieve the ball. "It's not that the kids play in the streets, or even that the ball goes inside my yard," she said, grappling for the right phrase. "It's that instead of good words, they say bad words to me. *¡Los muchachos no tienen respeto!*" The boys have no respect.

The chief of police, a Puerto Rican from New York City, replied that with all the problems his eight men face—marijuana smokers, paint-sniffers, and worse—this complaint must take a low priority. "Besides," he went on, "I don't want the first contact these kids have with the police to be a negative one."

"Pues," responded Señora Torrez, *"quizás son marijuaneros por la*

At work on the Central Arizona
Project, Picacho Pumping Plant
Site, 1985.
ANN SIMMONS–MYERS.

mañana, pero juegen béisbol por la tarde." Well, maybe they smoke marijuana in the morning, but in the afternoon they play baseball.

A different image is offered by the Ballet Folklorico Guadalupano, a group of fifty of the town's children, whose renderings of regional Mexican dances have won them acclaim in the United States, Mexico, and in Rome, where Pope John Paul II granted them a special audience in 1981.

The public will see more Guadalupanos as nearby tourist and resort facilities, including The Pointe at South Mountain, open their doors. To prepare themselves for their new neighbors, many townspeople take courses, underwritten by a state vocational education grant, in motel, restaurant, and resort operations. Tenacity still guides the people of Guadalupe.

Other Yaquis in the state live in communities at Marana, Scottsdale, Tucson, and southwest of Tucson on the Pascua Yaqui Reservation, which serves as official headquarters for the entire tribe. Tribal recognition by the federal government did not take place until the middle of Jimmy Carter's presidency.

•

The Navajo Indians gained a reservation while Andrew Johnson was president. Today that reservation, covering 25,209 square miles, is the country's largest. Mining leases, education programs, and economic development projects for the tribe's approximately 150,000 members are administered from the tribal headquarters at Window Rock. In 1982, after twelve years in office, tribal chairman Peter Mac-Donald was defeated in his third reelection bid. A man often viewed as a sophisticated and articulate diplomat, the tenth chairman of the Navajo tribe was also perceived as having lost touch with many of his constituents because of his urbanity. Among the problems handed over to his successor, Peterson Zah, were the amount of royalties paid by companies extracting minerals from beneath the reservation's surface and the dispute with the Hopi Indians over relocation and land use.

Hopi Indian land was carved from the interior of the Navajo Reservation in 1882. At the same time, the land was also assigned to "other Indians," a clause which ever since has caused intermittent disputes over cattle-grazing and homes on the Joint Use Area—land to which both tribes have had access. Barbed wire fences, militant demonstrations, and Acts of Congress have achieved little more than a perpetuation of animosities between the tribes, so it was with skepticism and curiosity that many greeted Zah's inaugural suggestion that instead of outside lawyers and bureaucrats trying to solve the problem, the two tribes engage in "a little feast in the shade of a tree and a lot of understanding."

Traditional Navajo culture takes many forms. To ensure that none of it is lost, Alfred Yazzie at the Navajo Curriculum Center, a night chanter and former law enforcement officer, had assisted in videotaping medicine men discussing tribal customs. "They compare our traditional culture with western culture and modern science—why we believe in harmony with nature, why certain ceremonies are held at particular times of the year. We want to make sure that the old fear doesn't come true—that some day our children will become our enemies and destroy us." The videotapes are shown at schools on the Reservation.

Videotaping is likewise practiced by the Hopi. Students at the Hotevilla Bacavi Community School on Third Mesa have taped a series of portraits which show continuity of the seasons and life. An elderly man talks in Hopi of the Buffalo Dance, followed by the dance itself; women, laughing and chatting, weave baskets; an eagle flies through the air, the ground receives new seedlings; dogs and horses, frisky from the chill, run through the snow, children sled on it. The tape closes with a scene of a mother stacking hundreds and hundreds of blue corn ears in a shed, enough to last her family through the winter. When word of the videotape reached the Hualapai Indians near Peach Springs, they asked the Hopi to come over and record their lives, too.

The Leupp Road passes Old Oraibi as it heads south from Hopiland through the Joint Use Area and the Navajo Reservation, and finally joins the main road into Flagstaff. The three Hopi Mesas take on a timeless grandeur as you descend from them.

On a summer drive not long ago, few cars and only one hitchhiker shared the road. His name was David, destination Flagstaff to help a friend work on his house, then on to Oklahoma for a while.

From the moment David got in the car he talked nonstop of his early childhood in Oklahoma, his youth on the Hopi Reservation, his initiation into Hopi ceremonialism, and tribal traditions and rituals. "I took part in the Tricentennial run," he said. "That was the hardest and most satisfying thing I've ever done."

The run took place in August 1980, three hundred years after the Pueblo Revolt, when Indians living in what is now called New Mexico rose in violent revolution to drive the Spanish from their midst. The Spanish, whose churches were destroyed and many of whose church-men were killed, retreated southward. To coordinate the uprising, Indian runners flew from pueblo to pueblo with the plans, noting the days left till the attack by the number of knots on a rawhide strip they carried. The commemorative run in which David took part started in Taos, New Mexico, passed through the New Mexico Pueblos, and finished five days later in Arizona at the Hopi Cultural Center on Second Mesa. The couriers ran in teams, each one passing a leather pouch on to his successor before being trucked to his next starting point. Each pouch contained a message and a strip of knotted rawhide. In addition to celebrating the great Pueblo Revolt, the participants reaffirmed the role of running as an integral part of Native American culture.

David continued his story at a cafe in Sunrise, telling of his family, his wood-working, and friends debilitated by alcoholism. "My Dad wanted me to become a surveyor, but I didn't want to go through all that training. Carpentry's been good, though." He patted the canvas knapsack which held his tools. "I've been carving Kachinas for a while, and people seem to really like them. I'm starting to sell some."

He went back to the car to retrieve some sweet corn bread. "My Mom made it for me before I left. We call it 'kneel down bread.' She didn't want me to hitchhike today. She said, 'What if a Navajo picks you up?' I told her I'd watch myself."

When David got out at the Monte Vista Hotel in Flagstaff, he wrote down his address. He included a drawing of three sets of deer prints, next to which he wrote his full name. "When my great-grandfather had to fill out some government forms in Oklahoma once," David explained with a grin, "the Indian Affairs man couldn't pronounce his last name. So they gave him a new one—Washington."

•

Askie Yazzie grew up at Kin-Li-Chee on the Navajo Reservation. When he was twenty-four, a recruiter for the copper mines asked if he'd like to work at Morenci, 150 miles south. No, he said, I have to harvest this year's corn crop. After the corn was in, she asked again.

When Yazzie retired from the mines in 1982 after forty years as a truckdriver and pipefitter, he was among the last of the Navajo recruited during World War II still living in the Clifton-Morenci area. Throughout the years he gained a reputation for his oil paintings of horses and mountains. His greatest contribution to the community was a mural painted on the wall of the United Steel Workers Local #616 meeting room during a lengthy strike in the late 1960s. His union hall art, painted as strike duty in lieu of picketing, depicts the Metcalf Mine and the smelter from a miner's point of view. It took two months to complete. His children accompanied him every day.

"I'm real proud of the painting and the way the kids helped," said Yazzie, living his retirement years in a mobile home anchored southwest of Clifton. "I can't really explain how I feel about it inside. Looking back, I just want to cry about the way things are now."

As he spoke, the strike which began in 1983 was underway, as cataclysmic to the state's mining towns as the Colorado River floods had been to its surroundings the same year. Unlike previous strikes, Phelps Dodge kept its gates open this time, and slowly but surely, jobs once held by well-compensated union men and women were filled by workers who signed on under company conditions. Many were union members who, in effect, crossed their own picket line. Like the legendary brothers in the Civil War—"one wore blue, the other wore gray"—the bitter labor conflict split families down the middle. The question of whether to stay loyal to the labor union or to cross the picket line pervaded every walk of life; local teachers saw it in their students, barkeeps saw it in their patrons. Strikers spent their days and evenings at the Oasis in Clifton or at the Open Pit Bar just down the road from the mine's main gate in Morenci. The most popular tune on the jukebox was George Jones's 1962 tearjerker, "Open Pit Mine," about a Clifton miner who kills his wife for cheating on him, then shoots himself as well.

ARCHITECTURE IN A RUGGED LAND

In the winter of 1982, architect Kenneth Frizzell conceived a breathtaking design for one of those junctions of desert and mountain that cradle the city of Tucson. He made a painting and gave it a name: *Troglodytic Futurismo*.

Hundreds of tightly packed earth-brown habitats filled the painting, jostling heroic rock outcroppings and cascading down the mountainside. It was a man-made honeycomb nestling in eaves sculpted by the hand of God. Frizzell made it into his Christmas card, placed the Star of Bethlehem in the indigo sky far above, and appended a scripture—Luke 1:2 – 7: "It seemed good to me also, having had perfect understanding of all things from the very first. . . ."

We would not allow it to be built.

Six years earlier the Pima County Board of Supervisors had enacted a "slope ordinance" to halt the subdividers' march up the mountainsides with their white Spanish Colonial mini-haciendas. It did that; it also forced Frizzell to level his dream. Loews Ventana Canyon, the luxury resort he had been commissioned to design, became a building that local architects agree is a lovely complement to its site, but it is not the mountainside Oz that it could have been.

Frizzell, an architect with a grand—some would say grandiose—vision, paid for the sins of the people who had built on the mountain with no vision at all.

This is a recurring theme of architecture in Arizona. We have not learned to harmonize our buildings with the land. The desert, especially, is a fragile stage set. In it, a skyscraper is a sore glass-and-concrete thumb. A rambling suburban ranch house is a creature from outer space. Great architecture here can be meek and respectful, or it can be bold and visionary, but it must learn its forms and textures from the land around it.

The Sinagua Indians did exactly that on a high, barren basin in northern Arizona some 900 years ago. Their masonry houses, in what we now call Wupatki National Monument, bud from their sites on sandstone outcroppings with such fluidity that it is as if Nature had turned to man and said, "Okay, I'm tired of working on this rock; you finish the job."

Frank Lloyd Wright told us to go study our rocks, reptiles, and cacti, and then make our buildings. "The Arizona desert is no place for the hard box walls of the houses of the Middle West and East," he wrote in *Arizona Highways* in May 1940. "Here all is sculptured by wind and

LAWRENCE W. CHEEK

water, patterned in color and texture...a desert building should be nobly simple in outline as the region itself is sculptured...."

Wright designed the archetype: Taliesin West, in Scottsdale. No other Arizona building evokes so much emotion; no other Arizona building, as architect Pietro Belluschi says, captures so fully "the mood of the land."

Wright's instruction largely has been ignored. A few architects have tried to copy his aesthetics, generally with embarrassing results. A few others have echoed his ethics.

In those same years of the building of Taliesin West, an architect named Margaret Spencer designed a guest ranch comprising sixteen rock cottages in what was then lonely desert several miles west of Tucson. Local legend has it that she drew the floor plans on the ground with a stick, letting topography and whim have their way. The red-gray stone for the walls was quarried a mile from the site. Fifty years later, Rancho de las Lomas has been almost encircled by subdivisions, but the modest little stone cottages still look as though the desert itself had given birth to them.

Bennie Gonzalez, an acclaimed Phoenix architect, installed one of his most dramatic desert buildings in the middle of a grassy park in downtown Scottsdale, next to a pond where swim the municipal swans, Winnie and Pooh. All this seems at first like an attempt to repeal the local environment rather than savor it. But the qualities of the buildings themselves are abstracted from those of the desert and mountains. The forms are stark and powerful. There is a counterpoint of light and shadow, but the light is dominant. And there is an insinuation of prehistoric architecture, quietly linking this Scottsdale City Hall and Library of 1968 to the Native Americans' utterly organic architecture of centuries past.

And there is The Boulders Resort of Carefree, a $200 million playground skirting a 600-foot-high pile of rocks northeast of Phoenix. Wright hardly would approve of the water-gulping eighteen-hole golf course; nor of the buildings' forms, which are not-too-distant cousins of the Taos Pueblo style. Wright loathed "style." But he would have to appreciate the way that the rhythmic, orderly chain of buildings reaches out and embraces the jumbled, grumpy boulders and makes perfect peace with them. He might even admire the philosophy of architect Bob Bacon, who, when asked what he would have designed for this site had the assignment been a cathedral instead of a resort, gave this answer: nothing.

LAWRENCE W. CHEEK

LAWRENCE W. CHEEK

Life in mining towns is entirely dependent upon "the company," whether Phelps Dodge, Anaconda, Kennecott, or a smaller one-town company. The company is landlord, paymaster, politician, government, doctor, and shopkeeper. It controls its workers from before birth at the company hospital to after death at the company cemetery. (In the early 1970s, Kennecott's open-pit mine at Ray was expanded to such an extent that the company moved the entire town, cemetery and all, to nearby Kearny.)

When a few Phelps Dodge officials rode down Tombstone Canyon into Bisbee one September morning, they were shocked to see a Mexican strung up from a cottonwood tree at Castle Rock. The previous evening he had been evicted from a bar and returned later to shoot some people. Aghast at what they saw, the mine barons decided that Bisbee needed a quick dose of civilization. When they returned to New York, the executives shipped hundreds of books out to the wild west, enough to give Bisbee its first library in 1883. The Copper Queen library moved from site to site until 1907, when it settled into its present location above the post office on Bisbee's Main Street. P-D gave its library to the city when it pulled out of town in the mid-1970s.

The county library system serves the area's outback. In the town of Cochise the post office doubles as the county branch library. At Cascabel, a community on the San Pedro River in the county's far northwest, patrons visit the second floor of an old ranch house. Readers in Sunsites get their books from a new county library built of rammed earth. Thirty-five more communities get monthly visits from the Cochise County bookmobile, a GMC Step Van once used to deliver bread. From the highway at Nicksville (second Monday of the month, mornings) to the water tower at Dragoon (first Wednesday, afternoons), two thousand books park themselves every weekday at dusty crossroads, grocery stores, and post offices. At Curtis Flats Road (third Tuesday, afternoons) a rancher shows up with his wheelbarrow. It is filled with books that he and his wife have read the previous month. He spends twenty minutes browsing the bookmobile's shelves and takes out enough to refill his wheelbarrow for the walk home. This is how rural Arizona gets its food for thought.

All you had to know to be the bookmobile driver was how to shift gears on a four-speed truck, so the county library staff was delighted when sixty-year-old John Kuehn applied for the job in 1981. He could drive *and* he knew all about books. Kuehn, who lived in a German town near the Polish border until the age of three, had been in the area once before, dining at Bisbee's Copper Queen Hotel when he was stationed thirty miles west at Ft. Huachuca. For many years he and his family lived in a farmhouse outside of Rockford, Illinois, where he owned a bookstore. "Our driveway was covered with snow four months of the year. One day in 1978 Grace and I said to hell with it." They joined the ranks of emigres swelling the Sunbelt's population. Once they settled in Bisbee, Grace sold real estate, and John opened a used and rare book shop on Brewery Gulch.

Below: The Cochise County bookmobile entering Texas Canyon.
RICHARD BYRD.

Overleaf: Lightning over Tucson.
RALPH WETMORE.

"The yucca are starting to bloom," remarked Mrs. McCauley as she handed John a sack of books to reshelve. The bookmobile's first stop of the day was Barrow's Trailer Park on U. S. 80. "I saw a snake in the road this morning," she continued, looking over the romance books. "The first of the season." Before leaving, Mrs. McCauley requested a book about the structural geology of the Santa Rita Mountains.

"You know, it always surprises me how many people don't read," John mentioned during a mini-mart coffee stop. "You suggest to someone that he read a book and he says sorry, I just don't have the time." John parked the van in St. David in front of the Church of Jesus Christ of Latter-Day Saints. A couple in their early twenties drove up and asked for library cards. "We were just passing through from Ohio a few days ago," the wife said, "and we liked it here. We're job-hunting now, but one of the first things we wanted to do was to get library cards."

John smiled and handed them a pen and a form to fill out. "We like to get as many people as possible. That way we can go to the Board of Supervisors at budget time and tell them we've got six thousand new

voters signed up." A teenager walked across the highway to return a book about the Tet offensive. He borrowed a copy of *Catch-22*.

Books became controversial in St. David in 1981 when school authorities removed John Steinbeck's *Of Mice and Men* and Joseph Conrad's *Lord Jim* from the reading list of a high school English class. A county librarian described a meeting she had attended in St. David: "They were considering a particular text on U. S. history. Well, someone went through it very carefully, making a note each time there was a reference to women, and brought it up at the meeting. 'Women belong in the home,' she said. 'Not in history.' And they rejected the book."

"It's a funny thing about these communities," John commented as he drove to the local schoolyard. "You can never tell why one type of book is popular at one place, and another type is popular just a few miles away. At McNeal [second Thursday of the month, mornings] wildlife books are very big. But at Double Adobe [fourth Tuesday, mornings] war books are in demand."

Lisa and Marissa were waiting when John drove up. They hopped into the van and scrambled over to the children's section. "Look," Lisa exclaimed, waving a book in the air. "They have *Heidi* in Spanish!" Marissa leaned over to see. "I can speak Spanish," she said. "But I can't read it."

By day's end, county residents had taken out 137 books to enjoy for a month, and in its parking space next to the old high school in downtown Bisbee, the bookmobile rumbled to a halt.

•

From Bisbee the long route to Tucson passes through Sonoita and Patagonia, over to Nogales, and north past Green Valley and the San Xavier Mission. One billboard advertised the state lottery, another promoted the Yaqui bingo hall, yet another commanded THIS VACATION, DO ARIZONA. Roadside fleamarkets and backyard satellite dishes made for odd neighbors. Highway signs on Interstate 19 between the Mexican border and Tucson measure distance solely in kilometers—the only roadway in the country to do so.

Rampant growth is often thought to have smothered the qualities which give Tucson its distinctive flavor. The characteristics which attracted outsiders two decades ago are barely visible, yet those settling in Tucson today will likely make the same observation twenty years from now. A downtown statue honoring Mexico's revolutionary bandit Pancho Villa still generates controversy. Sophisticated desert-dwellers will always gaze in wonder at arroyos and riverbeds when sudden rains fill them dangerously beyond capacity. The nationwide movement to provide church-sponsored sanctuary for Central American refugees started in Tucson, making the city a major switching point on the modern underground railway. Collegiate football scandals lend a touch of big-city notoriety, while movies are cranked out which feature a mock frontier ambience. Weekend country-swing dancers wear western clothes, but in contemporary Tucson and throughout Arizona, even drugstore cowboys are getting hard to find.

REFERENCE MATERIAL

SUGGESTED READINGS

INTRODUCTION/VIGNETTES
10. MODERN ARIZONA

Surprisingly few books about recent life in Arizona can be found; perhaps it's a subject which changes too fast to be afforded the permanence of a book. For a healthy understanding of the more traditional aspects of current Indian life, these can be useful: *Indian Running*, by Peter Nabokov (Santa Barbara: Capra Press, 1981); *Between Sacred Mountains: Navajo Stories and Lessons From the Land*, compiled by the Rock Point School Community (Tucson: Sun Tracks/The University of Arizona Press, 1984); and *American Indian Myths and Legends*, selected and edited by Richard Erodes and Alfonso Ortiz (New York: Pantheon, 1984).

Two statistical profiles of the state, updated regularly, give a good look at our annual ups and downs: *Arizona Statistical Review*, by the Valley National Bank of Arizona Economic Planning Division (Phoenix), and *Arizona Economic Indicators*, by the University of Arizona College of Business and Public Administration Division of Economic and Business Research. To follow modern activities well requires a healthy knowledge of history, for which *Historical Atlas of Arizona* by Henry P. Walker and Don Bufkin (Norman: University of Oklahoma Press, 1979) serves as both map and guide. Learning about life which preceded the written word is important in understanding history. *Those Who Came Before: Southwestern Archeology in the National Park System*, by Robert H. Lister and Florence C. Lister (Globe: Southwestern Parks and Monuments Association, softbound, 1983; Tucson: The University of Arizona Press, hardbound, 1984), does an admirable job discussing Arizona's prehistory.

More has been written about the Colorado than any other river in the country, except perhaps the Mississippi. For a direct and informative introduction, look at *The Colorado River in Grand Canyon—A Guide*, by Larry Stevens (Flagstaff: Red Lakes Books, 1983). A terrific view of the state's desert and those who live by it can be found in *The Desert Smells Like Rain: A Naturalist in Papago Indian Country* by Gary Nabhan (Berkeley: North Point, 1982). Details of the research about Arizona's land carried out by Forrest Shreve and others are published in *Discovering the Desert: The Legacy of the Carnegie Desert Botanical Laboratory*, by William G. McGinnies (Tucson: The University of Arizona Press, 1981). Shreve himself wrote *The Cactus and Its Home* (Williams and Williams Co., Baltimore, 1931).

A slew of books and magazine articles positively gushing with praise and hyperbole about Arizona were published in the latter part of the nineteenth century and on into the beginning of the twentieth century. Among them: *A Tour Through Arizona* by J. Ross Browne (1864) (reprinted by Tombstone Nugget Publishing Co., no date given); *Arizona: Its Resources and Prospects* by Richard McCormick (1865) (reprinted by Territorial Press, Tucson, 1968, with a new introduction by Sydney B. Brinkerhoff); *The Resources of Arizona* by Patrick Hamilton (1881) (reprinted by Piñon Press, Tucson, 1966); and *Across Arizona in 1883* by William Henry Bishop (reprinted by Outbooks, Olympic Valley, Ca., 1977). In the twentieth century, *Alluring Arizona* by William Hamilton Nelson (self-published, San Francisco, 1929) shows an author punch-drunk with love for the state as he rhapsodizes for 133 pages. *The Arizona Story* by Joseph Miller (New York: Hastings House, 1952) contains almost one hundred tales about Arizona as culled from its newspapers, dating back to the mid-nineteenth century, with cogent comments by the author.

Franklin D. Roosevelt's New Deal brought some writing and art work to the state. First, there was *Arizona: A State Guide*, part of the Writers' Program of the Work Projects Administration (New York: Hastings House, 1940). The book, revised sixteen years later to include innovations in farming, mining, industry, and the changes in Arizona wrought by World War II, was one of the precursors to the volume you're now holding. The Roosevelt years also gave us government-subsidized art, a benefit we still enjoy, some of which was collected in *The New Deal in the Southwest* by Peter Bermingham (Tucson: The University of Arizona Museum of Art, no year given). The book shows some of the art from the Public Works of Art Project and the Federal Art Project of the Works Project Administration. A more comprehensive and less bureaucratic look at artistic impressions of Arizona is found in the impressive *Visitors to Arizona 1846 to 1980* by James K. Ballinger and Andrea D. Rubinstein (Phoenix Art Museum, 1980). The book, really the catalog to a major exhibit curated at the Phoenix Art Museum, shows paintings, sketches, photographs, and other graphic art work carried out in Arizona over a 134-year period. *Hopi Photographers/Hopi Images*, compiled by Erin Younger and Victor Masayesva (Tucson: Sun Tracks/The University of Arizona Press, 1983), shows how one slice of the state's population, long accustomed to others looking at it, looks at itself.

Two labors of love are these collections of writings about Arizona: *Arizona in Literature* by Mary G. Boyer (Arthur H. Clark Co., Glendale, Ca., 1934), and *Arizona Anthem*, compiled by Blair Morton Armstrong (The Mnemosyne Press, Scottsdale, 1982). The first includes excerpts from works of fiction, non-fiction, poetry, and autobiography from early Spanish conquistadors to the late 1920s. The second, a bewildering and ambitious anthology of poetry about Arizona, fills its 600 pages with works from Gaspar de Villagra in the early seventeenth century to contemporary poets Alberto Ríos and Drummond Hadley.

Finally, sufficiently lightweight to carry in your back pocket is *Grand Canyon to Mexico Bicycle Route* by Ed Stiles and Lori Stiles (Tucson: Breakaway Press, 1982).

The author extends grateful appreciation to the Arizona Commission on the Arts for a travel-assistance grant enabling him to research the vignettes and Chapter 10.

1. MOUNTAIN ISLANDS

One of the most interesting accounts dealing with the relationship between mountains and deserts and their respective plant and animal inhabitants can be found in Frederick R. Gehlbach's *Mountain Islands and Desert Seas: A Natural History of the U.S. — Mexican Borderlands* (Texas A & M University Press, College Station, Texas, 1981). The book is a personalized summary of more than two decades of natural history exploration throughout the topographic extremes of the borderlands area. *Pleistocene Extinctions: A Search for a Cause,* by P. S. Martin and H. E. Wright, Eds. (Yale University Press, New Haven, 1967), and *Quaternary Extinctions: A Prehistoric Revolution,* by P. S. Martin and Richard G. Klein, Eds. (The University of Arizona Press, Tucson, 1984) are two books which give a very thorough review of the vegetative and faunal changes that have taken place throughout the state and elsewhere over the past 15,000 or more years.

Some landmark ecological studies that were performed many years ago are deserving of mention here. Harry S. Swarth's publication, "The Faunal Areas of Southern Arizona: A Study in Animal Distribution" (*Proc. Cal. Acad. Sci.* 18(12):267–383, 1929), has important ecological information and is easy and interesting reading as well. Forrest Shreve published many papers during the early 1900's on the vegetation of the Arizona landscape, including the following: "The Physical Control of Vegetation in Rain-Forest and Desert Mountains" (*Plant World* 20(5):135–141, 1917); "A Comparison of the Vegetational Features of Two Desert Mountain Ranges" (*Plant World* 22(10):291–307, 1919); and "Conditions Indirectly Affecting Vertical Distribution on desert mountains" (*Ecology* 3(3):181–268, 1922).

For an accounting of major habitat changes within the state brought on mostly by the "hand of man" within the past one hundred years, see *The Changing Mile* by J. R. Hastings and R. Turner (The University of Arizona Press, 1965).

Other sources consulted:

Brown, J. H. 1971. Mammals on Mountaintops: Nonequilibrium Insular Biogeography. *Amer. Natur.* 105:467–478.
Hoffmeister, D. F. 1956. Mammals of the Graham (Pinaleno) Mountains, Arizona. *Amer. Mid. Natur.* 55: 257–288.
Little, E. L. 1941. Alpine Flora of San Francisco Mountain, Arizona. *Madroño* 6:65–81.
Moore, T. C. 1965. Origin and Disjunction of the Alpine Tundra Flora on San Francisco Mountain, Arizona. *Ecology* 46:860–864.
Patterson, B. D. 1980. Montane Mammalian Biogeography in New Mexico. *Southwest Natur.* 25:33–40.
Whittaker, R. H., and W. A. Niering. 1964. Vegetation of the Santa Catalina Mountains, Arizona. I. Ecological Classification and Distribution of Species. *J. Ariz. Acad. Sci.* 3:9–34.
———. 1965. Vegetation of the Santa Catalina Mountains, Arizona: A Gradient Analysis of the South Slope. *Ecology* 46:429–452.
———. 1968a. Vegetation of the Santa Catalina Mountains, Arizona. III. Species Distribution and Floristic Relations on the North Slope. *J. Ariz. Acad. Sci.* 5:3–21.
———. 1968b. Vegetation of the Santa Catalina Mountains, Arizona. IV. Limestone and Acid Soils. *J. Ecol.* 56:523–544.

2. THE COLORADO PLATEAU

The best book on the Colorado Plateau as a place—and as a place in history—is Wallace Stegner's *Beyond the Hundredth Meridian: John Wesley Powell and the Second Opening of the West* (Houghton Mifflin, Boston, 1954). This will also lead you to Powell's protégé Clarence Dutton, perhaps the most impressive Grand Canyon writer yet (*Tertiary History of the Grand Canyon District,* U. S. Geological Survey, 1882).

For general summaries of plateau geology, biology, and history, see my book *The Bright Edge: A Guide to the National Parks of the Colorado Plateau* (Museum of Northern Arizona Press, Flagstaff, 1979).

To put the plateau in perspective geologically, see Charles B. Hunt, *Natural Regions of the United States and Canada* (W. H. Freeman, San Francisco, 1974). More regional is David A. Rahm, *Reading the Rocks: A Guide to the Geologic Secrets of Canyons, Mesas, and Buttes in the American Southwest* (Sierra Club Books, San Francisco, 1974). For more detail, go on to Halka Chronic, *Roadside Geology of*

Arizona (Mountain Press, Missoula, Montana, 1983) and *Geology of Arizona* by Dale Nations and Edmund Stump (Kendall/Hunt, Dubuque, Iowa, 1981).

No literature exists for the Navajo Country comparable to the many books written on Grand Canyon natural history. *Between Sacred Mountains: Navajo Stories and Lessons from the Land* helps (Sam and Janet Bingham, editors, University of Arizona Press, Tucson, 1984). For the Grand Canyon, start with the chapter by Steven Carothers and Nancy Goldberg in *The Grand Canyon: Up Close and Personal* (Western Montana College Foundation, 1980), and *The Colorado River in Grand Canyon: A Guide* by Larry Stevens (Red Lake Books, Flagstaff, 1983).

Regional understanding—and considerable detail on plants—comes from *Biotic Communities of the American Southwest—United States and Mexico*, David E. Brown, editor (*Desert Plants* Volume 4, 1982). A good introduction to desert ecology is Peggy Larson's *A Sierra Club Naturalist's Guide to the Deserts of the Southwest* (Sierra Club Books, San Francisco, 1977).

The Museum of Northern Arizona quarterly magazine *Plateau* contains a wealth of information on all aspects of plateau natural history. Recent issues focus on plateau dinosaurs, water, the Verde Valley, and the San Francisco Peaks.

Some of the best writing about the plateau landscape can be found in less technical books. See the books I quote from, and in particular, Willa Cather's *Death Comes for the Archbishop* (1927; reprinted by Vintage Books, New York) and *The Song of the Lark* (1915; reprinted by University of Nebraska Press, Lincoln), Philip Fradkin's *A River No More: The Colorado River and the West* (Knopf, New York, 1981; University of Arizona Press, Tucson, 1984), and Eliot Porter's *Glen Canyon: The Place No One Knew: Glen Canyon on the Colorado* (Sierra Club Books, San Francisco, 1963).

Other sources consulted:

Babbitt, Bruce. 1978. *Grand Canyon: An Anthology.* Northland Press, Flagstaff. (quote from Haniel Long, *Piñon Country.* Duell, Sloan & Pearce, 1941).

Dutton, Clarence E. 1880. *Geology of the High Plateaus of Utah.* U. S. Geological Survey, Washington.

Lanner, Ronald. 1981. *The Piñon Pine: A Natural and Cultural History.* University of Nevada Press, Reno.

Leopold, Aldo. 1949. *A Sand County Almanac and Sketches Here and There.* Oxford University Press, New York.

Loving, Nancy. 1981. *Along the Rim: A Road Guide to the South Rim of Grand Canyon.* Grand Canyon Natural History Association. (Gertrude Stevens quote)

Priestley, J. B. 1940. *Midnight on the Desert: Chapters of Autobiography.* Readers' Union Limited/William Heinemann, London.

Rusho, W. L., and C. Gregory Crampton. 1975. *Desert River Crossing: Historic Lee's Ferry on the Colorado River.* Peregrine Smith, Salt Lake City. (Escalante quote)

Waters, Frank. 1946. *The Colorado.* Holt, Rinehart & Winston, New York.

Wolfe, Thomas. 1939. *A Western Journal.* University of Pittsburgh Press.

D 3. THE MOJAVE DESERT

Dale Nations and Edmund Stump's *Geology of Arizona* (Kendall/Hunt, Dubuque, 1981) provides a highly readable general introduction to geologic terms, events, and Arizona strata and geomorphology. W. R. Dickinson's 1981 paper, "Plate Tectonic Evolution of the Southern Cordillera" (*Arizona Geological Society Digest* 14:113 − 135), is a challenging discussion of mountain-building events and geologic upheaval in the Southwest. An excellent review of late Cenozoic geologic events in the eastern Mojave Desert is Ivo Lucchitta's "Late Cenozoic Uplift of the Southwestern Colorado Plateau and Adjacent Lower Colorado River Region," which appeared in 1979 in the journal *Tectonophysics* (61:63 − 95). Paul Martin and R. G. Klein's *Quaternary Extinctions* (University of Arizona Press, Tucson, 1984) provides controversial scientific discussions of Pleistocene-Holocene climatic, floral, and faunal changes in the western United States.

The best introduction I've seen to weather is Vincent Schaefer and John Day's *A Field Guide to the Atmosphere* (Houghton Mifflin Co., Boston, 1981). Arizona, including Mojave, weather is discussed in detail in W. D. Sellers and R. H. Hill's *Arizona Climate, 1931 − 1972,* second edition (University of Arizona Press, Tucson, 1974).

A large volume of literature exists on the American deserts. An excellent sourcebook on the North American deserts is S. G. Wells and D. R. Haragan's edited volume *Origin and Evolution of Deserts* (University of New Mexico Press in Albuquerque, 1983), especially the chapters by C. B. Hunt, D. I. Axelrod, and T. VanDevender. The most concise description of the Mojave Desert I have found is in Forrest Shreve's 1942 paper in *Botanical Review* (8:195 − 246).

Desert Life has been the subject of much scientific and popular attention. G. W. Brown Jr.'s *Desert Biology* in two volumes (Academic Press, New York, 1968) is a good scientific introduction to the field. Popular writing on the Mojave includes E. C. Jaeger's third edition of *The California Deserts,* (Stanford University Press, Stanford), and Larson and Larson's *A Sierra Club Naturalist's Guide to the Deserts of the Southwest* (Sierra Club Books, San Francisco, 1977). Specific field guides to Mojave flora and fauna have not yet appeared, but Walter McDougall's *Seed Plants of Northern Arizona* (Museum of Northern Arizona, Flagstaff, 1973), T. H. Kearney's, and R. H. Peebles's *Arizona Flora*, second edition (University of California Press, Berkeley, 1973), L. Benson's *The Cacti of Arizona* (University of Arizona Press, Tucson, 1950), Stebbins's *A Field Guide to Western Reptiles and Amphibians* (Houghton Mifflin Co., Boston, 1966), and the Peterson and other guides to western wildflowers, birds, and mammals are useful.

The history of Arizona's Mojave Desert is best explored through the writings of Mohave County historian Roman Malach. In particular, his *Mohave County: Sketches of the Early Days* (1974) and his *Hualapai Mountains* (1975) both published in Kingman by the author, make good reading. Other useful works include R. C. Bond's Ph.D. dissertation, *Settlement Patterns of the Eastern Mojave Desert* (University of California at Los Angeles, 1972); Casebier's *Camp El Dorado, Arizona Territory* (Arizona Historical Foundation Monograph Number 2, Tempe, 1970); and John Nicholson's well-edited book, *The Arizona of Joseph Pratt Allyn* (University of Arizona Press, Tucson, 1974). Phillip Fradkin's *A River No More: The Colorado River and the West* (Knopf, New York, 1981; University of Arizona Press, Tucson, reissued in 1984) provides the best discussion of the history, politics, and importance of the Colorado River to the people of the lower Colorado River basin.

4. THE SONORAN DESERT

The Sonoran Desert has been eloquently described in writing for decades, and some of these early essays have been reissued. See John Van Dyke's *The Desert* (1901; reprinted by the Arizona Historical Society in collaboration with Arizona Silhouettes, Tucson, 1976) and William Hornaday's *Camp-Fires in Desert and Lava* (1908; reprinted by University of Arizona Press, Tucson, 1983). Highly acclaimed natural historian/philosopher Joseph Wood Krutch continued this tradition with *The Desert Year* (1952; reprinted by the University of Arizona Press, Tucson, 1983). A more "modern" evolutionary ecologist's approach to the desert natural history essay can be found in John Alcock's *Sonoran Desert Spring* (University of Chicago Press, Chicago, 1985). My own ecological essays, complementing George Huey's photographs, take a similar approach in *Sketches on Saguaro* (Southwestern Parks and Monuments Association, 1985).

For a historic review of Sonoran Desert studies, I recommend William McGinnies's *Discovering the Desert* (University of Arizona Press, Tucson, 1982). Although it is somewhat dated, there is much pertinent geographic data in Roger Dunbier's *The Sonoran Desert: Its Geography, Economy and People* (University of Arizona Press, Tucson, 1968). As a field guide to common wildlife and showy flora, the best available volume is James MacMahon's *Deserts* (Audubon Society Nature Guides, Random House, New York, 1985).

For an ecology of the Sonoran Desert that includes people, I recommend Charles Bowden's *Killing the Hidden Waters* (University of Texas Press, Austin, 1977) and Bernard Fontana's *Of Earth and Little Rain* (Northland Press, Flagstaff, 1981). Paul Mirocha and I have attempted to extend this human ecology perspective to desert dwellers in addition to the Papago in *Gathering the Desert* (University of Arizona Press, Tucson, 1985).

Other sources consulted:

Bayham, Frank. 1982. A Diachronic Analysis of Prehistoric Animal Exploitation at Ventana Cave. Ph.D. dissertation, Arizona State University, Tempe.
Berger, J. M. 1898. Report of the Farmer in Charge of San Xavier Papago Reservation. Annual Reports of the Department of Interior, Washington, D. C.
Cornejo, Dennis. 1982. "Night of the Spadefoot Toad." *Science '82*, 44–48.
Emory, W. H. 1857. Report on the United States and Mexico Boundary Survey, Executive Document 108. U. S. House of Representatives, 34th Congress, Washington, D. C.
Gaillard, D. D. 1894. The Papago of Arizona and Sonora. *American Anthropologist* 7:293.
Haury, Emil W. 1975. *The Stratigraphy and Archaeology of Ventana Cave*. University of Arizona Press, Tucson.
Lumholtz, Carl S. 1912. *New Trails in Mexico*. Scribners, New York.
McGee, W. J. 1897. "Sheetflood Erosion." *Bulletin of the Geological Society of America* 8:105.
Martin, William E., Helen M. Ingram, Nancy K. Laney, and Adrian H. Griffin. 1984. *Saving Water in a Desert City*. Resources for the Future, Washington, D. C.
Rea, Amadeo M., Gary Paul Nabhan, and Karen L. Reichhardt. 1983. "Sonoran Desert Oases: Plants, Birds and People." *Environment Southwest* 503:5–9.
Shreve, Forrest, and Ira Wiggins. 1964. *Vegetation and Flora of the Sonoran Desert*. Stanford University Press, Stanford.
Solbrig, Otto T. 1978. "The Strategies and Community Patterns of Desert Plants," in G. Orians and O. Solbrig, eds., *Convergent Evolution in Warm Deserts*. Dowden, Hutchinson and Ross, Stroudsburg, Pa., pp. 67–106.
Treutlein, Theodore, trans. 1949. *Pfeffercorn's Description of Sonora*. University of New Mexico Press, Albuquerque.

Van Devender, Thomas. No date. Packrat Middens from the Castle Mountains, Arizona. Unpublished report, Arizona Sonora Desert Museum, Tucson.

Wyllys, Rufus Kay. 1931. Padre Luis [sic] Velarde's Relacion of Pimeria Alta, 1716. *New Mexico Historical Review* 6:111 – 157.

social history of the Chihuahuan region, both before and after arrival of European settlers, in *Cycles of Conquest* (University of Arizona Press, Tucson, 1962). For a closer look at the early days of Anglo-American settlement, read J. G. Bourke's journal of his experiences in the Apache campaign *On the Border With Crook* (University of Nebraska Press, Lincoln, reprinted 1971).

A 5. THE CHIHUAHUAN DESERT

good general description of the landscapes and natural history of the northern Chihuahuan Desert region is provided by F. R. Gehlbach's *Mountain Islands and Desert Seas: A Natural History of the U. S.—Mexico Borderlands* (Texas A & M University Press, College Station, Texas, 1981). For a more detailed discussion of the plants and their distributions, the early work of Forrest Shreve is still unequalled, particularly "Observations on the Vegetation of Chihuahua" (*Madroño* 5:1 – 12, 1939) and "Grasslands in Northern Mexico" (*Madroño* 6:190 – 198, 1942). The unusual vegetation of desert dunes of the Chihuahuan Desert as well as other North American dunes is explored by Jan Bowers in "The Plant Ecology of Inland Dunes in Western North America" (*Journal of Arid Environments* 5:199 – 220, 1981). Almost every aspect of the flora and fauna of the Chihuahuan Desert region is covered by the technical volume *Transactions of the Symposium on the Biological Resources of the Chihuahuan Desert Region, United States and Mexico*, edited by R. H. Wauer and D. H. Riskind (U. S. National Park Service Transactions and Proceedings Series No. 3, 1974).

R. H. Schmidt, Jr., examines the climate of the Chihuahuan Desert and the numerous difficulties encountered in defining a desert in "A Climatic Definition of the Real Chihuahuan Desert" (*Journal of Arid Environments* 2:243 – 250, 1979). The physical setting of a Chihuahuan playa is described by J. F. Schreiber, Jr., in "Geology of the Willcox Playa, Cochise County, Arizona" (*New Mexico Geological Society Guidebook*, 29th Field Conference, pages 277 – 282, 1978).

The paleo-history of the region, covering approximately the last ten to fifteen thousand years, is investigated in considerable detail by Paul Martin in *The Last 10,000 Years—A Geochronology of Pluvial Lake Cochise* (University of Arizona Press, Tucson, 1964) and by Tom Van Devender and Geoff Spaulding in "Development of Vegetation and Climate in the Southwestern United States" (*Science* 204:701 – 710, 1979).

Edward Spicer presents an excellent summary of the

S 6. THE ELUSIVE INTERIOR

tart with Captain John G. Bourke's *On The Border With Crook* (University of Nebraska Press, Lincoln, reprint of 1891 edition), still the best introduction to the land and history of Apachería. Edwin Corle's *The Gila* (University of Nebraska Press, Lincoln, 1951) also is good background.

For geology, use *Geology of Arizona* by Dale Nations and Edmund Stump (Kendall/Hunt, Dubuque, Iowa, 1981) and Halka Chronic, *Roadside Geology of Arizona* (Mountain Press, Missoula, Montana, 1983). Also see Louis L. Jacobs's article on Verde Valley geology and fossils in *Plateau* 53(1):2 – 5, 1981.

Chaparral ecology is summarized in *Arizona Chaparral: Plant Associations and Ecology* by R. S. Carmichael, O. D. Knipe, C. P. Pase, and W. W. Brady (U. S. Forest Service Research Paper RM-202, 1978). Aldo Leopold's pioneering work appears in his "Grass, Brush, Timber, and Fire in Southern Arizona" (*Journal of Forestry* 22(6):1 – 10, 1924). See also *Biotic Communities of the American Southwest—United States and Mexico*, David E. Brown, editor (*Desert Plants*, Vol. 4, 1982) and Howard Scott Gentry, *The Agaves of Continental North America* (University of Arizona Press, Tucson, 1982).

For more information on Apaches and the Changing Woman story, see *Handbook of North American Indians, Volume 10: The Southwest* (Smithsonian, 1983) and *The Cibecue Apache*, by Keith Basso (Holt, Rinehart & Winston, New York, 1970). My telling of the story is based in part on a recounting of it by Philip Cassadore, a San Carlos Apache medicine man.

Other sources consulted:

Grey, Zane. 1924. *Call of the Canyon*. Pocket Books, New York.

Lowe, Charles H. 1964. *The Vertebrates of Arizona*. University of Arizona Press, Tucson.

Priestley, J. B. 1940. *Midnight on the Desert: Chapters of Autobiography*. Readers' Union Limited/William Heinemann, London.

7. INDIANS OF ARIZONA

The literature on Indians of the Southwest, including Arizona, is enormous. Fortunately, all the best of it has been drawn upon and correlated into a superbly edited single work—Volumes 9 (1979) and 10 (1983) of the Smithsonian Institution's *Handbook of North American Indians*, published by the federal government in Washington, D.C. These two volumes, covering all the Indians of the Southwest, have it all—archaeology, anthropology, ethnology, ethnohistory, pre-history, history, linguistics, religion, mythology, world views, fine arts, poetry, music, modern-day status—everything that one would wish to know about the different tribes. Far and away, these recently published volumes in the Smithsonian's series are the best source available for further reading on Arizona's Indians. Another fine collection of books is published by the Indian Tribal Series in Phoenix and covers ten of Arizona's seventeen tribes. They are available in most libraries.

For general, overall treatments that deal wholly, or in part, with Arizona's Indians, try *Indians of Arizona: A Contemporary Perspective,* edited by Thomas Weaver (Tucson: University of Arizona Press, 1974); Edward H. Spicer's classic and highly-readable *Cycles of Conquest* (Tucson: University of Arizona Press, 1962); Bertha P. Dutton's *Indians of the American Southwest* (Englewood Cliffs, N.J.: Prentice Hall, 1975) and Chapter 16 ("The Indians of the Southwest") in Alvin M. Josephy, Jr.'s *The Indian Heritage of America* (New York: Alfred A. Knopf, 1968).

In the fields of archaeology and early pre-history, I suggest the following: first, the very lucid *Those Who Came Before* by Robert H. and Florence C. Lister (Tucson: University of Arizona Press, 1983). Then, *The Archaeology of Arizona: A Study of the Southwest Region* by Paul S. Martin and Fred T. Plog (Garden City, N.Y.: Doubleday Natural History Press, 1973); Emil W. Haury's fascinating *The Hohokam, Desert Farmers and Craftsmen: Excavations at Snaketown, 1964–1965* (Tucson: University of Arizona Press, 1976); and Gordon R. Willey's *An Introduction to American Archaeology. Volume One: North and Middle America* (Englewood Cliffs, N.J.: Prentice Hall, 1966). Willey's book has a huge sweep, but it provides a marvelous context for an understanding and appreciation of Arizona's early Indian cultures.

Now we come to the individual tribes. Leading off with the Hopis, I recommend: Frank Waters's *Book of the Hopi* (New York: Viking Press, 1963) and his *Masked Gods* (Albuquerque: University of New Mexico Press, 1950); Harry C. James's *Pages From Hopi History* (Tucson: University of Arizona Press, 1974); Harold Courlander's *The Fourth World of the Hopis* (New York: Crown Publishers, 1971); Richard O. Clemmer's *Continuities of Hopi Culture Change*

(Ramona, Calif.: Acoma Books, 1978). In addition, for a stupendous bibliography on just about everything ever written on Hopis, see W. David Laird's annotated *Hopi Bibliography* (Tucson: University of Arizona Press, 1977).

On Navajos, there are Clyde Kluckhohn's and Dorothea C. Leighton's *The Navaho* (Cambridge, Mass.: Harvard University Press, 1946); Peter Iverson's *The Navaho Nation* (Westport, Ct.: Greenwood Press, 1981); *Navajo History*, ed. by Ethelou Yazzie (Many Farms, Ariz.: Navajo Community College Press, 1971), a Navajo version of the people's creation; Frank McNitt's *Navajo Wars: Military Campaigns, Slave Raids and Reprisals* (Albuquerque: University of New Mexico Press, 1972); and Donald L. Parman's *The Navajos and the New Deal* (New Haven, Ct.: Yale University Press, 1976). Not to be overlooked, also, is Ruth Underhill's basic *The Navajos* (Norman: University of Oklahoma Press, 1967).

On the Pimas, there are the re-edition of Frank Russell's *The Pima Indians,* edited by Bernard L. Fontana (Tucson: University of Arizona Press, 1975), and George Webb's *A Pima Remembers* (Tucson: University of Arizona Press, 1959). For the Yaquis, see Edward H. Spicer's *The Yaquis: A Cultural History* (Tucson: University of Arizona Press, 1980) and Dolores G. Valenzuela's *The Emerging Pascua Yaqui Tribe* (Tucson: The Pascua Tribe, 1981).

Works on the Papagos include Bernard L. Fontana's *Of Earth and Little Rain: The Papago Indians* (Flagstaff, Ariz.: The Northland Press, 1981); the Papago Tribe's own publications, *Tohono O'odham: Lives of the Desert People* (1984) and *Tohono O'odham: History of the Desert People* (1985); and Ruth Underhill's *Singing For Rain: The Song Magic of the Papago Indians of Southern Arizona* (Berkeley, Calif.: University of California Press, 1938).

Jack D. Forbes's work, *Warriors of the Colorado: The Yumas of the Quechan Nation and Their Neighbors* (Norman: University of Oklahoma Press, 1965), deals authoritatively with the Colorado River tribes. Interesting, also, is Douglas W. Schwartz's "The Havasupai, 600 A.D.–1955 A.D.: A Short Culture History" in *Plateau,* 28(4), 77–85, and Henry P. Ewing's "The Pai Tribes," edited by Robert C. Euler and Henry F. Dobyns in *Ethnohistory,* 7 (1), 61–80, 1960.

Works on the Apaches include Keith Basso's *The Cibecue Apache* (New York: Holt, Rinehart and Winston, 1970) and his *Western Apache Raiding and Warfare: From the Notes of Grenville Goodwin* (Tucson: The University of Arizona Press, 1971); and Donald E. Worcester's *The Apaches, Eagles of the Southwest* (Norman, University of Oklahoma Press, 1979).

Specialized works on Indian-white relations during the Hispanic period include Herbert E. Bolton's *Rim of Christendom* on Father Kino (Tucson: University of Arizona Press, 1985) and Elizabeth A. H. John's *Storms Brewed in Other Men's Worlds: The Confrontation of Indians, Spanish, and French in the Southwest, 1540–1795* (College Station: Texas

A and M Press, 1975) and Jack D. Forbes's *Apache, Navajo, and Spaniard* (Norman: University of Oklahoma Press, 1960).

For more recent Indian-white relations, see Jerry Kammer's *The Second Long Walk: The Navajo-Hopi Land Dispute* (Albuquerque: University of New Mexico Press, 1980) and Alvin M. Josephy, Jr.'s, *Now That the Buffalo's Gone* (New York: Alfred A. Knopf, 1982).

8. HISPANIC HERITAGE

For those interested in learning more about the history of Arizona, the available material can be divided into three groups according to historical period: Spanish exploration and settlement; Mexican independent rule; and the Anglo-American domination of the area.

For a closer look at what is today Arizona during the period of Spanish exploration and colonization (1539 – 1821), the best works include *El Antiguo Régimen: Los Reyes Católicos y los Austrias* (Madrid, Alianza Edit. 1973) by Antonio Domínguez Ortiz which provides a complete overview of all aspects of activity during this period; *Naufragios* (Mexico, edit. Premiá 1977) by Alvar Nuñez Cabeza de Vaca and other expeditionary chronicles such as those of the Fray Marcos de Niza, Pedro Castañeda de Nájera, and Antonio de Espejo expeditions which can be found in *La colección de documentos inéditos relativos al descubrimiento, conquista y colonización de las antiguas posesiones españolas en América y Oceanía* (1885 – 1900), edited by Joaquin F. Pacheco, F. Cárdenas y Luis Torres de Mendoza (Madrid, Manuel B. Quirós 1864). See also *The History of Arizona and New Mexico* in *The Works of Hubert Howe Bancroft* (San Francisco, 1889) which contains a compendium of the most salient points of the colonial history of the state.

For more information about the period of Mexican independent rule (1821 – 1853) see *A Documentary History of the Mexican Americans* (New York, Praeguer Publishers 1971) by Wayne Moquin and Charles van Doren and *El gran despojo* (México, ed. Diégenes 1976) by Manuel Median Castro. You can read nineteenth century prose in the intriguing diary of a native Tucsonan in *Diario de las operaciones militares . . .* (1838) by Jose Cosme Urrea.

To read about the coming of Anglo Americans to this region, it is helpful to divide areas of interest into social, political, economic, and cultural history. In the area of social history, one might read *Operation Wetback: The Mass Deportation of Mexican Undocumented Workers in 1954* (1980) by Juan García.

For political history see Rodolfo Acuna's *Occupied America* (San Francisco, Canfield Press 1972) and Carey McWilliam's *North from Mexico* (New York, Greenwood Press 1968). In the area of economics, the fundamental study is J. Gomez Quinones' and David Maciel's *La clase obrera en la historia de México: Al norte del Río Bravo (pasado lejano 1600 – 1930) y (pasado inmediato 1930 – 1980)*, a two-volume work published in 1981 (Mexico, edit. Siglo XXI).

For cultural and educational history Octavio Paz's "México y los Estados Unidos: Posiciones y contraposiciones" serves as an introductory article (published in *La Opinión*, Sept. 7, 1980). Also helpful are *Los Chicanos: Segregación y educación* (México, edit. Nueva Imagen, 1981) by Ellen Bilbao and M. A. Gallart, Rosemary Gipson's "The Mexican Performer: Pioneer Theater Artists of Tucson" published in *The Journal of Arizona History* in 1972, Nicolas Kanellos's "El teatro professional hispánico: Orígenes en el suroeste" published in *La Palabra* in 1980 and Tino Villanueva's *Chicanos: Antología histórica y literaria* (Mexico, F.C.E. 1980), and Cecil Robinson's *Mexico and the Hispanic Southwest in American Literature* (University of Arizona Press, Tucson, 1977).

For a unique look at the history of Arizona from the Mexican American point of view, read *El Sol,* a Spanish-language newspaper published in Phoenix since 1900.

9. ANGLO SETTLEMENT

There is very little good analytical history of Anglo Arizona. Jay J. Wagoner's two books—*Early Arizona: Prehistory to Civil War* and *Arizona Territory, 1863 – 1912: A Political History* (University of Arizona Press, Tucson, 1977, 1970)—provide a competent outline of the major personalities and events up to statehood. Lawrence Clark Powell's *Arizona: A Bicentennial History* (W. W. Norton & Company, New York) serves as an elegantly written meditation upon the course of human events within Arizona's boundaries. But a definitive economic and social history of Arizona since the Gadsden Purchase remains to be written.

Nevertheless, a few historians and anthropologists have begun to probe beneath Arizona's guntotin', cowboy mystique. The most incisive work to date is James Byrkit's *Forging the Copper Collar: Arizona's Labor-Management War of 1901 – 1921* (University of Arizona Press, Tucson, 1982). Byrkit argues that the copper companies, particularly Phelps Dodge, destroyed Arizona's progressive coalition of small businessmen and workers, turning the state into an internal colony of the corporations.

The second best book on late nineteenth and early

twentieth century Arizona remains unpublished: Joseph Park's master's thesis, "The History of Mexican Labor in Arizona during the Territorial Period" (Department of History, University of Arizona, 1961). The thesis, available from the University of Arizona's main library, details some unsettling truths about ethnic relations in Arizona.

A number of scholars have published excellent books and monographs on the ecological history of Arizona since it became a part of the United States. These works include Jay J. Wagoner's "History of the Cattle Industry in Southern Arizona, 1540–1940" (*Social Science Bulletin* No. 20, University of Arizona, Tucson, 1952); James R. Hastings's and Raymond M. Turner's classic *The Changing Mile* (University of Arizona Press, Tucson, 1965); Ronald Cooke's and Richard Reeves's *Arroyos and Environmental Change in the American South-West* (Clarendon Press, Oxford, 1976), and Charles Bowden's *Killing the Hidden Waters* (University of Texas Press, Austin, 1977). All these works discuss the hidden and not-so-hidden costs of Anglo Arizona's insatiable hunger for grasslands, farmlands, and water.

Robert Sharp provides a delightful first-hand account of life on one of Arizona's largest ranches in his *Big Outfit: Ranching on the Baca Float*. Courtland Smith's *The Salt River Project* (University of Arizona Press, Tucson, 1974) and Rich Johnson's *The Central Arizona Project* (University of Arizona Press, Tucson, 1977) describe the evolution of water control in modern Arizona. Bradford Luckingham's article "Urban Development in Arizona: The Rise of Phoenix" (*Journal of Arizona History* 22[2]:197–234, 1981) traces the outline of that metropolis's phenomenal growth, while

C. L. Sonnichsen's *Tucson: The Life and Times of an American City* (University of Oklahoma Press, Norman, 1982) furnishes a witty and informal history of Arizona's oldest non-Indian urban center.

The *Journal of Arizona History (JAH)* contains articles on nearly all aspects of the state's history. I have relied on Sue Abbey's "The Ku Klux Klan in Arizona, 1921–1925" (*JAH* 14[1]:10–30, 1973) and Dick Hall's "Ointment of Love: Oliver E. Comstock and Tucson's Tent City" (*JAH* 19[2]: 111–30, 1978). Other major scholarly journals that publish articles on Arizona history include *Arizona and the West, New Mexico Historical Review*, and the *Western Historical Quarterly*.

Charles Poston's rather fanciful account of his life and times can be found in *Building a State in Apache Land* (Aztec Press, Tempe, 1963). An even better and more colorful description of early Anglo Arizona is J. Ross Browne's *Adventures in the Apache Country* (University of Arizona Press, Tucson, 1974). Browne in particular conveys a sense of Arizona myth-making in process—rattlesnakes and ghost towns, Apache raids and doughty pioneers.

Finally, for a remarkable portrait of one of Arizona's most intriguing pioneer groups, turn to Charles S. Peterson's *Take Up Your Mission: Mormon Colonizing Along the Little Colorado River, 1870–1900* (University of Arizona Press, Tucson, 1973). If you have time for only two books, read Peterson and Byrkit. The two authors rather neatly split the state in half, Byrkit discussing the mining communities of the south, Peterson the agrarian communities of the north.

ABOUT THE AUTHORS

TOM MILLER is the author of *On the Border: Portraits of America's Southwestern Frontier* (UA Press, 1985) and *The Panama Hat Trail: A Journey From South America* and is coauthor of *The Interstate Gourmet: Texas and the Southwest*. His numerous reports about conflict and culture in the Southwest and Latin America have appeared in *The New York Times* and many other publications, as well as on national television and radio programs. He has also taught writing to students from grade-school level through college in both the United States and Mexico.

STEVEN W. CAROTHERS, president of SWCA, Inc., an environmental consulting firm in Flagstaff and Tucson, Arizona, has written on a variety of biological topics. His articles have appeared in *Natural History, American Zoologist, Wilson Bulletin, Journal of Environmental Management*, and other popular as well as scientific publications. His special research interests are focused on the Grand Canyon and Colorado River, and he is a coauthor of *Grand Canyon Birds* (UA Press).

ALVIN M. JOSEPHY, JR., has been a nationally known student of American Indian affairs and history for more than thirty years. Among his prize-winning books are *The Patriot Chiefs, The Nez Perce Indians and the Opening of the Northwest*, and *The Indian Heritage of America* which was a National Book Award nominee. A former editor-in-chief of American Heritage, he is now president of the National Council of the Museum of the American Indian in New York City and a contributing editor of *American West Magazine*.

ARMANDO MIGUÉLEZ is an assistant professor of Spanish at the University of Arizona. He is a native of Leon, Spain, who has spent the last several years studying the literary tradition of the Mexican Americans. His original research has produced a wealth of new documentation that traces the literary tradition of the Hispanic in the Southwest of the United States through 400 years of development. He received his doctorate in Spanish language and literature from Arizona State University in 1981.

GARY PAUL NABHAN is the author of *The Desert Smells Like Rain: A Naturalist in Papago Indian Country* and *Gathering the Desert* (UA Press, 1985), and of many popular and technical articles. An ethnobotanist and plant genetics specialist, he is cofounder of Native Seeds/SEARCH, an organization which maintains seed banks of indigenous southwestern plants. Since receiving his doctorate in 1983, he has held a research position at the University of Arizona's Office of Arid Land Studies.

CECIL SCHWALBE has been herpetologist for the Arizona Game and Fish Department since 1984. He has taught classes on the ecology and herpetology of the Southwest and has consulted on national and regional films, videotapes, and articles on southwestern natural history. He received his doctorate in zoology from the University of Arizona in 1981.

THOMAS SHERIDAN is the author of *Los Tucsonenses: The Mexican Community of Tucson from the Gadsden Purchase to World War II* (UA Press, 1986), as well as of numerous articles about the history and anthropology of northwestern Mexico and the southwestern United States. He received his doctorate in anthropology at the University of Arizona in 1983, and from 1982 to 1984 he was director of the Mexican Heritage Project at the Arizona Heritage Center. Since 1985 he has been assistant ethnohistorian at the Arizona State Museum.

LARRY STEVENS is the author of *The Colorado River in Grand Canyon: A Guide*, and has been a biologist and commercial whitewater guide in Grand Canyon since 1973. He has written popular and scientific articles on subjects ranging from river-running skills to the insect pests of Hopi Indian stored foods. A doctoral candidate in ecology at Northern Arizona University in Flagstaff, Stevens has carried out research on water in the Great Basin Desert.

STEPHEN TRIMBLE's commitment to writing and photography grew out of his experiences as a park ranger in the Southwest. Among his many books on western national parks and landscape are *The Bright Edge: A Guide to the National Parks of the Colorado Plateau; Longs Peak: A Rocky Mountain Chronicle;* and *The Sagebrush Ocean: Biogeography of the Great Basin*. He was primary photographer and interviewer for the soundtrack of "Our Voices, Our Land," the audio-visual introduction to the permanent collection on Southwest Indians at the Heard Museum, Phoenix.

PETER WARREN has studied the plants and animals of the arid parts of Arizona and northern Mexico since the 1970s. His interest in vegetation ecology ranges from rings around kangaroo rat mounds to zonation on mountainsides in Grand Canyon National Park. As research assistant at the University of Arizona's Office of Arid Lands Studies, he has authored many technical reports about vegetation of the Southwest, and he has taught classes about the natural history of desert areas.

INDEX

(Page numbers in italics refer to illustrations.)

Acacia
spindly, 117
white-thorn, 121, 123
Agave, 104, 139, *141,* 142, 151
Age of Fishes, 149
Agriculture, 96, 98, 113, 209, 223,
236 – 43, 247, 256 – 58, 264. *See
also* Water projects, irrigation
and the Indians, 95, 167 – 70, 173, 178
workers in, *235, 259*
Agua Fria River, 144
AiResearch, 98, 247
Ajo Mountains, 32 – 33, 90
Ajo Peak, 32
Ajo perityle, 33
Ak-Chin Indian Reservation, 188, 190
Akimel O'odham Indians, 180
Alamo Canyon, 41
Alarcón, Hernando, 255
Alfalfa, 96, 98, 256, 265
Alianza Hispanoamericana, 194, 207
All American Protective League, 211
Allosaurus (dinosaur), 54
Alluring Arizona (Nelson), 252
Allyn, Joseph Pratt, 74
Alpine zone. *See* Tundra
Aluminum Corporation of America, 247
Amargosa River, 72
American Federation of Labor, 232
A-Mountain, 212
Anaconda, 274
Anasazi Indians, 135, 167 – 71, 173, 175
Anglos, 158, 247
Hispanic relations with, 200, 206 – 7,
210 – 13, 226 – 27
Indian relations with, 74, 173, 177, 179,
182 – 83, 186, 226, 244
Animal life, 262. *See also* Birds;
Fish; Insects; Lizards; Snakes
in the Chihuahuan Desert, 125, 127,
129 – 31
on the Colorado Plateau, 62, 70
in the Mojave Desert, 80 – 81, 83, 85,
102
in mountain regions, 28, 31 – 32,
34 – 35, 41 – 43
prehistoric, 78, 89, 92, 123, 149,
151, 165. *See also* Dinosaurs;
Fossils
in the Sonoran Desert, 92 – 93, 95,
102 – 4, 107
Anthel, 76, 80
Anthropologists and anthropology, 134,
138
Anti-miscegenation laws, 10
Antler Orogeny, 77
Apache County, 9

Apache Indian Reservation, 154
Apache Indians, 117, 144, 155, 161, 178
Athapascan, 175
ceremonies of, *133, 156,*
173 – 74, *175*
Changing Woman, legend of, 132,
136, 142, 153
Chiricahua, 135, 171 – 72, 180,
182 – 83, 221
Cibecue, 184
contemporary economy of, 190 – 191
and migration to Arizona, 134, 171
Northern Tonto, 183 – 84
and raiding, 114, 139, 173, 181 – 82, 199,
220 – 21
San Carlos Tontos, 184
Western, 183 – 84, 221
White Mountain, 184
Apache plume, 70
Apachería, 134, 136, 144, 149, 153, 219,
226
Apache-Sitgreaves National Forests, 36
Aquarius Mesa, 142
Aquarius Mountains, 76
Archaeologists and archaeology, 92, 95,
111, 165, 167
Archaic period, 167
Architecture, 272 – 73
Arizona, 158. *See also* Animal life;
Vegetation
climate of, 23, 25, 39. *See also*
Rainfall
and Constitutional Convention
(1910), 229
economy of, 201, 209, 223, 228, 235,
247
maps of, *3, 15, 159*
multi-ethnic background of, 158,
160 – 61, 229.
See also Anglos; Blacks;
Hispanics; Indians of the
Southwest; Jews
name origin of, 177
political boundaries of, 49 – 50
population of, 163, 264
promotion of, 5 – 7
sky of, 50, 76, 260. *See also*
Astronomy
songs about, 11
and statehood (1912), 2, 5 – 6, 14
territory of, 2, 200 – 201, 221
Arizona Biltmore Hotel, 98
Arizonac ("little spring"), 177
Arizona City. *See* Yuma
Arizona Cotton Growers Association,
209
Arizona cypress, 38 – 39, 41, 141 – 42

Arizona Place Names, 255
Arizona Republic, 7, 210
Arizona rosewood, 33, 38
Arizona Strip, 64, 74, 171
"Arizona—The Sun-Kissed Land"
(territorial song), 11
Arizona walnut, 62, 142
Arroyo, 17, 236, 239, 277. *See also*
Washes
Art and artists, 48, 95, 217. *See also*
Basketry; Pottery
Asia and Asians, 161, 209, 244, 258.
See also Chinese Americans
Asparagus, 256 – 58
Aspen, *19,* 28, 32
Astronomy, 153, 260
Athapascan Indians. *See* Apache
Indians, Athapascan
Austin, Mary, 164
Awatovi, 179
Aztec Land and Cattle Company, 223,
238

Baboquivari Mountains, 39
Baboquivari Peak, 17, 90, *166*
Bagdad (mining town), 139, 149
Baja California, 92, 214
Barberry, 92, 139
Barfoot Lookout, 117 – 118
Barrel cactus, 79, 92
The Barrio, *6,* 204
Basalt, 58 – 59
Basin Province, 17, 77, 90, 100, 151
Basketry, 167, 190
Bayham, Frank, 95, 109
Beale, Edward Fitzgerald, 18, 74
Bear Canyon, 41
Beardtongue. *See* Penstemon
Bears, 78, 151
grizzly, 31, 62
Beaver, 62
Beaver Creek, 62
Beets, 256, 265
Belluschi, Pietro, 273
Berger, J.M., 111
Betatakin, 169
Between Sacred Mountains (Rock Point
School), 8
Beyond the Hundredth Meridian
(Stegner), 71
Bicycling, 68
Bidahochi formation, 52, 55
Big Sandy River, 144
wash, 72
Big Surf, *266*
Bill Williams Mountains, 58, 171
Bill Williams River, 74, 144, 171

Biologists and biology, 22 − 23, 28, 33
Birch, 28
Birds, 31, 36, 60, 71, 89, 107, 262. *See also* names of specific birds
   desert regions, 76, 80 − 81, 83, 103 − 4
   evolution, 22 − 23
Birdwatching, 33
Bisbee, 11, 120, 201, 207, 229, *233,* 234, 274, 277
Bisbee Deportation (1917), 230 − 31, *232*
Bisbee Workman's Loyalty League, 231
Bison, 78, 165, 171
Black, John A., 5
Black Canyon City, 136
Black Draw, 121
Black Hills, 151
Blackjack Ben, 263
Black Jack Canyon, *135*
Black Mesa, 50, 52, 54 − 55, 162, 185
Black Mountains, 72
Black River, 135, 144, 148
Blacks, 98, 138, 158, 212, 215, 244
Blacksmith shop, *238*
Blue Ridge Reservoir, 144
Blue River, *147,* 148
Bobcats, *14,* 70, 262
Bobtail pigeons, 36
Boley, Ray, 108
Bolles, Don, 98
Bootettix grasshopper, 76, 85
Boothill Graveyard, 234
Bosque Redondo Indian Reservation, 183
Boulder Canyon Act (1928), 243
Boulder Canyon, Colorado, 241
Bourke, John G., 117, 135, 140, 150
Bowden, Charles, 223
Box elder, 25, 62, 142
Brichta, Bernabe, 207 − 8
Bridalveil Falls, *38*
Bristlecone pine, 28, *29,* 85
Brittlebush, 85, 92 − 93, 107
Brontosaurus (dinosaur), 54
Browne, J. Ross, 2, 219, 227
Bullhead City, 253
Bulrushes, 75
Burch, Carley, 151
Burro Creek, 72
Burroweed, 114, 142
Bursage, 76, 85, 90
Byrkit, James, 228, 232

Cabbage, 256, 265
Cabeza Prieta Wildlife Refuge, 113, *109*
Cactus. *See* names of specific cacti; Vegetation
Cactus wren, 76, 89, 103, *105*
Calhoun, J.O., 231 − 32
California, 2, 72, 199, 234, 258, 262, 265

Indians of, 170, 182, 191
   Mojave Desert in, 74, 79
   overland trails in, 156, 221, 255
   Sonoran Desert in, 92
Call of the Canyon (Grey), 151
Camels
   military use of, 18, 74
   prehistory of, 78, 151, 165
Cameron Trading Post, 52
Camp Verde, 149 − 50, 184
Canyon de Chelly, 49, 52, *54,* 169, 183
Canyon Lands, 45 − 47, 49
CAP. *See* Central Arizona Project
Carleton, James H., 183
Carpenter, Edwin F., 260
Carrasco, José, 201
Carrillo, Leopoldo, 236
Carrillo Elementary School, 204
Carrillo Gardens, 203
   concert scene, *205*
Carrizo Mountains, 50
Carson, Kit, 153, 183
Castillo, Mae Chee, 178
Castle Mountains, 90, 92
Castle Rock, 274
Cataract Canyon, 192
Catclaw, 70, 92 − 93, 139
Cathedral of St. John the Divine, 248
Cather, Willa, 50, 59
Catholics, 180, 212, 215, 244, 265. *See also* Dominicans; Franciscans; Jesuits
Cattails, 75
Cattle, 32, 89, 247. *See also* Ranchers and ranching
Cenezoic era, 66, 85, 149
Central Arizona Project (CAP), 86, 98, 190, 240, 253
   workers in the, *268*
Century plant, 104
Cerbat Mountains, 72, 142
Cerro Colorado, 226
Chandler, 240, 244, 264 − 65
Chandler, Alexander J., 264 − 65
Chandler Heights, *86*
The Changing Mile (Hastings and Turner), 222
Chaparral, 31, 38 − 39, 41, 136, 139 − 40, 153
Chemehuevis Indians, 191
   Shoshonean, 74
Chicano movement, 215 − 17
Chicken scratch music, 108
Chihuahua, 114, 117, 167, 201
Chihuahuan Desert. *See also* Animal life; Vegetation
   boundaries, 33 − 34, 114, 128 − 29, 134
   climate, 17, 117 − 18
Chimichanga, 214
Chinese Americans, 10, 161, 204
   portrait of, *160*

Chinle formation, 52 − 53, 149
Chinle Hills, *55*
Chinle Wash, 50, 53
Chiricahua Indians. *See* Apache Indians, Chiricahua
Chiricahua Mountains, 33, 35, 117 − 118
   Chiricahua Peak in, 118
   Lookout Point in, *119*
Cholla teddy bear cactus, 79, 85, 90, *101*
Chorizanthe (buckwheat), 76
Christianity, 95, 165, 167, 177, 185, 197
Chuckwagon, *220*
Chuckwalla, *81,* 102
Chulo. *See* Coatimundi
Church of Jesus Christ of Latter Day Saints. *See* Mormons
Chuska Mountains, 43, 50, 58
Cibecue Indians. *See* Apache Indians, Cibecue
Cibecue Mountains, 171
Citrus fruits, 240, 243, 258
Civilian Conservation Corps, 262
Clarkdale, 149, 184
Clark's nutcracker, 60
Claypool-Kinney Bill, 210
Cliffrose, 139
Clifton, 36, 149, 154, 190, 201, 229, 271
Climate. *See* Arizona; Rainfall
Coal, 54 − 55, 185, 193
Coal Mine Canyon, 53
Coatimundi, *35*
Cochise County, 9
   Jewish population of, 234
Cochise Head, *115*
Cochise Indians, 167 − 68
Cocomaricopa Indians, 256
Coelophysis (dinosaur), 53
Colorado, 2, 28, 44, 49, 199, 241, 248
The Colorado, 46
Colorado chub fish, 125
Colorado Plateau, 17, 58, 68, 71, 144, 149, 222, 238. *See also* Animal life; Vegetation
   boundries of, 44, 57, 64, 72, 134, 136
Colorado River, 34, 44 − 47, 50, 62, 144, 237, 262
   exploration of, 18, 74
   Grand Canyon section of, 63 − 64, 69
   and the Indians, 165, 171, 181 − 82, 191
   marshland scene on the , *75*
   Mohave Desert section of, 72, *73,* 74 − 77
   naming of, 255 − 56
   river running in, 49, 248, *250*
   Sonoran Desert section of, 92, 100, 113
   and water resources, 240 − 43, 248 − 55, 271
Colorado River Basin, 48

Colorado River Compact, 241–42
Colorado River Indian Reservation, 191
Colorado Storage Project, 248
Columbine, 67
Columbus, New Mexico, 231
Community Development Block
    Grants, 266
Conchos Indians, 117
Conrad, Joseph, 277
Cooke, Col. Phillip St. George, 220–21
Coolidge Air Force training field, 262
Coolidge Dam, 144
Copper, 120, 154–55, 158, 190, 201, 207,
    227–32, 247
Copper Queen mine, 274
    smelter, 228
Copper Queen Hotel, 274
Copper Queen Mining Company, 228
Coppery-tailed trogon, 33
Coral beans, 114
Cordes Junction, 142
Corn, 139, 235–36, 265, 271
Coronado, Francisco Vasquez de, 74,
    134, 196–97, 255
Cotton, 98, 209–10, 240, 243, 247, 265
Cottonwood (town), 149
Cottonwoods (trees), 25, 28, 62, 80, 142
Cottonwood Wash, 74
Cougars, 70
Covered Wells, 90
Cowboys, 138–39, 221,
    223, 224–25
Coyote gourds, 104
Coyotes, 70, 76, 89, 102, 262
Coyotes (mixed descent), 195
Creosotebush, 9–10, 31, 44, 72, 76, 83,
    85, 87, 90, 107, 121, 128,
    136, 139
Cretaceous period, 52, 54
Crinoids, 123
Crook, George, 117, 121, 135, 184
Crook Trail, 150
Crops, 95, 98, 139, 167, 209–10,
    235–36, 240, 243, 247, 256–58,
    265, 271
Cross, Edward, 6
Crystal Creek, 70

Daily Arizona Miner, 10
Dams. See Water projects
Darwin, Charles, 22–23
Datura, 72, 81
Davis, Arthur, 241
Davis, Lew, 8
Davis Dam, 253–54
Davis-Monthan Air Force Base:
    aircraft maintenance scene, 261
Dawes Allotment Act (1887), 185
Death Comes for the Archbishop
    (Cather), 50
Deer, 70, 139, 262

Defiance Plateau, 50, 52
Desert, 17, 86, 111. See also
    Chihuahuan Desert; Mojave
    Desert; Sonoran Desert
criteria for defining the, 128
evolution of the, 23, 25–27
The Desert (Van Dyke), 245
Desert bighorn sheep. See Sheep,
    desert bighorn
Devonian period, 149
Díaz, Melchior, 255
Díaz, Porfirio, 209
Dinetah, 173
Dinosaur National Monument, 44
Dinosaurs, 50, 52–54, 67
    tracks of, 56
Dolomite, 77
Dominicans, 197
Dook'o'ooslid, 18. See also Mount
    Humphreys
"Dos Mujeres" (photograph), 208
Douglas, 121, 229, 234, 263
    barrio scene in, 6
Douglas, Walter, 230, 231, 232
Dragoon Mountains, 117–18, 234
Drought, 107, 113, 129, 222, 239–40
Dude ranches, 98, 247
Duels, 6–7
Dutton, Clarence, 44

Earth First!, 249
East Clear Creek, 62, 144
Easter ceremony (Yaqui), 177, 197
East Kaibab Monocline, 63
Echo Cliffs, 49, 53
Ecologists and ecology, 69, 107, 136,
    140–42, 249, 252
Education, 210, 215–16
Ehrenberg, Herman, 226
El Capitan Pass, 68
El Crepúsculo de la Libertad, 199
El Dorado Canyon, 74
Elections, 207–8, 229
Electricity, 252–54
    hydro, 240, 248
El Fronterizo, 161
El Tucsonense, 202
Emancipation Proclamation, 161
Emanuel, Abraham Hyman, 234
Environmental concerns, 249, 252
Eocene epoch, 77
Erosion, 149, 151
Escalante, Fray Silvestre Vélez de, 49
Escudilla Mountains, 62
Espejo, Antonio de, 134, 196, 201
Euraisian cheatgrass, 62
Evolution, 22–23, 25–27

Farfán de los Godos, Marcos, 134
Farmers, 199, 237, 253
Feldspar, 155
Federal reclamation project, 235

Films. See Motion pictures
Finger Rock, 40
Fink, Augusta, 164
Fire and firefighters
    and chaparral, 140–42
    control practices of, 36, 60–62, 129
    and manzanita, 141
First Mesa, 179
Fish, 70, 125
Flagstaff, 20, 68, 223, 271
    climate of, 14, 17
    ecology of, 28, 31, 57–60
    Indian population of, 168, 170, 172,
        186
    observatories in, 48, 260
Flooding, 113, 240
    of the Colorado River, 70, 354–55
    flash, 17, 53, 79, 111
    floodplains and, 235–36, 239,
        254–55
    prehistoric, 62
    of Rillito River, 255
Floodplains. See Flooding
Florence, 5, 155, 190, 218–19
Florence Junction, 136
Flores, Blas y Pauline, 216
Fores, Carlota, 214
Flycatcher, Sulphur-bellied, 33
Forging the Copper Collar (Byrkit),
    228
Fort Apache, 150, 178
    Indian reservation, 135–36, 138, 184,
        190. See also White Mountain
        Apache Indian Reservation
Fort Bowie, 114, 117, 128–29
Fort Huachuca, 227, 234, 274
Fort Mojave Indian Reservation, 191
Fort Whipple, 183
    as territorial capital, 200
Fossils, 52–54, 123, 149, 151
Four Corners, 8, 44, 169
Four Peaks, 36, 147
Fradkin, Philip, 67
Franciscans, 180, 182, 197
Fred Lawrence Whipple Observatory,
    260
Fredonia, 139, 263
Frizzell, Kenneth, 272
Frogs
    Tarahumara, 35

GABA. See Greater Arizona Bicycling
    Association
Gadsden, James, 200
Gadsden Purchase (1853), 100, 182,
    199–200, 218, 225, 235
Galapagos Islands, 22–23
Galiuro Mountains, 222
Galleta grass, 60
Garcés, Francisco, 180
García, Doña, 161
Gentry, Howard Scott, 139

Geologic time, 52 – 54, 63 – 65, 66, 77, 85, 140, 148 – 49, 155
Geologists, 44, 50, 63, 111, 136, 149
Geology, 14, 17, 153
  of the Colorado Plateau, 52
  of interior Arizona, 148 – 49
  of the Mojave Desert, 77
  of the Sonoran Desert, 113
Geronimo, 117, 121, 183
Gila Bend, 25, 178, 190
  gunnery range, 262
Gila City, 227
Gila Monster, 89
Gila Mountains, 136
Gila River, 2, 145, 199, 221, 227, 255
  and the Indians, 100, 117, 144, 168, 170 – 71, 180 – 82, 190
  and irrigation, 144, 151, 239 – 41
Gila River Indian Reservation, 8, 188
Gila Valley, 142, 149
Gila woodpecker, 103, 105
Glaciers, 27, 58, 77 – 78, 126, 140. See also Ice Age
Glen Canyon, 46 – 47, 49, 53, 249
Glen Canyon Dam, 69 – 70, 71, 248, 252, 254
Glendale, 240, 244
Globe, 8, 17, 68, 139, 149, 154, 228 – 29
Gloria de los Heroes de la Patria Mexicana, 203
Gold, 75, 153 – 55, 183, 221, 225 – 27
Gold rush, 256
Gompers, Samuel, 231
Goodyear Aircraft, 98, 164, 247
Graham family. See Pleasant Valley War
Grama grass, 60, 116, 129, 131
Granados, Rafael, 216
Grand Canyon, 14, 17, 27, 43 – 45, 57, 65, 74, 132, 248, 254
  ecology, 69 – 71
  geographic boundries of the, 47
  geology of the, 62 – 64, 66 – 67, 71
  Havasu Falls, 69
  and the Indians, 170 – 71, 181, 192
  Jaidito Canyon, 12 – 13
  Shoshone Point, 1
  South Kaibab trail, 66
  Supai, 188
Grand Canyon National Park, 192
Gran Desierto, 107
Grand Wash Cliffs, 46, 63 – 64, 78, 136
Granite, 37, 64, 71, 114, 140, 154 – 155
Granite Dells, 149
Granite Reef diversion dam, 240
Grasses. See names of specific grasses; Vegetation
Greasewood, 62
Great Basin, 37, 60, 171, 173
Great Basin Desert, 31 – 32, 57, 72, 77
Great Depression, 98, 138, 212 – 13
Greater Arizona Bicycling Association (GABA), 68

Great Plains, 44
Greene Cattle Company office, 224
Greenlee County, 9
Green Valley, 11, 277
Grey, Zane, 148, 151, 223
Groundwater. See Water
Guadalupe, 177, 265 – 67, 269
Guaymas, 6, 199
Gulf of California, 17, 64, 74, 77, 168, 180

Hakataya Indians, 135, 170 – 71
Hano, 179 – 80
Havasu Creek, 67
Havasu Falls, 69
Havasupai Indians, 67, 71, 171, 180, 256
  contemporary economy of the, 192
Hawks
  marsh, 104
  red-tailed, 36, 89
Hayden, Carl, 243
Hayes, Ira, 8
Health-seekers, 245, 247
Heard, Dwight, 98
Heat adaptation, 80 – 81, 83
  of plants, 104
Heintzelman, Samuel, 226
Heintzelman Mine, 201
Hispanics. See also Anglos, Hispanic relations; Chicano movement; Mexican Americans; Mexicans
  and the arts, 269
  and assimilation, 211 – 12
  employment of, 201, 207, 209, 226, 258
  fiesta days of, 203
  income of, 215
  Indian relations with, 182
Hodge, Hiram, 245
Hoffman, Abraham, 212
Hogans, 172, 176
Hohokam culture, 95 – 96, 135, 168, 170, 180, 239, 244
Holbrook, 55, 223
Hooker, Henry, 222
Hoover Dam, 253 – 54
Hopi Buttes, 50, 55
Hopi Cultural Center, 270
Hopi Indian Reservation, 27, 50, 270
Hopi Indians, 8, 54, 71, 191
  language of, 171
  Navajo conflict with, 193, 269 – 70
  portrait of, 163
  pottery of, 186
  religion of, 18, 58, 63, 162 – 63, 165, 179 – 80, 185 – 86, 270
Hopi Mesas, 270
Horsecamp Canyon, 143
Hotevilla, 162, 185
Hotevilla Bacavi Community School, 270

Huachuca Mountains, 33, 35
Hualapai Indians, 71, 74, 134, 144, 165, 171, 192 – 93, 270
Hualapai Mountains, 31 – 32, 72, 142
Hudges, M.A., 212
Hughes, Bill, 223
Hughes, Mack, 223
Hughes, Sam, 236
Hughes, Skeeter, 223
Hummingbirds, 33, 41, 104
Humphreys Peak, 58
Hunt, George W.P., 218, 229, 230
Hydroelectricity. See Electricity, hydro

Ice Age, 61, 70, 77 – 78, 92, 165 – 66
Immigration, 208 – 9, 211
Imperial National Wildlife Refuge, 262
Indian Reorganization Act (1934), 185
Indians of the Southwest, 98, 158, 256. See also Anglos, Indian relations; names of specific tribes; Paleo-Indians
  assimilation of, 185 – 86
  and the Central Arizona Project, 254
  language of, 100, 171
  migration to Arizona of, 164 – 65, 197
  music of, 108
  religious beliefs of, 162 – 65, 177
  reservation lands of, 178, 190, 221, 253, 269 – 70
Industrial Workers of the World (IWW/Wobblies), 230 – 32
Industry, 98, 247, 264
Insects, 76, 85, 88 – 89, 95, 130
Irrigation. See Water projects
Ives, Joseph Christmas, 72, 74
IWW. See Industrial Workers of the World

Jácome family portrait, 211
Jaidito Canyon, 12 – 13
James, George Wharton, 264
Javelina, 103
Jerome, 11, 149, 154 – 55, 226, 229, 231
Jesuits, 177, 180, 197
Jews, 234, 244
Joe Miguel and The Blood Brothers (music group), 108
Johnson, Charles, 74
Jojoba, 90, 139
Joshua trees, 44, 78, 79, 85, 88 – 89

Kachina ceremony, 186
Kaibab Plateau, 58, 63 – 64, 70
Kaibab Upwarp, 64
Kaighn, Richard, 256 – 58
Kayenta, 53, 57
Kayenta Formation, 53
Keet Seel, 169

Kennedy, John F., 215
Kingman, 31, 231, 263
Kino, Eusebio, 180
Kitt Peak, 90, 260
Kofa Mountains, 32
Kofa National Wildlife Refuge, 262, *263*
Kuehn, John, 274
Ku Klux Klan, 211, 244

La Cuarenta ("The Forty"), 265
Lai Ngan, 161
Lake Bidahochi, 55, 64
Lake Havasu, 253 – 54, *267*
Lake Mead, 17, 69 – 70, 72, 74, 77,
    253 – 54
Lake Mohave, 253 – 54
Lake Powell, 47, 49, 70, 249,
    253, 254
    Padre Bay on, *46*
The Land of Journey's Ending (Austin),
    164
Lange, Dorothea, 8
Lanner, Ronald, 60
Las Cruces, 117, 128 – 29
Lava, 55, 62, 107
Las Vegas, 14, 253
Lee's Ferry, 44, *45,* 46 – 47, 49,
    70, 237
Leopold, Aldo, 62, 140
Lettuce growing, 258, 265
Libraries, 98, 274 – 76
Life zones, 28, 58
Ligas Protectora Latina (LPL), 210. *See
    also* Mutual aid societies; Unions
Limestone, 77, 123, 127, 140, 155
    Kaibab, 47, 66 – 67, 151
    Muav, 71
    redwall, 67, 71
Little Colorado River, 49 – 50, 55,
    57 – 64, 138, 144, 237
Little Colorado Valley, 50, 60 – 62
Little Hatchet Mountains, 125
Livestock, 62, 129, 236. *See also*
    Cattle; Sheep
Lizards, 81, 83, 85, 89, 102, 118,
    125, 127, 130 – 31
Loews Ventana Canyon, 272
"The Long Walk," 183
Lord Jim (Conrad), 277
Lost Dutchman Mine, 155
Lowe, Charles H., Jr., 127, 136
Lowell, Percival, 260
Lowell Observatory, 260
Lower Granite Gorges, 63 – 64
Low Rider, *217*
Lukachukai Mountains, 43, 50
Lumholtz, Carl, 107
Lunar and Planetary Laboratory, 260
Lupine, *59*

MacDonald, Peter, 269
Made in America, 9

Mammoths, 78, 89, 123, 165
Manzanita, 139, 141
Maple, *43*
Marble Canyon, 46, 63 – 64
Maricopa County, 5, 239, 241, 244
Maricopa Indians, 171, 188
Marshlands, *75*
Mather Point, 63
Maxwell, George H., 241
Mazatzal Mountains, 43, 142, 147
Mazatzal Revolution, 149
McClintock, James H., *219*
McCormick, Richard C., 4
McFarland, Ernest, 243
McGee, W.J., 111
McGroarty, John S., 254
McNary, 138
McWilliams, Carey, 198
Meadow vole. *See under* Rodents
Melons, 256, 265
Merriam, C. Hart, 28, 58
Merriam's elk, 31
Merriam's Transition zones, 28
Mesa Verde, 44
Mesa Verde Rock Group, 52, 54
Mesozoic era, 52, 66, 149
Mesquite, 70, 80, 92, *93,* 103,
    121, 123, 129 – 30, 139, 142, 168
Mestizos, 195, 199
Metamorphic rocks, 64, 66, 149, 155
Meteor Crater, 62
Mexican Americans, 98, 265. *See also*
    Hispanics
Mexican American War (1846 – 48), 153,
    182, 199 – 200
Mexican Hay Lake, *134*
Mexicans, 98, 158, 265. *See also*
    Hispanics; Mexican Americans;
    Mexico; Yaqui Indians
    and the Indians, 173, 181 – 83
Mexican poppies, *94*
Mexican War of Independence
    (1810 – 21), 198, 209
    celebration of, *212*
Mexico, 167, 254, 269. *See also*
    Mexicans; Mexican War of
    Independence
    ecology of, 37, 92, 95, 100, 109, 114,
        127, 142
    and the Indians, 167 – 68, 177
    and influence in Arizona, 181 – 82,
        195,197, 205, 224, 265
Miami, Arizona, 149, 154, 229
Mice. *See* Rodents
Middle Granite Gorges, 63
Middle Holocene period, 93
Middle Verde Indian Reservation, 184
Midnight on the Desert (Priestley),
    132
Military, the, 201, 205, 256, 258, 261 – 62
Miners. *See* Mining, miners and
    prospectors

Mining, *154,* 162, 223, 247, 253
    and company towns, 227, 274
    development of, 225 – 33
    early exploration of, 74 – 75, 153
    Hispanic interests in, 199 – 201,
        205 – 6, 209 – 10
    miners and prospectors, 139, 153,
        182 – 83
Miocene epoch, 140
Mockingbirds, 22 – 23
Moenkopi formation, 149
Mogollon culture, 135, 167 – 68, 170, 173
Mogollon Rim, 36, 57 – 60, 62, 64, 68,
    100, 139, 142, 144, 147, 149 – 51
    upland forest scene, *148*
Mohave County, 9, 74
Mohave Indians, 72, 74, 171, 191
Mohave rattlesnake, 35, *87*
Mojave Desert, 74. *See also under*
    Animal life; Vegetation
    climate of, 17, 77 – 79
    ecology of, 17, 31, 44, 57, 67, 72, 102,
        142
    geology of, 77 – 79, 134
    Indian population in, 171, 191
Monsoons, 60, 62
Montezuma Castle, 170
Monument Upwarp, 52
Monument Valley, *9,* 14, 49, 52, 55
Moore, Alonzo "Lonnie," *120*
Morenci, 36, 139, 144, 149, 154, 190,
    229, 271
Mormons, 46, 74, 85, 138 – 39, 220, 244
    as farmers, 62, 237 – 39
    polygamist villages of the, 64
Morning glories, *93*
Morrow, William, 231
Motion pictures, 9, 14, 173
Motorola, 98, 247, 265
Mountain lion, *150*
Mountains, 17
    ecological variations of, 18, 20 – 22
    religious significance of, 18
    temperature variations in, 21 – 22
Mount Baldy, 28, 58, 148
Mount Graham, hiking scene, *21*
Mount Hopkins, 260
Mount Humphreys, 18, *20*
Mount Lemmon, 37 – 38
Mount Wrightson, *26*
Mowry, Sylvester, 6 – 7, 226
Muddy Creek formation, 77
Mulattos, 195, 197
Mule deer, *61,* 62, 95
Mutual aid societies, 207, 209 – 10. *See
    also Ligas protectoras;* Unions

Nabhan, Gary, 86
National Reclamation Act (1902), 98,
    239 – 40
Native Americans. *See* Indians of the
    Southwest

Native food plants, 60, 92, 95, 139, 168
Navajo Community College, 193
Navajo Country, 9, 45, 49 – 50, 52 – 55, 60, 66
Navajo Indian Reservation, 8, 27, 48, 62, 271
Navajo Indians, 17, 135, 139, 175 – 76, 270
   assimilation of, 71, 161, 185
   contemporary economy of, 193
   Hopi conflict with, 193, 269
   migration to Arizona of, 171, 173, 191
   raiding among, 180, 182 – 83
   religion of, 18, 50, 58
   Tribal Council of, 178
   portraits of, *176, 189, 191*
Navajo Mountains, 50
Navajo Power Plant, 55
Needles, 72, 191
The Needles (mountains), 76
Nelson, William Hamilton, 252
Nelson, Willie, 184
Nevada, 2, 72, 77 – 78, 171, 199, 253
New Mexico, 18, 36, 117, 144, 201, 231, 241, 248
   ecology of, 28, 127 – 29, 142
   geology of, 44, 149 – 50
   Indian population of, 135, 170 – 71, 173, 179, 183, 193, 270
   prehistory of, 125, 167
   territory of, 2, 199 – 200
New Oraibi, 162
New Pascua, 177
New Times, 7
A Night on Bald Mountain, 62
Nogales, 68, 111, 160 – 61, 177, 218, 277
Northern Tonto Indians. *See* Apache Indians, Northern Tonto
North from Mexico (McWilliams), 198
Nuvatukyaovi, 18. *See also* Mount Humphreys

Oak, *39,* 93, 114, 141
   Arizona white, 139, 141
   Emory, 123, 141
   evergreen, 25, 33, 38
   Gambel, 60
   Mexican blue, 123
Oak Creek, 62, 151
Oak Creek Canyon, 151, *279*
Oatman, 76, 85
Observatories, 48, 260
Ocotillo, 37, 76, 90, 104, 121, 123
Of Mice and Men (Steinbeck), 277
Old Oraibi, 185, 270
Old Pascua, 177, 214
Old Walpi Pueblo, *181*
Oñate, Juan de, 256
On the Border With Crook (Bourke), 117, 135, 140
Opatas Indians, 117
Oraibi, 170, 179

Organized labor. *See* Unions
Organ Pipe Cactus National Monument, 32, 90
Orientals. *See* Asia and Asians; Chinese Americans
ORO Ranch, 224
Oshara tradition, 167, 169
Owl, 76, *90,* 99

Pachuco movement, 213 – 15
Padre Bay, *46*
Painted Desert, 27, 48 – 50, 52 – 53, 57
   Chinle Hills, in the, *55*
Paiute Indians, 64, 256
   Southern, 74, 171, 175
Paleo-Indians, 92, 165 – 67
Paleontologists, 53 – 54, 123
Paleozoic era, 52, 63 – 64, 77, 149, 155
Palm Canyon, *112*
Paloverde, 25, 31, 37, 76, 90, 95, *99*
Papago Indians, 95, 107, 113, 117, 180 – 81, 183, 214, 260
   assimilation of, 161
   contemporary music of, 108
   language of, 171
   name change of, 190. *See also* Tohono O'odham
   religion of, 90, 164 – 65
   reservation lands belonging to, 90, 177 – 78, 182, 188, 190
Paradise Valley, 108
   country club scene, *10*
Paria Canyon, *51*
Paria River, 49, 63
Park, Levin, 202 – 3
Parker, 253 – 54
Parker Dam, *252,* 253 – 54
Pascua Yaqui Indian Reservation, 269
Patagonia, 226, 277
Pattie, James Ohio, 74, 153
Paul Winter Consort (music group), 248, *249*
Payson, 68, 136, 149, 184, 225
Pax, Octavio, 197
Peccary. *See* Javelina
Peloncillo Mountains, 43, 117, 121
Penstemon, *18,* 41
Peridots, 191
Peterson, Charles, 237 – 38
Petrified Forest National Park, 49, 52 – 53
Petroglyphs, 95, *162*
Pfeffercorn, Ignaz, 100
Pfeifer, Ed, *36*
Phelps, Dodge and Company. *See* Phelps Dodge Corporation
Phelps Dodge Corporation, 120, 144, 229 – 31, 271, 274
Philadelphia, 6, 210
Phoenix, 9, 25, 36, 40, 58, 68, 90, 96 – *97,* 100, 136, 138, 218, 260
   as agricultural center, 243 – 44

   capital of, 200 – 201
   courthouse scene in, *245*
   and Hispanics, 197, 207, 210, 212 – 13
   history of, 96, 98, 155, 205
   and the Indians, 168, 177, 180, 188, 190
   population of, 96, 98, 243 – 45, 247
   and water resources, 240, 243
Phoenix Gazette, 210
Pima Indians, 8, 117, 144, 165, 171, 173, 180, 182 – 83, 186, 190, 197, 219, 256
Pinacate lava flows, 113
Pinaleño Mountains, 21 – 22
Pincushion cactus, 90
Pine, 147
   Apache, 38
   Chihuahua, 38
   pinyon, 28, 31, 37 – 38, *44,* 58, 60, 80, 92, 139 – 40
   ponderosa, 27 – 28, 31 – 32, *56,* 58, *59,* 60, 107, 136, 138 – 39, 142, 153
Pinery Canyon, 118
The Pinon Pine (Lanner), 60
Pinyon jay, *57,* 60
Plant life. *See* Crops; Vegetation
Pleasant Valley War (1887), 147 – 48
Pleistocene epoch, 88, 123, 126, 140
Pliocene epoch, 52, 55, 77
Porcupines, 92
Porphyry, 154 – 55
Poston, Charles Debrille, 218 – 19, 226 – 27, 247
Poston's Pyramid, *219*
Pottery, 167 – 68, 170
Powell, John Wesley, 44, 46, 63, 248 – 49
Precambrian period, 66, 148 – 49, 155
Prescott, 58, 96, 139, 142, 149 – 50, 154, 168, 183 – 84, 207
   capital, 5, 200 – 201
Presidios, 197 – 98
Prickley pear cactus, 79, 95
Priestley, J.B., 63, 132, 153
Primrose Hill, 219
Pronghorn sheep. *See* Sheep, pronghorn
Prospectors. *See* Mining, miners and prospectors
Pueblo Colorado Valley, 50
Pueblo Indians, 135, 169 – 71, 175, 182
   Rio Grand Tewa, 179 – 80
Pueblo Revolt (1680), 175, 179, 270
Purdy, Samuel J., 6
Pusch Ridge Wilderness Area, 41 – 42
Pyramid Canyon, 253

Quail, 262
   Gambel's, 103, *105*
   harlequin, 33
Quartzsite, 147, 262 – 64
Quechan Indians, 171, 181, 191
Quitobaquito, 107, 109

Rabbits
  cottontail, 262
  jackrabbits, *80,* 89, 95
Railroads, 158, 200, 209 – 10. 222 – 23,
    225 – 29, 238
  and WWII workers, *213*
Rainbow Bridge, 249
Rainfall, 60 – 62, 113, 128, 151
  in the Chihuahuan Desert, 117 – 118
  and Indian religion, 17
  in the Mohave Desert, 79
  in the Sonoran Desert, 92 – 93, 104, 111
Ranchers and ranching, 201, 247, 253.
    See also Dude ranches
  and cattle, 62, 140, 158, 190, 199,
    220 – 25
Rancho de las Lomas, 273
Range Province, 90, 100, 151
Rats. *See* Rodents
Rattlesnakes. *See* Snakes
Ravens, 36, 71, 89
Red Lake, 72
Red Rock Country, 134, 142, 151
Reptiles. *See* Animal life,
    prehistoric; Lizards; Snakes
Resources of Arizona (Hamilton), 5
Rio Grande River, 116, 182
Rio Grande Tewa Indians. *See* Pueblo
    Indians, Rio Grande Tewa
Rio Grande Valley, 170, 179
*A River No More: The Colorado River and
    the West* (Fradkin), 67, 69
River runners, 49, 248, *250*
Roadrunners, 103, *105*
Rocks, 191, 249. *See also* names of
    specific rock types; Volcanic
    remains
  of the Colorado Plateau, 44, 47, 50,
    52 – 55, 66 – 67, 71
  in desert regions, 77, 114, 123, 127
  of the interior regions, 151, 154 – 55
Rocky Mountains, 44, 63, 77 – 78, 155,
    171, 254
Rodents, 89
  cottonrats, 151
  deer mice, 31
  kangaroo rat, 83, 85, 92, 102,
    127, 131
  meadow vole, 32, 125, 151
  pack-rats, 78, 92 – 93, 126
  pocket mouse, 85, 102
  woodrats, 23, 25, 139, 151
Roosevelt, Theodore, 240, *241.*
    See also Roosevelt Dam
Roosevelt Dam, 68, 98, 144, 240,
    242, 264
Rosa, José de la, 199
Rose Peak, 36

Sacatone alkali grass, 118, 128
Safford, 14, 21, 136, 149
Safford, Anson P. K., 4, 245

Sagebrush, 72, 92
Saguaro cactus, *2, 4,* 14, 25, 31, 37, 76, 90,
    91, 100, 103, 107, *110,* 128, 136, 202
St. David, 275, 277
St. Johns, 52 – 53
Salado Indians, 135, 168
Saltbush, 61, 72, 107, 121
Salt Creek Canyon, 151
Saltgrass, 62, 107, 121
Salt River, 96, 98, 144, *146,* 151, 153, 168,
    180, 240, *251*
Salt River Canyon, 149, 183
Salt River Indian Reservation, 188
Salt River Project, 98, 144, 240
Salt River Valley, 5, 138, 222, 239,
    240, 243 – 45, 247, 265 – 66
Salt River Valley Water Users
    Association, 98, 239
Samaniego family parlor, *203*
San Agustín Day, 203
San Augustin Cathedral, *202*
San Carlos Indian Reservation, 135, 142,
    184, 190 – 91
San Carlos Tontos Indians. *See* Apache
    Indians, San Carlos Tontos
San Carlos Valley, 149
Sanctuary movement, 277
Sand dunes, 113, 130 – 31
Sandhill cranes, *130*
San Dieguito-Armagosa culture, 167, 170
Sand People. *See under* Papago Indians
Sandstone
  Coconino, 67, 151
  De Chelly, 52
  Navajo, 47, 249
San Francisco Mountains, 25, 27, 58
San Francisco Peaks, 17 – 18, 20, 26 – 28,
    37, 57 – 58, 60, 170 – 71, 186
  Inner Basin scene in, *30*
Sangre de Cristo Mountains, 28
San Juan Basin, 50
San Juan Mountains, 28, 44
San Juan River, 49 – 50
San Marcos Hotel (Chandler), 264 – 65
San Pedro River, 114, 123, 180, 240, 274
San Pedro Valley, 166, 168, 180, 222
San Simon Valley, 117, 128, 222
Sand people (Papagos), 180, 183
Santa Catalina, 37 – 39, 41, 68
Santa Catalina Mountains, 20, 25
Santa Cruz Desert, 199
Santa Cruz River, 100, 111, 180 – 81,
    235 – 36, 240
Santa Cruz Valley, 168, 183, 222
Santa Rita Copper and Silver Mine, 201
Santa Rita Mountains, 33 – 34, 41, 123,
    127, 260
Santa Rosa, 90, 95
San Xavier del Bac Mission, 180, 190,
    197, *198,* 277
San Xavier Indian Reservation, 111, 113,
    177

Schist, 64 – 66, 71
Scottsdale, 108, 178, 244, 269, 273
  city hall scene, *272*
Second Mesa, 270
Sedimentary rock, 44, 64
Sedona, 9, 14, 58, 136, 149
Seligman, 58 – 59, 224
Sentinel Plain lava flow, 113
Shadscale deserts, 61
Shale, 54, 66
Sharp, Bob, 224 – 25
Sheep, 62
  desert bighorn, 31, 41, *42,*
    62, 95, 262
  pronghorn, 95
Shoshonean Chemehuevis Indians. *See*
    Chemehuevis Indians, Shoshonean
Shoshone Point, *1*
Show Low, 58, 152
Shreve, Forrest, 41, 72, 86, 100, 128 – 29
Shrubs. *See* names of specific shrubs;
    Vegetation
Sierra Ancha Mountains, 43, 147
Sierra Bonita Ranch, 222
Sierra Madre Mountains, 100, 114, 117
Sierra Nevada Mountains, 77 – 78
Sierrita Ranch scene, *200*
Silktassel, 139, 141
Silver, 75, 153 – 55, 177, 225 – 27
Silver Lake, 203
Sinagua Indians, 135, 168, 170, 272
Skeleton Cave, 184
Skull Valley, 142, 149
Skunks, *82*
Sloths, 89, 92, 123
  ground, 70, 78
Smith, John Y. T., 96
Snake Dance (Hopi raindance), 186
Snakes, 33, 102
  rattlesnakes, 35, *87,* 89, 114, 125
Snakeweed, 129, 139, 142
Snively, Jacob, 227
Snow, Erastus, 238
"Snowbirds," 256, *257*
Snow Bowl (San Francisco Mountains),
    27
Sobaipuri Indians, 180 – 81
Sociedades mutualistas. See Mutual
    aid societies
Society of United Workers, 207
The Song of the Lark (Cather), 59
Sonita, 107, 277
Sonora, 6, 92, 114, 167, 177, 180, 199,
    201 – 2, 218, 226, 235, 258, 265
Sonora Mining and Exploring
    Company, 218
Sonoran Desert, 262. *See also*
    Animal life; Vegetation
  boundaries of, 100, 102, 126, 128 – 29,
    136
  ecology of, 17, 31 – 32, 34, 44, 72,
    116 – 17, 134

Sonoran Desert (cont.)
  geology of, 77, 113
  prehistory of, 92–93, 95
  rainfall in, 17, 92–93, 111, 121
Soto, Ramón, 194, 203
  ranch scene, *196*
Sotol, 38, 139, 151
Southern Pacific Band (music group),
  205
Southern Pacific Railroad, 96, 160, 230
Southern Paiute Indians. *See* Paiute
  Indians, Southern
Southern Tonto Indians. *See* Apache
  Indians, Southern Tonto
Spaniards, 170–71, 220, 229, 236
  colonization of, 197–98
  exploration of, 46, 62, 74, 95, 139, 153,
    195–96, 256
  and the Indians, 173, 175, 177, 179–83,
    185, 270
  missionary work of, 180–82, 197–98
Springerville, 237, 263
Spruce, 28, 32
Squash, 95, 167, 256
Squirrel, 81, *82*, 83, 102
  Abert, 28, 35
  Apache fox, 35
  Harris antelope, 104
Steinfeld's Store, 194
Steward Observatory, 260
Sulphur Springs Valley, 114, 240
Suma Indians, 117
Sumac, 121, 139
Sunrise ceremony (Apache),
  156–*57*, 174–*75*
Sunset Crater, 27–28, 58, 68, 170
Supai, *188*
Superstition Mountains, 43, 153–55
Swarth, Harry (biologist), 34
Swilling, John W., 96
Sycamore, 25, 142
Sycamore Canyon, *16*, 62
  creek bed scene, *137*

Tactical Aircrew Combat Training
  System (TACTS), 262
Tale Told In Our Barrio (Carrillo
  School), 204
Taliesin West, 273
Taos, 153, 182, 270
Tarbush, 121, 123
Taylor, Jake, 262
Telescopes, 260
Tempe, 210, 244, 265
Temperatures, criteria for defining
  desert, 128
Tertulia movement, 205
Tewksbury family. *See* Pleasant Valley
  War
Texas, 127, 138, 199–200
Texas Canyon, 114, 117
The Territory of Arizona (Safford), 4

Third Mesa, 170, 270
Tiger salamander, 35, 125
Toads. *See also* Frogs and Toads
  horned, *126*
  Spadefoot, 125
Tobosa grass, 118, 121, 128
Tohono O'odham, 180, *187*, 260.
  See also Papago Indians
Tombstone, 194, 227, 234
Tombstone Canyon, 120, 274
Tombstone Epitaph, 6
Tombstone Hebrew Association, 234
Tombstone Historical Jewish Graveyard,
  Inc., 234
Tombstone Independent, 6
Tom Reed Mine, *84*
Tonto Apache Indian Reservation, 150
Tonto Basin, 58, 136, 142, 147, 149, 168
Tonto Creek, 147
Tonto Natural Bridge, 68
Tonto Platform, 66–67
Topock, 72, 75–76
Toroweap formation, 151
Toroweap Point, 64
To the Last Man (Grey), 148
Tourism and tourists, 9, 14, 98
Transition zone, 28, 136
Trapping and trappers, 74, 182
Treaty of Guadalupe-Hidalgo (1848), 2,
  199
Tree-ring dating, 83
Trees. See names of specific trees;
  Vegetation
Tricentennial run (Hopi), 270
Trout Creek, 72
Tsegi Canyon, *169*
Tsegi Mesa, 50
Tubac, 180, 197, 199, 218, 226, 229, 325
Tuberculosis patients, *244*, 245
Tucson, 9, 25, 37–38, 68, 90, 114, 117,
  150, 161, 178, 201, 212, 215,
  235–36, *246*, 260, 272, 277
  as capitol, 200–201
  climate of, 111, 121, 245
  and Hispanics, 177, 183, 194, 199,
    201–2, 207, 213–14, 229
  history of, 2, 155, 205
  and the Indians, 168, 177, 183, 269
  population of, 243–44, 247
  water resources of, 240
Tucson Mountains, *34*, 41
Tully, Carlos H., 201
Tumacácori, 197
  Mission, *195*
Tundra, 25–26, 28, 31, 58
Turkcy vultures, 36, 83

Udall, Morris K., 214, 252
Unions, 207, 210, 231–32. *See also*
  Ligas protectoras
  strikes, 229–30, 271

United States government agencies, 182,
  188, 190, 239–40
  Air Force, auxiliary training field, 262
  Army, 178, 258, 261–62
  Bureau of Indian Affairs, 178, 185
  Corp of Engineers, 178, 261
  Marine Corp, Yuma air station, 262
  Reclamation Service, 239–41
United Steel Workers Local 616, 271
University of Arizona, 127, 178, 214,
  257, 260
*Unwanted Mexican Americans in the Great
  Depression* (Hoffman), 212
Upper Sonoran zone, 28, 37
Uranium, 52, 75, 193
Urías, Isabel D., 204
Utah, 2, 32, 44–46, 49–50, 64, 78, 171,
  193, 199, 237, 241, 248–49
Ute Indians, 180

"Valley of the Sun," 98, 144, 247
Van Dyke, John C., 245
Vasek, Frank, 83
Vegetation, 165, 221–22. *See also*
  Crops
  in the Chihuahuan Desert, 114,
    117–18, 121, 123, 126–31
  on the Colorado Plateau, 44, 50,
    57–58, 60–62, 67, 70–71
  evolution of, 23, 25–27
  the "floristic approach" of, 128–29
  interior regions, 136, 138–42, 147, 153
  and life zones, 28
  Mojave Desert, 72, 75–76, 78–81,
    83, 85, 88–89
  and mountain regions, 23, 25–28,
    31–34, 37–38, 41
  of the Sonoran Desert, 90, 92–93, 95,
    100–104, 107, 113, 168
Velvet ash, 62, 142
Ventana Cave, 92, 95, 109, 111, 166
Verde formation, 151
Verde River, 144, 147, 150–51, 153, 168,
  171, 201, 240
Verde Valley, 58, 134, 136, 142, 149–50,
  168, 170, 172, 184
Vermillon Cliffs, *47*, 49
Villa, Ernesto, *206*
Villa, Pancho, 277
Virgin Mountains, 142
Volcanic remains, 27–28, 31–32, 37, 44,
  55, 58–59, 62, 64, 76, 91, 148–49,
  155
  and art, 48

Walapai Indians. *See* Hualapai Indians
Walnut Canyon, 170
Walnut Canyon National Monument, 60
Walpi, 179
Walz, Jacob, 155
Warner, Solomon, 236
Washes, 111. *See also* Arroyo

Water, 17, 57, 67, 235, 239, 240, 253 – 54.
    See also Flooding; Water
        projects
    and desert survival, 86, 107
    and Indian rights, 178, 188, 190
    and the Sonoran Desert, 107, 109, 111,
        113
    and tinajas, 33
Waterfowl, *75*
Water projects, 86, 144, 158, 190
    and dams, 248 – 54
    and irrigation, 62, 98, 235 – 36,
        239 – 40, 254, 257 – 58
Waters, Frank, 46
Watt, James, 252
West Clear Creek, *24*
Western Apache Indians. *See* Apache
    Indians, Western
Western Federation of Miners, 229
Western Federation of Workers, 207
A Western Journal (Wolfe), 55
Westward Ho Hotel, 98, 243
Wheat, 235 – 36
Whetstone Mountains, 123
White Dove of the Desert. *See* San
    Xavier del Bac Mission
White Mountain Indian Reservation,
    190
White Mountain Indians. *See* Apache
    Indians, White Mountain
White Mountains, 14, 134, 138, 225
    ecology of, 25, 28, 31, 58 – 59, 62
    geology of, 44, 148

White River, 135, 144, 148
Wickenburg, 96, 132, 136
Wickiup (town), 178
Wickiups (Indian shelter), 172
Wienker, Curtis, 138
Wildflowers. *See* names of specific
    wildflowers; Vegetation
Wildlife. *See* Animal life
Willcox, 36, 118
Willcox Playa, 107, 118, *124*
    prehistoric record of, 123, 125
Williams, 11, 58, 68
Willows, 70 – 71
Wilson, Woodrow, 231, 265
Window Mountains, 90, 92
Window Rock, 178, 269
Window Valley, 90, 95, 99
Winslow, 55, 60
Wiser, Jacob, 155
Wobblies. *See* Industrial Workers of
    the World
Wolfe, Thomas, 55
Wolves, 31, 35, 62, 70, 78
Woodland, 123, 127
World War I, 209, 229 – 30, 247
World War II, 8, 98, 138, 144, 191, 213,
    225, 247, 262, 264 – 65, 271
Wrens, 71
Wright, Frank Lloyd, 272 – 73
Wright, Harold Bell, 245
Wupatki, 68, 170
Wupatki National Monument, 272
Wyoming, 2, 199, 248

Yaqui Indians, 100, 171, 234, 265 – 67,
    269
    ceremonies of, 177, 197
    deer dancer of, *179*
Yavapai Indians, 134, 139, 171, 183 – 84
    religious beliefs of, 165
Yazzie, Alfred, 269
Yazzie, Askie, 271
Yellow-headed blackbirds, 76
Yellowthroats, 76
Young, Ewing, 153
Yucca, 34, 85, *88*, 117
    Mojave, 31, 85
Yuma, 107, 138, 144, 177, 227
    agriculture in, 256 – 58
    climate in, 5, 17, 111
    Crossing Cultural Park of, 256
    Custom House of, 256
    marine air station in, 262
    Proving Grounds of, 258, 261 – 62
    territorial prison in, 256
    water resources in, 254 – 55
Yuma County, 9, 111, 241
Yuma Indian Reservations, 191
Yuma Indians, 161, 171, 182, 191, 197

Zacatecas, 114
Zah, Peterson, 269
    inauguration scene, *192*
Zion, 219, 236, 238 – 39
Zoroastrianism, 219
Zuñi Indians, 179

Designed by Al Whitehurst.
Production coordinated by Harrison Shaffer.
Composed by Andresen's Tucson Typographic Service.
Printed and Bound by Kingsport Press.